TREATISE ON

INVERTEBRATE PALEONTOLOGY

Part B
PROTOCTISTA 1

Volume 1:
Charophyta

MONIQUE FEIST, COORDINATING AUTHOR

by MONIQUE FEIST, NICOLE GRAMBAST-FESSARD,
MICHELINE GUERLESQUIN, KENNETH KAROL, LU HUINAN,
RICHARD M. MCCOURT, WANG QIFEI, and ZANG SHENZEN

Prepared under Sponsorship of
The Geological Society of America, Inc.

The Paleontological Society   *SEPM (Society for Sedimentary Geology)*
The Palaeontographical Society   *The Palaeontological Association*

RAYMOND C. MOORE   ROGER L. KAESLER
Founder   Editor

JEAN BURGESS, JILL HARDESTY, JANE KERNS
MICHAEL CORMACK, DENISE MAYSE
Assistant Editors and Editorial Staff

THE GEOLOGICAL SOCIETY OF AMERICA, INC.
and
THE UNIVERSITY OF KANSAS
BOULDER, COLORADO, and LAWRENCE, KANSAS
2005

Library of Congress Catalogue Card Number 53–12913
ISBN 0–8137–3002–3

Distributed by the Geological Society of America, Inc., P.O. Box 9140, Boulder, Colorado 80301, www.geosociety.org, from which current price lists of parts in print may be obtained and to which all orders and related correspondence should be directed. Editorial office of the *Treatise:* Paleontological Institute, The University of Kansas, 1475 Jayhawk Blvd., Room 121, Lawrence, Kansas 66045-7613, www.ku.edu/~paleo.

Citation information: Kaesler, R. L., ed. 2005. Treatise on Invertebrate Paleontology, Part B, Protoctista (Charophyta), vol. 1. The Geological Society of America & The University of Kansas. Boulder & Lawrence. xvi + 170 p., 79 fig., 9 tables.

The *Treatise on Invertebrate Paleontology* has been made possible by (1) funding principally from the National Science Foundation of the United States in its early stages, from The Geological Society of America through the bequest of Richard Alexander Fullerton Penrose, Jr., from the Paleontological Society, and from The Kansas University Endowment Association through the bequest of Raymond C. and Lillian B. Moore; (2) contribution of the knowledge and labor of specialists throughout the world, working in cooperation under sponsorship of The Geological Society of America, the Paleontological Society, the SEPM (Society for Sedimentary Geology), the Palaeontographical Society, and the Palaeontological Association; (3) acceptance by The University of Kansas of publication without any financial gain to the University; and (4) generous contributions by our individual and corporate sponsors.

PART B

PROTOCTISTA 1

VOLUME 1: CHAROPHYTA
(Moellerinales, Sycidiales, Charales)

MONIQUE FEIST, NICOLE GRAMBAST-FESSARD, MICHELINE GUERLESQUIN,
KENNETH KAROL, LU HUINAN, RICHARD M. MCCOURT, WANG QIFEI, AND
ZANG SHENZEN

INFORMATION ON *TREATISE* VOLUMES

Parts of the *Treatise* are distinguished by assigned letters with a view to indicating their systematic sequence while allowing publication of units in whatever order each is made ready for the press. Copies can be obtained from the Publication Sales Department, The Geological Society of America, 3300 Penrose Place, P.O. Box 9140, Boulder, Colorado 80301, www.geosociety.org.

PUBLISHED VOLUMES

Part A. INTRODUCTION: Fossilization (Taphonomy), Biogeography, and Biostratigraphy, xxiii + 569 p., 169 fig., 1979.

Part C. PROTISTA 2 (Sarcodina, Chiefly "Thecamoebians" and Foraminiferida), Volumes 1 and 2, xxxi + 900 p., 653 fig., 1964.

Part D. PROTISTA 3 (Protozoa: Chiefly Radiolaria, Tintinnina), xii + 195 p., 92 fig., 1954.

Part E. ARCHAEOCYATHA and PORIFERA, xviii + 122 p., 89 fig., 1955.

Part E, Revised. ARCHAEOCYATHA, Volume 1, xxx + 158 p., 107 fig., 1972.

Part E, Revised. PORIFERA, Volume 2 (Introduction to the Porifera), xxvii + 349 p., 135 fig., 10 tables, 2003.

Part E, Revised. PORIFERA, Volume 3 (Demospongea, Hexactinellida, Heteractinida, Calcarea), xxxi + 872 p., 506 fig., 1 table, 2004.

Part F. COELENTERATA, xx + 498 p., 358 fig., 1956.

Part F. COELENTERATA, Supplement 1 (Rugosa and Tabulata), Volumes 1 and 2, xl + 762 p., 462 fig., 1981.

Part G. BRYOZOA, xiii + 253 p., 175 fig., 1953.

Part G, Revised. BRYOZOA, Volume 1 (Introduction, Order Cystoporata, Order Cryptostomata), xxvi + 625 p., 295 fig., 1983.

Part H. BRACHIOPODA, Volumes 1 and 2, xxxii + 927 p., 746 fig., 1965.

Part H, Revised. BRACHIOPODA, Volume 1 (Introduction), xx + 539 p., 417 fig., 40 tables, 1997.

Part H, Revised. BRACHIOPODA, Volumes 2 and 3 (Linguliformea, Craniiformea, Rhynchonelliformea [part]), xxx + 919 p., 616 fig., 17 tables, 2000.

Part H, Revised. BRACHIOPODA, Volume 4 (Rhynchonelliformea [part]), xxxix + 768 p., 484 fig., 3 tables, 2002.

Part I. MOLLUSCA 1 (Mollusca General Features, Scaphopoda, Amphineura, Monoplacophora, Gastropoda General Features, Archaeogastropoda, Mainly Paleozoic Caenogastropoda and Opisthobranchia), xxiii + 351 p., 216 fig., 1960.

Part K. MOLLUSCA 3 (Cephalopoda General Features, Endoceratoidea, Actinoceratoidea, Nautiloidea, Bactritoidea), xxviii + 519 p., 361 fig., 1964.

Part L. MOLLUSCA 4 (Cephalopoda: Ammonoidea), xxii + 490 p., 558 fig., 1957.

Part L, Revised. MOLLUSCA 4, Volume 4 (Cretaceous Ammonoidea), xx + 362 p., 216 fig., 1996.

Part N. MOLLUSCA 6 (Bivalvia), Volumes 1 and 2 (of 3), xxxvii + 952 p., 613 fig., 1969.

Part N. MOLLUSCA 6 (Bivalvia), Volume 3, iv + 272 p., 153 fig., 1971.

Part O. ARTHROPODA 1 (Arthropoda General Features, Protarthropoda, Euarthropoda General Features, Trilobitomorpha), xix + 560 p., 415 fig., 1959.

Part O, Revised. ARTHROPODA 1 (Trilobita: Introduction, Order Agnostida, Order Redlichiida), xxiv + 530 p., 309 fig., 1997.

Part P. ARTHROPODA 2 (Chelicerata, Pycnogonida, Palaeoisopus), xvii + 181 p., 123 fig., 1955 [1956].

Part Q. ARTHROPODA 3 (Crustacea, Ostracoda), xxiii + 442 p., 334 fig., 1961.

Part R. ARTHROPODA 4, Volumes 1 and 2 (Crustacea Exclusive of Ostracoda, Myriapoda, Hexapoda), xxxvi + 651 p., 397 fig., 1969.

Part R. ARTHROPODA 4, Volumes 3 and 4 (Hexapoda), xxii + 655 p., 265 fig., 1992.

Part S. ECHINODERMATA 1 (Echinodermata General Features, Homalozoa, Crinozoa, exclusive of Crinoidea), Volumes 1 and 2, xxx + 650 p., 400 fig., 1968 [1967].

Part T. ECHINODERMATA 2 (Crinoidea), Volumes 1–3, xxxviii + 1,027 p., 619 fig., 1978.

Part U. ECHINODERMATA 3 (Asterozoans, Echinozoans), xxx + 695 p., 534 fig., 1966.

Part V. GRAPTOLITHINA, xvii + 101 p., 72 fig., 1955.

Part V, Revised. GRAPTOLITHINA, xxxii + 163 p., 109 fig., 1970.

Part W. MISCELLANEA (Conodonts, Conoidal Shells of Uncertain Affinities, Worms, Trace Fossils, Problematica), xxv + 259 p., 153 fig., 1962.

Part W, Revised. MISCELLANEA, Supplement 1 (Trace Fossils and Problematica), xxi + 269 p., 110 fig., 1975.

Part W, Revised. MISCELLANEA, Supplement 2 (Conodonta), xxviii + 202 p., frontis., 122 fig., 1981.

THIS VOLUME

Part B, Part B. PROTOCTISTA 1 (Charophyta), xvi + 170 p., 79 fig., 9 tables, 2005.

VOLUMES IN PREPARATION

Part B. PROTOCTISTA 1 (Chrysomonadida, Coccolithophorida, Diatomacea, Pyrrhophyta, etc.).

Part E, Revised. PORIFERA (additional volumes).

Part F, Revised. CNIDARIA (Scleractinia).

Part G, Revised. BRYOZOA (additional volumes).

Part H, Revised. BRACHIOPODA (additional volumes).

Part K, Revised. MOLLUSCA 3 (Nautiloidea).

Part L, Revised. MOLLUSCA 4 (Ammonoidea) (additional volumes).

Part M. MOLLUSCA 5 (Coleoidea).

Part O, Revised. ARTHROPODA 1 (Trilobita) (additional volumes).

Part Q, Revised. ARTHROPODA 3 (Ostracoda).

Part R, Revised. ARTHROPODA 4 (Crustacea Exclusive of Ostracoda).

Part T, Revised. ECHINODERMATA 2 (Crinoidea).

Part V, Revised. GRAPTOLITHINA.

Part W, Revised. TRACE FOSSILS.

EDITORIAL PREFACE

ROGER L. KAESLER

[The University of Kansas]

From the outset the aim of the *Treatise on Invertebrate Paleontology* has been to present a comprehensive and authoritative yet compact statement of knowledge concerning groups of invertebrate fossils. Typically, preparation of early *Treatise* volumes was undertaken by a small group with a synoptic view of the taxa being monographed. Two or perhaps three specialists worked together, sometimes co-opting others for coverage of highly specialized taxa. Recently, however, both new *Treatise* volumes and revisions of existing ones have been undertaken increasingly by teams of specialists led by a coordinating author. This volume has been prepared by such a team.

Given the aim of the *Treatise*, one might be excused for wondering about our decision, following the earlier lead of Raymond C. Moore when he first organized the project, to include in the *Treatise on Invertebrate Paleontology* the phylum Charophyta. Invertebrates, after all, are defined as animals without backbones. Of all the kinds of organisms that are likely to make it into the *Treatise*, the charophytes are perhaps the least animal-like. On the contrary, they are among the most plantlike of the algae, and indeed some authors have regarded the charophytes as the basal group of kingdom Plantae.

The present arrangement, of course, stems from Moore's sense of practicality and his interest in completeness. From the outset his plan was to include a number of taxa of protists in the *Treatise*. Some of the groups that are related to the charophytes—in the same kingdom at least—are among the most useful and intensively studied kinds of fossils. To have omitted the order Foraminiferida from the *Treatise*, for example, would have done a great disservice to paleontology as a whole.

Part C of the *Treatise* covers the order Foraminiferida, now regarded by MARGULIS and SCHWARTZ (1998) as class Foraminifera of the phylum Granuloreticulosa. Part D, a rather slim volume, details the radiolarians, which comprise two classes of the phylum Actinopoda (MARGULIS & SCHWARTZ, 1998). Part B, of which this is the first volume, is intended to deal with all the plantlike protists: calcareous nannoplankton, benthic calcareous algae, dinoflagellates, silicoflagellates and ebridians, diatoms, and, herein, the charophytes.

We have departed from Moore's original plan in one major way that may disturb some systematists. The part of the *Treatise* that deals with foraminifera (in two volumes) is labeled formally as C Protista 2[(1)] and C Protista 2[(2)]. The radiolarian *Treatise* is D Protista 3. Clearly Moore intended the present volume and others that deal with the plantlike protists to be formally B Protista 1. We have, instead, labeled this volume B Protoctista 1, following MARGULIS and others (1990), MARGULIS, MCKHANN, & OLENDZENSKI (1992), MARGULIS & SCHWARTZ (1998), and L. MARGULIS (personal communication, 2004). BROWN (1993, p. 2,389), in a widely used dictionary defined protist as follows: "A member of the kingdom Protista of simple organisms regarded as intermediate between or distinct from animals and plants, including protozoans, algae and (now less commonly) bacteria and fungi; *esp.* a unicellular eukaryote, a protozoan or single-celled alga."

MARGULIS and SCHWARTZ (1998, p. 112) pointed out that for more than one hundred years the term protist has connoted a single-celled organism. The basis for grouping single-celled organisms separately from multicellular forms is no longer tenable for at least two reasons. First, the single-celled prokaryotes and the single-celled eukaryotes are organized biologically in fundamentally different ways and ought not to be classified together in the kingdom Protista. Second, many of the predominantly single-celled eukaryote phyla have multicellular members that have evolved independently of each other. MARGULIS and SCHWARTZ (1998, p. 112) capped their argument by pointing out that COPELAND (1956) along with numerous 19th-century biologists recognized "the absurdity of referring to giant kelp by the word 'protist,' a term that had come to imply unicellularity and, thus, smallness." Use of the kingdom Protoctista obviates this absurdity, and we have adopted herein the term for that reason.

Users of previous volumes of the *Treatise* have found in the Editorial Preface details pertaining to use of the *International Code of Zoological Nomenclature* (RIDE & others, eds., 1999; please refer to the most recent *Treatise* volume, Part E(R), vol. 3, 2004, for guidance about preparation of manuscript according to zoological nomenclature). The charophytes, of course, are governed by the *International Code of Botanical Nomenclature* (GREUTER & others, 2000), the provisions of which are in many instances quite unlike those of the *ICZN*. In delving into the use of the botanical code, we on the *Treatise* editorial staff have been assisted by E. L. Taylor, C. H. Haufler, both of The University of Kansas, and M. Feist, the coordinating author of this volume. Nomenclatorial codes tend to be rather legalistic and difficult to navigate. Fortunately, a number of sources are available that guide the interested invertebrate paleontologist who is dealing with the *ICBN* for the first time. One source that we found to be most useful is the set of notes by FENSOME and WILLIAMS (2004).

The charophyte *Treatise* has had a rather interesting history. R. E. Peck was the original author of the volume. He worked with both R. C. Moore and Curt Teichert. In 1983 Peck turned over his manuscript and responsibility for the volume to R. M. Forester, who enlisted the help of M. Feist and N. Grambast-Fessard. Dr. Peck died in 1984, and in 1991 pressure from his other work necessitated that Dr. Forester resign his *Treatise* responsibilities. In 1995 J. A. Eyer offered to assist with the project but given the active work of Drs. Feist and Grambast-Fessard did not get involved further. Dr. Feist, as coordinating author, and her team made steady progress. They were assisted by the preliminary editorial work of R. M. McCourt.

Some languages, most notably the Polish and Czech languages, are enriched with the use of diacritical marks that provide enhanced alphabetical diversity. While celebrating diversity, we have nevertheless elected to omit such marks from Polish and Czech geographical terms used in the *Treatise*. We continue to insert diacritical marks into authors' names. Two factors have led us to this editorial decision. First, we in the *Treatise* editorial office typeset electronically all the pages, and such diacritical marks must be inserted by hand into the final computer-prepared pages. This is a costly and time-consuming operation that is fraught with the possibility of introducing errors. Second, in the burgeoning information age of the new millennium, databases and schemes for information retrieval will be of critical importance in managing paleontological information. Stability and uniformity of terminology are requisites of database-management systems, and the use of diacritical marks and computer technology are likely to remain incompatible for some time to come. We hope that linguistic purists will be tolerant of this transgression, which we have undertaken solely in the interest of expediency, consistency, and information retrieval.

In this volume we have taken special pains to acknowledge authorship of chapters and subsections. Readers citing the volume are encouraged to pay close attention to the actual authorship of a chapter or subsection.

Stratigraphic ranges of taxa have been compiled from the ranges of lower taxa. In all instances, we have used the *range-through* method of describing ranges. In instances, therefore, where the work of paleontology is not yet finished, some ranges of higher taxa will not show gaps between the ranges of their subtaxa and may seem to be more complete than the data warrant.

While editor of the *Treatise*, the late Professor Curt Teichert once remarked that a published *Treatise* volume is a progress report and should by no means be regarded as the last word on the systematics and paleontology of the organisms discussed. All of us associated with publishing this volume hope that it will stimulate a burst of activity of research on the charophytes.

ACKNOWLEDGMENTS

The Paleontological Institute's Assistant Editors for Text, Jean Burgess and Jill Hardesty, and the Assistant Editor for Illustrations, Jane Kerns, have faced admirably the formidable task of moving this volume through the various stages of editing and into production. In this they have been assisted ably by other members of the editorial team including Mike Cormack with his outstanding computer skills, Chasity Gaultney with her work on illustrations, and Denise Mayse with general support. Jill Krebs, the remaining member of the Paleontological Institute editorial staff, is involved with preparation of PaleoBank, the paleontological database for future *Treatise* volumes, and has not been closely involved with this volume.

It is quite unlikely that this volume would have been published without the efforts of Monique Feist. She was the driving force behind the volume and has been a paragon as a coordinating author. Her synoptic view of the charophytes, her skill in bringing together an international team of specialists, and her careful attention to detail have made the work of the editors much easier. We are grateful to her for her dedication.

Roger L. Kaesler
Lawrence, Kansas
May 3, 2005

REFERENCES

Brown, L. 1993. The New Shorter Oxford English dictionary, vol. 2. Clarendon Press. Oxford. p. i–viii, 1,877–3,801.

Copeland, H. F. 1956. The Classification of Lower Organisms. Pacific Books. Palo Alto, California. 302 p.

Fensome, R. A., & G. L. Williams. 2004. The Lentin and Williams Index of Fossil Dinoflagellates, 2004 edition. American Association of Stratigraphic Palynologists Contributions Series 42:909 p.

Greuter, W., J. McNeill, F. R. Barrie, H. M. Burdet, V. Demoulin, T. S. Filgueiras, D. H. Nicholson, P. C. Silva, J. E. Skog, P. Trehane, N. J. Turland, & D. L. Hawksworth. 2000. International Code of Botanical Nomenclature (Saint Louis Code). Koeltz Scientific Books. Königstein, Germany. 474 p.

Margulis, L, J. O. Corliss, M. Melkonian, & D. J. Chapman. 1990. Handbook of Protoctista. Jones and Bartlett Publishers. Boston. 914 p.

Margulis, L., H. I. McKhann, & L. Olendzenski. 1993. Illustrated Glossary of Protoctista. Jones and Bartlett Publishers. Boston. 288 p.

Margulis, L., & K. V. Schwartz. 1998. Five Kingdoms. An Illustrated Guide to the Phyla of Life on Earth, 3rd ed. W. H. Freeman and Company. New York. 520 p.

Ride, W. D. L., H. G. Cogger, C. Dupuis, O. Kraus, A. Minelli, F. C. Thompson, & P. K. Tubbs, eds. 1999. International Code of Zoological Nomenclature, 4th ed. International Trust for Zoological Nomenclature. London. 306 p.

STRATIGRAPHIC DIVISIONS

The major divisions of the geological time scale are reasonably well-established throughout the world, but minor divisions (e.g., subseries, stages, and substages) are more likely to be provincial in application. The stratigraphic units listed here represent an authoritative version of the stratigraphic column for all taxonomic work relating to this volume. They are adapted from the International Stratigraphic Chart, and units are approved by the International Commission on Stratigraphy (ICS) and ratified by the International Union of Geological Sciences (IUGS). A copy of the comple chart can be obtained at the following website: http://www.iugs.org/iugs/pubs/intstratchart.htm.

Cenozoic Erathem
  Neogene System
     Holocene Series
     Pleistocene Series
     Pliocene Series
     Miocene Series
  Paleogene System
     Oligocene Series
     Eocene Series
     Paleocene Series
Mesozoic Erathem
  Cretaceous System
     Upper Cretaceous Series
     Lower Cretaceous Series
  Jurassic System
     Upper Jurassic Series
     Middle Jurassic Series
     Lower Jurassic Series
  Triassic System
     Upper Triassic Series
     Middle Triassic Series
     Lower Triassic Series

Paleozoic Erathem
  Permian System
     Lopingian Series
     Guadalupian Series
     Cisuralian Series
  Carboniferous System
     Pennsylvanian Subsystem
     Mississippian Subsystem
  Devonian System
     Upper Devonian Series
     Middle Devonian Series
     Lower Devonian Series
  Silurian System
     Pridoli Series
     Ludlow Series
     Wenlock Series
     Llandovery Series
  Ordovician System
     Upper Ordovician Series
     Middle Ordovician Series
     Lower Ordovician Series
  Cambrian System
     Furongian Series
     Middle Cambrian Series
     Lower Cambrian Series

COORDINATING AUTHOR'S PREFACE

MONIQUE FEIST

[Université Montpellier II, France]

The Charophyta, commonly called charophytes or stoneworts, are green algae that occur worldwide, sometimes abundantly, in fresh and brackish water. Long considered a distinctive group, recent morphological and molecular studies have shown conclusively that charophytes are members of the evolutionary lineage of green algae that gave rise to land plants. Their importance is enhanced by a fossil record more complete and well studied than nearly any other calcareous algae, with the exception of the Dasycladales.

Extant charophytes are of little commercial importance; however, they are of great scientific value. Their primary importance is as model organisms in studies of membrane electrophysiology and cell physiology; and ecological studies are often in relation to recent problems of water management (see chapter on Ecology, p. 29).

Although fossil charophytes were reported as early as the 18th century (SCHREBER, 1759), most charophyte research has been performed within the last century. After the first attempts to establish a coherent classification of the group (see chapter on Classification, p. 83) authors paid attention to the description of assemblages, first in the Paleozoic of Russia (KARPINSKY, 1906) and in the Paleozoic and Mesozoic of North America (PECK, 1934a, 1934b, 1938). Studies of Tertiary charophyte floras started in England (REID & GROVES, 1921); then they were developed in Germany (MÄDLER, 1955), Sweden (HORN AF RANTZIEN, 1959b), France, England, Belgium (GRAMBAST, 1958, 1959b, 1962), and in the former USSR (MASLOV, 1966a).

At the same time, new observations of particular characters of the gyrogonite (basal plate, apical aperture, and ornamentation) facilitated the distinction of genera and species (GRAMBAST, 1956a, 1956c, 1957).

GRAMBAST (1964) also revealed the existence of phylogenetic relationships within the charophytes and especially within the family Clavatoraceae, whose lineage to the plant kingdom is quite remarkable (see chapter on Evolutionary History, p. 60).

Charophytes are represented in the fossil record mainly by the calcified female fructifications, consisting of the gyrogonite and utricle. These fructifications are broadly spherical bodies, ranging from 200 to 3,500 μm. Fossil charophytes provide an excellent source of stratigraphic data, which have numerous applications in paleontology. Their distribution in space and time has provided the basis for establishing biozonal scales (see chapter on Stratigraphic Distribution, p. 39).

Research developed in the last twenty years has been concerned primarily with the application of cladistic analyses and molecular biology to infer phylogenetic relationships both within the Charophyta and the plant kingdom (see chapters on Evolutionary History and Molecular Phylogeny, p. 60 and p. 77, respectively).

Fossil and extant charophytes are often studied independently by different groups of researchers. The present volume brings together knowledge of fossil and extant forms; it is thus intended to be a synthesis that is useful to a wide variety of scientists who study charophytes. The group comprises 86 genera, 12 families, and 3 orders, which are described in this volume, the first edition of the *Treatise* to include coverage of this important group.

We wish to thank the following colleagues who have given permission to reproduce illustrations and in many cases have provided original artwork: Dr. Jean-Pierre Berger, Institut de Geologie, Fribourg, Switzerland; M. Hagen Has and Dr. Hans Kerp, Forschungsstelle für Paläobotanik, Westfälische Wilhelms-Universität, Münster, Germany; Dr. Dieter Korn, Department of Invertebrate Palaeontology, Humboldt Museum, Berlin, Germany; Dr. Lu Huinan and the late Dr. Wang Zhen, Nanjing Institute of Geology and Palaeontology, Nanjing, China; Dr. Carles Martin-Closas, Facultat de Geología; University of Barcelona, Spain; Dr. Eduardo Musacchio, Universidad Nacional de la Patagonia San Juan Bosco, Comodoro Rivadaria, Argentina; Dr. Michael Schudack, Institut für Paläontologie, Freie Universität Berlin, Germany; Dr. Ingeborg Soulié-Märsche, Laboratoire de Paléontologie, Université Montpellier II, Montpellier, France; Dr. Gajendra Pratap Srivastava, Birbal Sahni Institute of Palaeobotany, Lucknow, India; Dr. Yang Guodong, North-West China Bureau of Petroleum Geology, Ulumqi, China; and Dr. Zhang Zerun, Petroleum Geology, Ministry of Geology and Mineral Resources, Zhengzhou, China.

We are grateful to Dr. Gilbert Klapper, Department of Geology, University of Iowa, Iowa City, USA, and to Dr. Richard McCourt, Academy of Natural Sciences, Philadelphia, USA, for reviewing portions of the manuscript. We thank M. Michel Pons who assisted with photography, and Jacqueline Courbet and Laurence Meslin for preparing original drawings, all from the Laboratoire de Paléontologie, Université Montpellier II, Montpellier, France.

REPOSITORIES AND THEIR ABBREVIATIONS

Abbreviations and locations of museums and institutions holding type material, which are used throughout the volume, are listed below.

AGE: Archiv für Geschiebekunde, Geologisch-Paläontologisches Institut, Hamburg, Germany

AI: Institute of Geological Sciences, Polish Academy of Sciences, Kraków, Poland

AMNH: American Museum of Natural History, New York City, New York, USA

AM or AMu: Australian Museum, Sydney, Australia

BGMRH: Bureau of Geology and Mineral Resources of Henan, Henan, China

BGR: Bundesanstalt für Geowissenschaften und Rohstoffe, Hannover, Germany

BGS: British Geological Survey, MPK collection, Nottingham, United Kingdom

BIG: Beijing Institute of Geology, Beijing, China

BM: Berlin Museum, Berlin, Germany

BMNH: British Museum (Natural History), London, United Kingdom

BMS: Buffalo Museum of Science, Buffalo, New York, USA

BPGNC: Bureau of Petroleum Geology of North China, Zhengzhou, Henan, China

BPNWC: Bureau of Petroleum of North West China, Wulumuqi, Xinjiang, China

BSPGM: Bayerische Staatssammlung für Paläontologie und historische Geologie, München, Germany

BYU: Geology Department, Brigham Young University, Provo, Utah, USA

CCG: Chengdu College of Geology (now Chengdu University of Technology), Chengdu, Sichuan, China

CEGH-UNC: Cátedra de Estratigrafía y Geología Histórica, Universidad Nacional de Córdoba, Córdoba, Argentina

CSGM: Central Siberian Geological Museum, United Institute of Geology, Geophysics, & Mineralogy, Siberian Branch of the Russian Academy of Sciences, Novosibirsk, Russia

CU: University of Cincinnati, Cincinnati, Ohio, USA

CUG: Colgate University, Geology Department Collections, Hamilton, New York, USA

CPC: Bureau of Mineral Resources, Canberra, Australia

CRICYT: Centro Regional de Investigaciones Científicas y Tecnológicas, Mendoza, Argentina

DNPM: Departamento Nacional da Produçao Mineral, Rio de Janeiro, Brazil

FEGI: Far East Geological Institute, Russian Academy of Sciences, Vladivostok, Russia

FM: Field Museum (Natural History), Chicago, Illinois, USA

FUB: Freie Universität Berlin, Institut für Geologische Wissenschaften, Fachrichtung Paläontologie, Berlin, Germany

GII: Institut für Geologie und Paläontologie der Universität Innsbruck, Innsbruck, Austria

GIK: Geologisch-Paläontologisches Institut, Universität zu Köln, Köln, Germany

GISO: Geological Institute of Shengli Oil Field, Dongying, Shandong, China.

GMU: Geological Museum, Ukrainian Academy of Sciences, Kiev, Ukraine

GPIMH: Geologisch-Paläontologisches Institut und Museum der Universität Hamburg, Hamburg, Germany

GSC: Geological Survey of Canada, Ottawa, Canada

GSM: British Geological Survey (formerly Geological Survey Museum; Institute of Geological Sciences, London), Keyworth, Nottinghamshire, United Kingdom

GSS: Geological Survey of Scotland, Edinburgh, United Kingdom

GSWA: Geological Survey of Western Australia, East Perth, Australia

HM: Hunterian Museum, University of Glasgow, Glasgow, United Kingdom

IGASB: Institute of Geology, Academia Sinica, Beijing, China

IGPTU: Institut und Museum für Geologie und Paläontologie, Tübingen Universität, Tübingen, Germany

IPFUB: Institut für Paläontologie, Freie Universität, Berlin, Germany

IPPAS: Institute of Palaeobiology, Polish Academy of Sciences, Warsaw, Poland

IPM: Institut de Paléontologie du Muséum national d'Histoire naturelle de Paris, Paris, France

IPUB: Institüt für Paläontologie, Universität Bonn, Bonn, Germany

IPUM: Instituto di Paleontologia, Università di Modena, Modena, Italy

IRSNB: Institut Royal des Sciences naturelles de Belgique, Brussels, Belgium

ISM: Illinois State Geological Survey, Urbana, Illinois, USA, formerly at Illinois State Museum, Springfield, Illinois, USA

IU: Indiana University, Bloomington, Indiana, USA

JPI: Jianghan Petroleum Institute, Jingsha, Hubei, China

KIGM: Institute of Geology and Mineral Deposits, Kraków, Poland

KUMIP: University of Kansas, Lawrence, Kansas, USA

LGI: Leningrad Mining Institute, Leningrad, Russia

MCCA: Museo Comunale in Cortina d'Ampezzo, Cortina d'Ampezzo, Italy

MCZ: Museum of Comparative Zoology, Harvard University, Cambridge, Massachusetts, USA

MFGI: Museum Far Eastern Geological Institute, Vladivostok, Russia

MGSB: Museo Geologico, Seminari Conciliar, Barcelona, Spain

MHGI: Museum of the Hungarian Geologic Institute, Budapest, Hungary

MIGT: Museum, Institute of Geology, Dushambe, Tajikistan

MLGIN: Micropalaeontological Laboratory, Geological Institute, Academy of Sciences, Moscow, Russia.

MLP: Collection Paleobotanica, Museo de la Plata, La Plata, Argentina

MMMN: Manitoba Museum of Man and Nature, Winnipeg, Canada

MMF: Geological and Mining Museum, Sydney, Australia

MNCN: Museo Nacional de Ciencias Naturales, Madrid, Spain

MNHN: Muséum National d'Histoire Naturelle de Paris, Paris, France

MNMPB: Magyar Nemzeti Museum, Budapest, Hungary

MNS: Museum für Naturkunde, Stuttgart, Germany

MUZ IG: Museum of the State Geological Institute, Warsaw, Poland

NHM: Natural History Museum, London, United Kingdom

NIGP: Nanjing Institute of Geology and Palaeontology, Nanjing, China

NIGPAS: Nanjing Institute of Geology and Paleontology, Academia Sinica, Nanjing, China

NIUPGAS: Nanjing Institute of Geology and Paleontology, Academia Sinica, Nanjing, China

NMV: National Museum of Victoria, Melbourne, Australia

NRM: Naturhistoriska Riksmuseet (Swedish Museum of N atural History), Stockholm, Sweden

NYSM: New York State Museum, Albany, New York, USA

ODM: Old Dominion College, Norfolk, Virginia, USA

OSU: Ohio State University, Department of Geology, Columbus, Ohio, USA

OUZC: Ohio University Zoological Collections, Athens, Ohio, USA

PDMNH-P: Paleontological Department of the National Museum, Museum of Natural History, Prague, Czech Republic

PIUB: Paleontological Institute of the University of Bonn, Bonn, Germany

PIUFB: Paläontologisches Institut, Freie Universität Berlin, Berlin, Germany

PIUW: Paläontologichen Instituts, Universität Wien, Vienna, Austria

PIUZ: Paleontological Institute, University of Zürich, Zürich, Switzerland

PIW: Institut für Paläontologie der Universität Würzburg, Würzburg, Germany

P-MD: Provincial Museum of Danzig, Danzig, Germany

PMUK: Palaeontological Museum, University of Kiev, Ukraine

PRM: Peter Redpath Museum, Montreal, Canada

PU: Princeton University, Princeton, New Jersey, USA

ROM: Royal Ontario Museum, Toronto, Canada

RMS: Palaeobotanical Department, Riksmuseum, Stockholm, Sweden

SAM: South Australian Museum, Adelaide, Australia

SGIP: Sammlung des Geologisch-Paläontologichen Institutes der Universität Palermo, Palermo, Italy

SGS: Geological Collection, Swedish Geological Survey, Uppsala, Sweden

SMF: Natur-Museum und Forschungs-Institut, Senckenberg, Germany

SPIE: Sammlung des Institut für Paläontologie, Universität Erlangen-Nürnberg, Erlangen, Germany

SPIML: Sammlung des Paläontologischen Institutes der Universität Marburg, Lahn, Germany

SPIT: Sammlung des Paläontologischen Institutes der Universität Tübingen, Tübingen, Germany

SSPHG: Staatliches Sammlung für Paläontologie und historische Geologie, München, Germany

SSSBGF: Stratigraphische Sammlung der Sektion Geowissenschaften der Bergakademia Freiberg, Freiberg, Germany

SUP: Sydney University, Department of Geology, Sydney, Australia

TMM: Texas Memorial Museum, University of Texas, Austin, Texas, USA

TsNIGER: Ts NIGER Museum, Russia

UA: University of Alberta, Edmonton, Alberta, Canada

UAF: University of Alaska, Fairbanks, Alaska, USA

UC: University of Cincinnati, Cincinnati, Ohio, USA

UCC: Chicago Natural History Museum, formerly in Walker Museum, Chicago, Illinois (see also FM), USA

UCM: Universidad Complutense de Madrid, Madrid, Spain

UG: University of Göttingen, Göttingen, Germany

UL: Lodz University, Institute of Geography, Lodz, Poland

UM: University of Minnesota, Minneapolis, Minnesota, USA

UMC: University of Missouri-Colombia, Colombia, Missouri, USA

UMG: University of Montana, Department of Geology, Missoula, Montana, USA

UMP: University Montpellier II , Department of Paleontology, Montpellier, France. C, L. Grambast Collection; CF, M. Feist Collection; CM, M. Massieux Collection; CSM, I. Soulié-Märsche Collection

UNE: University of New England, Armidale, New South Wales, Australia

UPLGS: Université de Paris, Laboratoire de Géologie de la Sorbonne, Paris, France

USGS: U.S. Geological Survey, Type algae collection, Denver, Colorado, USA

USNM: U.S. National Museum, Washington, D.C., USA

U-SK: Universitäts-Sammlung zu Kiel, Germany

UTBEG: University of Texas, Bureau of Economic Geology, Austin, Texas, USA

VK: Theo Van Kemper Collection, Amsterdam, The Netherlands

WAGS: Western Australia Geological Survey, Perth, Australia

WAM: Western Australia Museum, Perth, Australia

WIF: Wadi Institute of Himalayan Geology, Dehra Dun, India

WMC: Woodwardian Museum, University of Cambridge, Cambridge, United Kingdom

WMNM: Wesfälisches Museum für Naturkunde, Münster, Germany

YaFAN: Institute of Geology, Yakut Branch, Siberian Division AN SSR, Yakutsk, Russia

YPM: Yale Peabody Museum, New Haven, Connecticut, USA

ZPAL: Institute of Paleobiology, Polish Academy of Sciences, Warsaw, Poland

MORPHOLOGY

MICHELINE GUERLESQUIN and MONIQUE FEIST

[Université Catholique de l'Ouest, Angers, France; and Université Montpellier II, France]

MORPHOLOGY OF LIVING CHAROPHYTA

The extant charophytes belong to a single family, the Characeae, which includes seven genera with more than 400 microspecies (*sensu* WOOD & IMAHORI, 1964–1965). Species have a wide range of geographic distributions from local endemics to cosmopolitan. All the extant genera are also known as fossils; however, the fossil record of *Nitella,* whose fructifications are uncalcified, is quite limited.

Living charophytes possess highly specialized morphological features that distinguish them from other green algae, especially in the complexity of the thallus and gametangia. These and other such features as the phragmoplast type of cell division and molecular phylogenetic analyses suggest a close relationship with higher plants.

THALLUS
Structure

The oospore germinates into a short filamentous structure called the protonema, a cladom approximately 1 mm long, which gives rise to the adult (Fig. 1.1). The thallus consists of one or more main axes with regularly alternating nodes and internodes (Fig. 2*a*–2*b*). Each node consists of several small cells that give rise to lateral branchlets. The internodes are elongated, multinucleate single cells generally 1 to 4 cm long, reaching 15 cm in the largest species.

Cortication

Some species have an external layer of narrow cells (cortex) surrounding the internodal cells and at the base of the nodal branchlets (phylloids). Such cortication (Fig. 3) is well developed in most species of *Chara,* incomplete in *Lychnothamnus,* and absent from *Chara* section *Charopsis, Lamprothamnium,* and the subfamily Nitelloideae.

Some corticate species possess spine cells, short pointed cells projecting from the cortical cells. Spine cells occur singly or in clusters on the main axes. In *Chara, Lamprothamnium, Lychnothamnus,* and *Nitellopsis sarcularis* ZANEVELD, single-celled stipulodes originating from nodal cells occur in one or two tiers at the base of the branchlet whorls (Fig. 2b). Stipulodes are absent from *Tolypella* and *Nitella.* These appendages are very useful in the classification of living forms.

The cortex consists of an external layer of 6 to 14 thin cortical cells surrounding the internodal cells and at the base of the nodal branchlets. The cortication (Fig. 3.1–3.3) is **haplostichous** when the primary cortical cells are arranged so as to correspond one-to-one to the branchlets. In this instance, they may be **contiguous** (*Chara canescens* DESVAUX & LOISELEUR-DESLONGCHAMPS) or **noncontiguous** [*Lychnothamnus barbatus* (MEYEN) LEONHARDI]. When the cortical cells are subdivided, the cortication is **diplostichous** if the primary tubular cells under the phylloids alternate with one row of secondary tubular cells; spine cells, which occur only on primary tubes, are a useful character to distinguish both kinds of cortical cells.

Cortication is called **triplostichous** when two rows of secondary cortical cells are intercalated between the primary tubular cells; in this instance, the cortication is styled **isostichous** (as in *Chara globularis* THUILLER) if primary and secondary tubes have the same size and **anisostichous** [as in *Chara globularis* var. *virgata* (KÜTZ) R. D. WOOD] when the primary tubes have a larger diameter in section. The diameter of the cortical cells is also taxonomically significant. The cortex is said to be **aulacanthous** when the primary tubular cells are smaller in diameter than the secondary ones. It is **tylacanthous** in the reverse instance. In the extant forms, subdivision of the cortical cells occurs only in the genus *Chara.*

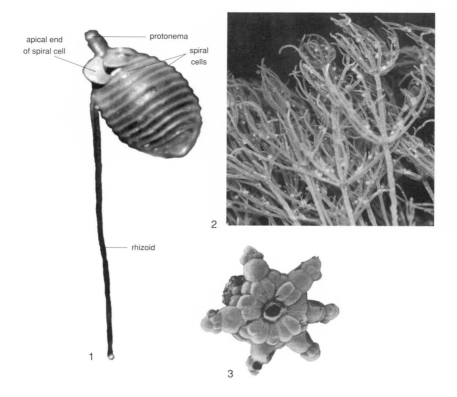

FIG. 1. *1*, Germination of oosporangium of a *Chara* species, ×70 (Kiss & Staehelin, 1993); *2, Chara vulgaris* f. *contraria* (A. BRAUN *ex* KÜTZING) R. D. WOOD; general view of several specimens bearing antheridia, ×4 (Corillion, 1994); *3, Nitellopsis obtusa* (DESVAUX in LOISELEUR-DESLONGCHAMPS) J. GROVES; stellate bulbil, ×92 (Feist & Grambast-Fessard, 1991, fig. 4b).

Branching

In the extant subfamily Charoideae, axes as well as branchlets are divided into nodes and internodes (Fig. 4). The branchlets are not divided dichotomously. As is shown by transverse sections, nodes have two central cells surrounded by two layers of numerous peripheral cells (Fig. 3.4–3.6). In *Lamprothamnium* the central cells are subdivided. In the extant subfamily Nitelloideae transverse sections of nodes have four central cells surrounded by only one row of a small number of peripheral cells (BHARATHAN, 1980) (Fig. 3.6). In *Nitella* branchlets bifurcate one to five times. Only main axes are subdivided into nodes and internodes. In *Tolypella* the branching is more complex, with divided primary and secondary rays. Bract cells,

originating from nodal cells of branchlets, are more or less elongate elements that occur around the gametangia but are rudimentary on or absent from the sterile nodes. Bracteoles are single cells, quite similar to the bract cells but derived from antheridial primordia. Two bracteoles adjoin the oogonium (Fig. 2c–2d). Bracteoles are sometimes represented as casts at the base of encrusted fossils of the family Characeae.

Rhizoids

Charophytes are fixed on the substratum by the rhizoids. These are very thin and colorless filaments (Fig. 1.1, 4.3), and they are irregularly organized in nodes (with ramifications) and internodes. Besides attachment, the rhizoids are involved in the absorption of nutrients.

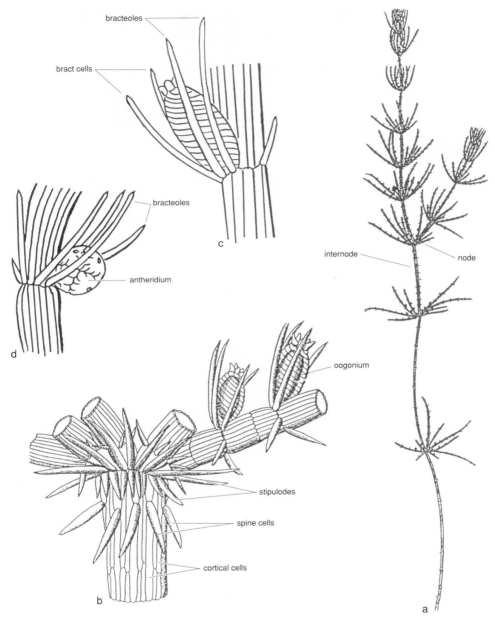

FIG. 2. *a–b, Chara zeylanica* f. *elegans* (A. BRAUN *ex* T. F. ALLEN) H. & J. GROVES; *a,* habit, ×1; *b,* axial node with stipulodes in 2 tiers on the main axis, corticated axis, base of branchlets and solitary spine cells, ×23 (Wood & Imahori, 1964 in 1964–1965, pl. 95,*1,4*); *c–d, Chara* sp., fertile nodes of a dioic species, ×40 (Corillion, 1975, pl. III, f, g).

Bulbils

Bulbils are multicellular tuberous growths, either isolated or aggregated on the rhizoids. In *Nitellopsis obtusa* (DESVAUX in LOISELEUR-DESLONGCHAMPS) J. GROVES, stellate bulbils are modified branchlet whorls situated on the lower axial nodes (Fig. 1.3). Bulbils function in vegetative propagation.

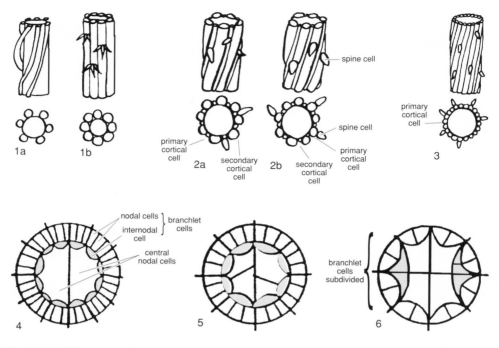

FIG. 3. *1–3,* Different types of cortication; *1,* haplostichous; *a,* incomplete (noncontiguous), *b,* complete (contiguous); *2,* diplostichous and anisostichous; *a,* aulacanthous, *b,* tylacanthous; *3,* triplostichous and isostichous (Corillion, 1957, pl. 1,*4–8*); *4–6;* transverse sections of nodes showing origin of branchlets by subdivisions of central nodal cells; *4, Chara (C. zeylanica); 5, Lamprothamnium (L. papulosum); 6, Nitella (N. acuminata)* (adapted from Bharathan, 1980, fig. 20, sections 1, 5, 9).

Calcification

It has been shown that the thallus and gyrogonite have two types of calcification (FLAJS, 1977; SOULIÉ-MÄRSCHE, 1989). For the thallus, the calcium deposit is external and generally not resistant. Incrustation of thalli occurs independently of the biocycle, provided the temperature is high enough for precipitation of calcium carbonate. In corticated forms calcite may be included in the elongated filaments around the internodal cells; this external calcified layer strengthens the thallus and allows its preservation, usually in the form of unconnected fragments in the sediments.

REPRODUCTIVE ORGANS

Oosporangium

Development.—The oosporangium (female gametangium, oogonium, Fig. 5, 6.1–6.2) originates from a nodal cell on the lowest nodes and sometimes at the base of the branchlets. The nodal cell divides into three: the upper cell enlarges to form the oosphere and its sister cell(s); the lowest cell often forms a short stalk. The central cell divides to produce five elongate cells that spiral sinistrally around the oosphere and subdivide apically to produce the coronula (one tier of five cells in the subfamily Charoideae and two tiers in the subfamily Nitelloideae).

Morphology.—In the family Characeae, which includes the seven extant genera, the oosporangium consists of five spiral cells enclosing the oosphere or, after fertilization, the oospore (Fig. 6.1–6.2). The spiral cells are joined at the apex along a broken line, and the base of the oosporangium is obturated by one to three sister cells of the oosphere, which constitute the basal plate. The apex is surmounted by one (in the

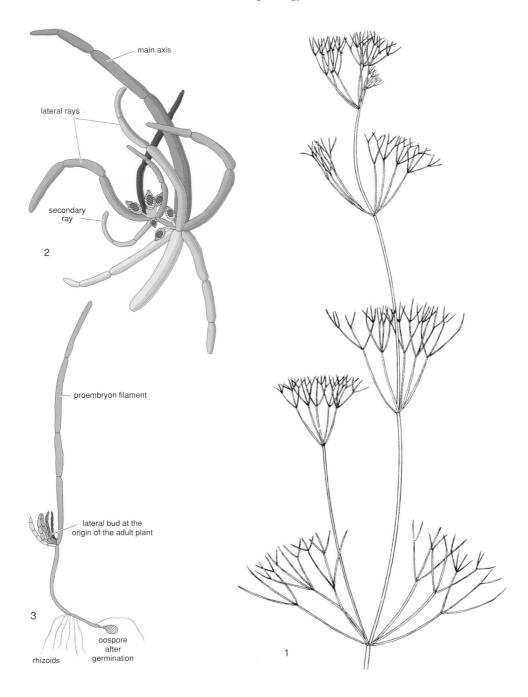

Fig. 4. *1. Nitella bifurcata* subsp. *mucronata* (A. Braun) R. D. Wood; habit, ×1 (Wood & Imahori, 1964 in 1964–1965, pl. 224,*6*); *2, Tolypella nidifica* var. *glomerata* (Desvaux in Loiseleur-Deslongchamps) R. D. Wood, ×12; fertile branchlet with 1 ray node bearing 5 lateral rays, the left one bearing 3 secondary rays (adapted from Wood & Imahori, 1964 in 1964–1965, pl. 382,*8*); *3, Chara* sp., proembryon (Corillion, 1975, pl. I,*C*).

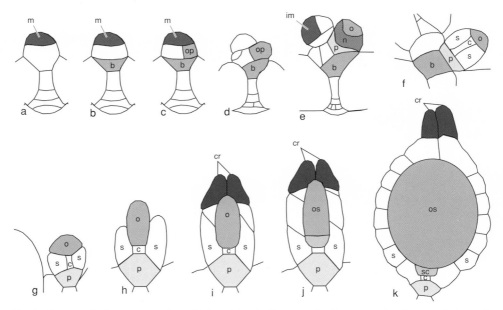

FIG. 5. Ontogenesis of an oosporangium of *Chara; b,* basal cell; *c,* central cell; *cr,* coronula cell; *im,* immature male gametangium; *m,* male gametangial primordium; *n,* oosporangial node; *o,* oosphere mother cell; *op,* oosporangial primordium; *os,* oosphere; *p,* pedicell cell; *s,* spiral cell; *sc,* sterile cell (adapted from Leitch, John, & Moore, 1990, fig. 1).

subfamily Charoideae) or two (in the sub-family Nitelloideae) rows of five coronula cells (Fig. 6.3). In most representatives of the subfamily Charoideae, the spiral cells and the basal plate become calcified; in all species, the oospore is included in an organic wall containing sporopollenin.

The basal plate.—The oosphere sister cell remains undivided in the Charoideae and in *Sphaerochara;* it subdivides into three (rarely two) cells in *Nitella* and *Tolypella.* The sister cell (or cells) becomes the basal plate in calcified species. Basal-plate morphology provides useful characters in the classification of fossils.

The gametangial wall.—After fertilization, the walls ensheathing the oosporangium thicken and undergo biochemical changes to form a hermetic and resistant envelope around the newly formed oospore. This complex wall is composed of three groups of layers (Fig. 7; HORN AF RANTZIEN, 1956b).

(1) In contact with the oospore is an organic transparent layer, the **sporine**, split into endosporine and ectosporine.

(2) Closely united with the ectosporine is the **sporostine**, a pigmented layer that is composed mainly of sporopollenin and cellulose (SHAW, 1971) and colored by a melanin-like compound (DYCK, 1970). The sporostine includes two layers, often indistinguishable, the endosporostine and the ectospostine, called by LEITCH (1989) a pigmented helicoidal layer and an ornamented layer respectively (Fig. 8.1). There is a lack of unanimity about the origin and position of the sporostine. HORN AF RANTZIEN (1956b), DYCK (1970), and LEITCH (1989) judged the sporostine to be produced by the inner walls of the spiral cells, whereas SOULIÉ-MÄRSCHE (1989) considered this layer to be an intercellular substance that covers all the parts of the oospore as well as its sister cells or basal plate and is independent of the spiral cells.

The surface of the sporostine may be smooth or marked by ornamentation of different shapes and disposition. GROVES and BULLOCK-WEBSTER (1920) defined three types of decoration that were also recognized

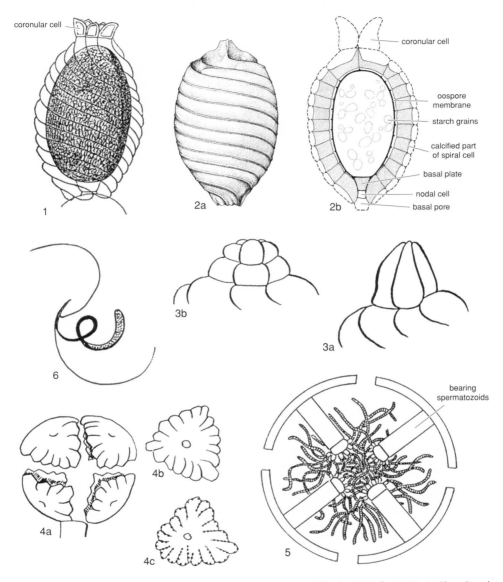

FIG. 6. Reproductive organs of the Characeae. *1,* Oosporangium, ×50 (Migula, 1897, fig. 27-7); *2, Chara hispida* L. *emend.* R. D. WOOD; *a,* gyrogonite (calcified oosporangium), *b,* same, longitudinal section; *dotted lines,* uncalcified part of spiral cells and of coronula cells, not preserved in fossils, ×40 (Feist & Grambast-Fessard, 1991, fig. 1A–1B); *3,* coronula cells; *a,* in *Chara, b,* in *Nitella* (Corillion, 1975, pl. IV,*d, f*); *4,* antheridium; *a,* external view of an antheridium open, showing 4 shield cells, *b,* isolated shield cells in *Chara, c,* in *Nitella; 5,* equatorial transversal section of antheridium showing 4 shield cells with their manubrium bearing spermatozoids; *6,* isolated biflagellate spiraled spermatozoid (Corillion, 1975, pl. V,*c,d,f,j*).

by HORN AF RANTZIEN (1959b). Electron microscopy has induced a renewal of investigations of the oospore membrane. JOHN and MOORE (1987) established a key to the *Nitella* species based on 21 categories of oospore. In *Chara,* which is less diversified, only seven categories have been determined (JOHN, MOORE, & GREEN, 1990). SOULIÉ-MÄRSCHE (1989) presented a synopsis of the oospore in the seven extant genera as well as

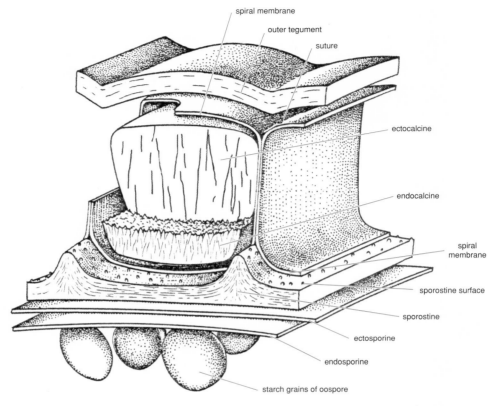

FIG. 7. Schematic representation of calcified oosporangial wall (Soulié-Märsche, 1989, fig. 8A).

in two Oligocene species, *Chara* sp. and *Stephanochara ungeri* FEIST-CASTEL. Features of the oospore were thought as early as the second half of the last century to be useful in recognizing species (DE BARY, 1875; NORDSTEDT, 1889). Although new investigations have revealed the usefulness of these characters in several taxonomic problems at the specific or infraspecific levels, their use is limited: the ornamentation varies according to the degree of maturity of the oospore, which is difficult to recognize; and the same ornamentation can occur in different species (JOHN & MOORE, 1987; SOULIÉ-MÄRSCHE, 1989; JOHN, MOORE, & GREEN, 1990). Following are some types of oospore ornamentation in extant species that also occur, more or less similarly, in fossil forms.

(a) Granulate, when the diameter of the ornamentation elements is less than 1 μm (*Chara globularis* var. *aspera* f. *galioides,* Fig. 8.2).

FIG. 8. Oospore membrane; *1, Chara hispida* L. *emend.* R. D. WOOD; section of compound oosporangial wall, ×4,000; labels: spiral cells: 1, spiral cell primary wall, 2, crystine, 3, pigmented helicoidal layer, 4, ornamentation layer; labels: oospore: a, oospore primary wall, b, amorphous layer, c, helicoidal layer, d, microfibrillar layer (Leitch, 1989, fig. 3); *2–7,* ornamentation of ectosporostine; *2, Chara globularis* var. *aspera* f. *galioides* (DE CANDOLLE) R. D. WOOD; granulate ornamentation (new); *3, Nitella syncarpa* var. *capitata* (NEES) KÜTZING; bristling tuberculate ornamentation, ×600 (Soulié-Märsche, 1989, pl. VI,*3*); *4–5, Nitellopsis obtusa* (DESVAUX in LOISELEUR-DESLONGCHAMPS) J. GROVES; lamellate endocalcine masking ectosporostine, ×240, ×1,200 (Soulié-Märsche, 1989, pl. IV,*3–4*); *6, Nitella gracilis* subsp. *gracillima* f. *robusta* (IMAHORI) R. D. WOOD; granulate-perforate ornamentation (Soulié-Märsche, 1989, pl. VI,*8*); *7, Lamprothamnium papulosum* (WALLROTH) J. GROVES; tuberculate ornamentation, ×600 (Soulié-Märsche, 1989, pl. V,*3*).

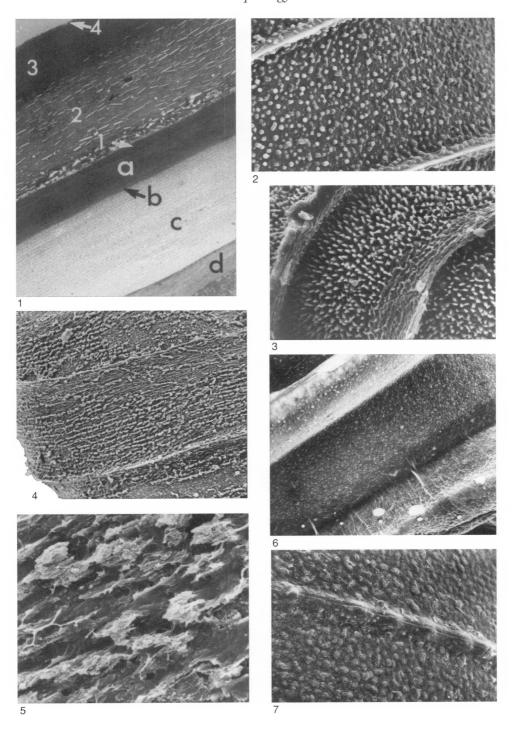

FIG. 8. *For explanation, see facing page.*

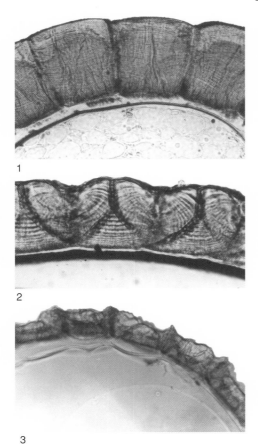

FIG. 9. Structure of calcified wall in axial longitudinal sections; *1,* parallel lamination in *Nitellopsis obtusa* (DESVAUX in LOISELEUR-DESLONGCHAMPS) J. GROVES, Gouwzee Lake, The Netherlands, ×120; *2,* Y-lamination in *Lamprothamnium papulosum* (WALLROTH) J. GROVES, Marseillan, Hérault, France, ×210; *3,* nitelloid calcification in *Tolypella intricata* f. *prolifera* (ZIZ ex A. BRAUN) R. D. WOOD, Juignée Lake, Maine-et-Loire, France, ×250 (new).

(b) Tuberculate, when the diameter of the ornamentation elements is greater than 1 μm [*Lamprothamnium papulosum* (WALLROTH) J. GROVES, Fig. 8.7]. Granules and tubercules can be perforated [*Nitella gracilis* subsp. *gracillima* f. *robusta* (IMAHORI) R. D. WOOD, Fig. 8.6].

(c) Reticulate (see Fig. 78,*1d,* Systematics, herein p. 144).

(d) Vermiculate, as in *Nitella syncarpa* (SOULIÉ-MÄRSCHE, 1989, pl. VI,*2*).

In *Nitellopsis obtusa,* the sporostine is masked by lamellate ectocalcine (Fig. 8.4– 8.5).

Lamprothamnium and *Lychnothamnus* have the same types of ornamentation as *Chara;* in *Tolypella* the surface of the oospore is smooth (SOULIÉ-MÄRSCHE, 1989). In uncalcified forms (*Nitella, Tolypella* section *nidifica,* and some species of *Chara*) the spiral cells are not preserved, and oospores are propagated covered only with the ecto-sporostine, which is, however, particularly resistant. PROCTOR (1962) has shown that such oospores retain their vitality when passing through the digestive tract of migratory water birds.

(3) The **calcine** (HORN AF RANTZIEN, 1956b) is the main constituent of calcified oosporangia. The crystals are disposed according to three types, discussed below.

Parallel lamination is the most common (Fig. 9.1). The calcine is differentiated into two zones, the internal one or **endocalcine**, having concentric organic lamellae, and, toward the exterior of the cell, the **ectocalcine**, massive and generally devoid of lamination. The lamination may occupy all the thickness of the cell.

Y-calcification (Fig. 9.2) occurs in some halophilic species, such as *Lamprothamnium papulosum.* Here, a system of radial convergent lines occurs in addition to the usual concentric lamination. These lines depart from the sutures and from the adaxial wall, going toward the median part of the spiral cell. In the middle of the cell the limit of these radial stripes outlines a letter Y, the fork of which is directed toward the center of the gyrogonite. Species with Y-calcification are found preferentially in somewhat saline environments, but it cannot be said that there is a causal relationship between these two facts. The meaning of this peculiar structure remains enigmatic (FEIST & GRAMBAST-FESSARD, 1984; LEITCH, 1989; SOULIÉ-MÄRSCHE, 1989).

Nitelloid calcification (Fig. 9.3) of the wall of the extant nitelloid gyrogonites of *Sphaerochara* WOOD has a characteristic powdery aspect, the origin of which is not clear. It has been observed generally that the outer part of the calcareous shell consists of a granular layer of loosely connected calcium carbonate particles, different in its structure from the calcine of the other Characeae (MIGULA, 1897; HORN AF RANTZIEN, 1959a). The more complete calcification of the fossil representatives of the genus does not differ fundamentally from the types of calcification in the extant forms.

Sporostine and calcified spiral cells form a thick and resistant envelope that protects the egg during unfavorable conditions, which may last from a few months to several years. After disintegration of the living cells, only the calcified walls remain, sometimes with the internal sporostine and basal plate intact. All these resistant parts of the oogonium constitute the gyrogonite, which can be preserved as a fossil.

Antheridium

The antheridium is usually composed of eight shield cells, which are closely joined together to form a sphere (Fig. 6.4). A stalklike cell (manubrium) protrudes into the sphere from the inner surface of each shield cell. Each manubrium bears from one to four filaments that produce about 200 biflagellate spermatozoids (Fig. 6.5). The complex structure of the antheridium is unique in the biologic world. Antheridia are not calcified, but casts of them have been found in fossil representatives of the Clavatoraceae and Pinnoputamenaceae. These casts have internal features quite similar to those of extant species.

Monoecy and Dioecy

The presence of both sex organs on the same individual (monoecy) or on different individuals (dioecy) is a species-specific character. In the monoecious species, the male and female gametangia may be present at the same nodes (conjoined species) or at different nodes (sejoined species). The distinction between monoecious and dioecious forms cannot be detected generally in fossils except among the Clavatoraceae and Pinnoputa-

menaceae, which display clear examples of conjoined monoecy.

REPRODUCTION AND LIFE CYCLE OF CHAROPHYTA

Oogamy

The large oogonium (up to 1,400 μm) fixed on the thallus is fertilized by a small biflagellate spermatozoid. The spermatozoids share morphological characters that clearly ally them with other advanced green algae (Charophyceae *sensu* MATTOX & STEWART, 1984) and higher plants (GARBARY, RENZAGLIA, & DUCKETT, 1993). The zygote, filled with reserves and surrounded by resistant walls, falls to the bottom where it remains dormant until germination.

Parthenogenesis

Parthenogenesis is known in only one living species, *Chara canescens* DESVAUX & LOISELEUR-DESLONGCHAMPS, the females of which are more widely distributed than the males.

Vegetative Reproduction

As in most cryptogams, vegetative reproduction plays an important role in the Charophyta. Bulbils and axillary nodes enable widespread and rapid dispersal of vegetative propagules. Such structures seem likely to have played the same role in fossil taxa as suggested by the co-occurrence of calcified nodes and gyrogonites in sediments.

Development and Biocycle

It is generally recognized that after fertilization, meiosis occurs at the first division of the zygote. After a variable period of dormancy, the egg germinates into a haploid protonema on which the thallus develops. The diploid phase is restricted to the egg, and the green thallus is haploid. Thus the life cycle is monogenetic haplophasic. According to an alternative hypothesis (TUTTLE, 1926; SOULIÉ-MÄRSCHE, 1989), the four cells (oospore and sister cells) issuing from the first divisions during the development of the oogonium of *Nitella* were suggested to be the products of meiosis. If so, meiosis occurred in the diploid thallus before the formation of gametes. Recent cytological and chromosome studies (GUERLESQUIN, 1984; MICHAUX-FERRIÈRE & SOULIÉ-MÄRSCHE, 1987), however, have confirmed the haploidy of the thallus.

Polyploidy

Polyploids occur in most living species. The multiplication of the euploid chromosome number may increase the possibilities of adaptation of the species to new biotopes and thus favor the widening of their geographic distribution.

SPECIAL ASPECTS

Charophytes have three unique features. They have a vegetative apparatus with regular alternation of a giant polynucleate cell (produced by endomitosis) and a multicellular node made of several small uninucleate cells; the giant cells make charophytes useful as model systems for cell biology. They have a fairly large female gametangium made of an oosphere surrounded by a multicellular wall (five elongated cells) of vegetative origin. A complex male gametangium produces numerous helicoidal spermatozoids with two flagella inserted at the anterior end; their ultrastructure is similar in some respects to that of bryophyte spermatozoids.

Use of the charophytes by humans has varied during different periods. Silicified and calcified thalli were used in the past as natural abrasives. Crushed charophytes favoring colloid flocculation were used formerly to clarify fruit juices. Fresh or naturally dried specimens are used as green fertilizer in Africa and Asia.

The thallus is used as a support by epiphytes, as food by aquatic herbivores and waterbirds (ducks and moorhens), and as a calcium source by crayfish during ecdysis (molting of the carapace). Their dense vegetation provides sites for spawning by animals as well as shelter from predators.

MORPHOLOGY OF FOSSIL CHAROPHYTA

MORPHOLOGY OF FOSSIL VEGETATIVE REMAINS

Small fragmentary nodes and internodes of thalli are frequently found in nonmarine sediments, generally together with gyrogonites. Their state of preservation varies, and as a result the stem material may have different external characters. The most important in number, size, and diversity occur among the Clavatoraceae. Preservation adequate to provide information on the organism's habit is rare.

Calcified Species

Calcified thallus remains consist of nodes and portions of axes having the axial canals surrounded by small tubes (cortical cells) parallel to the main axis or coiled around it (Fig. 10). In fossil Characeae, the cortex is similar to those of the extant forms (see p. 1 herein), but the Clavatoraceae have a more complete cortication in which spine cells often cover the characean cortex. Just as in living species, different types of cortication may be present within a single fossil species (CORILLION, 1975). The following types of cortication have been reported so far from the fossil record: haplostichous, including isostichous noncontiguous (Fig. 10.2) and isostichous contiguous (Fig. 10.1, 10.4); anisostichous diplostichous (Fig. 10.6); and isostichous diplostichous (Fig. 10.7). The incomplete preservation of nodes does not allow the use of the cortication characters in systematics as it does for extant species.

Uncalcified Species

Vegetative parts of uncalcified taxa are rarely preserved as fossils. Silicified remains are the best preserved, such as in *Palaeonitella cranii* (KIDSTON & LANG) PIA; thalli enclosed in the silicates of the Rhynie Chert are visible in relief in thin sections (Fig. 11.1). These uncorticated thalli, bearing whorls of branchlets separated by internodes devoid of any appendages, are similar to the extant

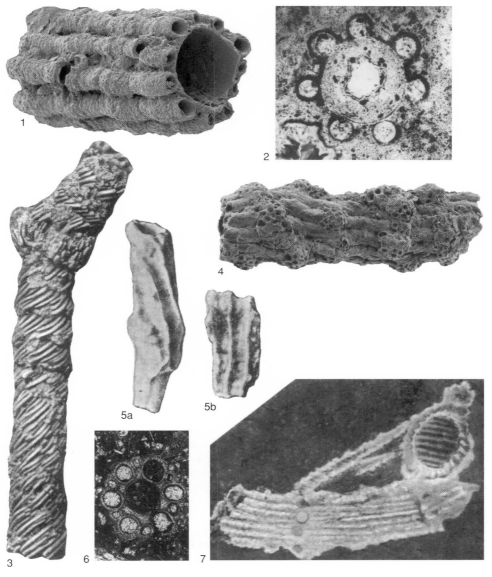

Fig. 10. *1*, Thallus internode showing central axis surrounded by cortical cells; associated with several species of Characeae, Bartonian, Paris basin, France, UMP C105-15, ×75 (new); *2*, thallus fragment associated with *Gyrogona medicaginula* Lamarck, Oligocene, Ireland; transverse section of node, showing 7 noncontiguous isostichous cortical cells, ×65 (Corillion, 1994, fig. 4); *3, Echinochara spinosa* Peck; node and part of internode showing arrangement of spine cells, Upper Jurassic, Colorado, USA, ×5 (Peck, 1957, pl. I,*17*); *4*, thallus internode showing cortical cells partly covered by spiralized swollen belt bearing numerous spine-cell scars, Berriasian, Germany, ×18 (new); *5a–b*, thallus fragments associated with *Sycidium panderi minor* Karpinsky, Devonian, Russia, external views showing incomplete cortication; *a*, slightly spiralized cortical cells and uncorticated portion of thallus, ×25, *b*, straight cortical cells, ×30 (Karpinsky, 1906, fig. 63, 65, 67); *6*, thallus fragment associated with *Clavator reidi* Groves, Lower Cretaceous, Jura Mountain, Switzerland; transverse section of node, showing alternating large and small cortical cells, ×30 (Mojon & Strasser, 1987, fig. 10D); *7, Chara sausari* Sahni & Rao; Deccan Intertrappean Beds, early Paleogene, Chindwara, C.P., India; external view of connected thallus and gyrogonite, showing contiguous isodiametrical cortical cells, ×30 (Sahni & Rao, 1943, fig. 2).

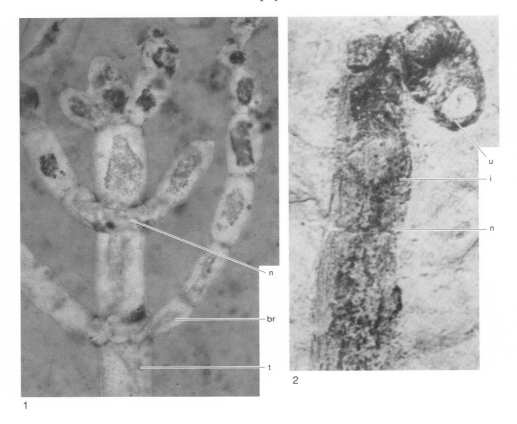

Fig. 11. *1, Palaeonitella cranii* (KIDSTON & LANG) PIA, Pragian, Lower Devonian, Rhynie Chert, Scotland; thin section showing uncorticated thallus (*t*) with branchlets (*br*) originating from nodes (*n*), ×125 (new); *2, Praesycidium siluricum* T. & A. ISHCHENKO, Ludlow, Silurian, Slasky Formation, Ukraine; cast showing corticated thallus with nodes (*n*) and internodes (*i*), bearing a utricle (*u*) at top right, ×5 (Ishchenko & Ishchenko, 1982, pl. 5*g*).

Nitella, although no characters typical of the genus have been observed so far.

Preservation as casts may provide images of thalli in connection with gyrogonites or utricles. A cast of *Praesycidium siluricum* T. & A. ISHCHENKO, one of the oldest representatives of Charophyta, shows a haplostichous isostichous cortication (Fig. 11.2). Similarly, casts of the Eocharaceae from the Upper Devonian of South Africa (GESS & HILLER, 1995) have verticillate thalli bearing structures presumed to be gyrogonites.

Fossil remains of the thallus are too scarce and fragmentary to legitimize a formal taxonomy, although species names have been given to some of them. In most cases, isolated fragments of the thallus are simply mentioned without names being given.

MORPHOLOGY OF FOSSIL REPRODUCTIVE ORGANS
Gyrogonite

The term gyrogonite was used for the first time by LAMARCK (1801) for fossil shells of undetermined nature that LEMAN (1812) recognized later as remains of charophytes. The classification of fossil charophytes is based on characters of the gyrogonite or of the utricle. The **gyrogonite** consists of calcium carbonate that is deposited in both the enveloping cells (i.e., **spiral cells, spiral units, spirals**), which spiral around and enclose the oospore, and the **basal plate**, representing the calcified sister cell of the oosphere. In the Clavatoraceae and the Sycidiales, a calcareous outer covering or **utricle** covers the gyrogonite, and many types of disposition may result

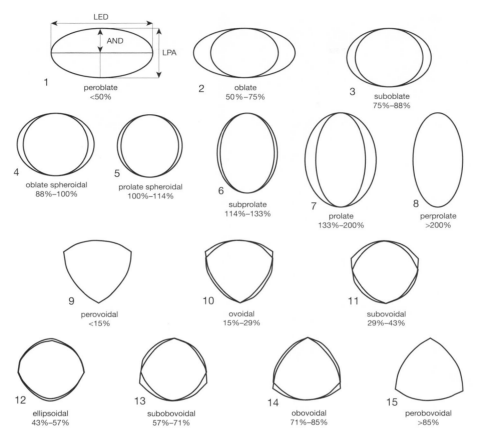

Fig. 12. Terminology of charophyte shapes; *1–8,* isopolar specimens, LPA/LED, ×100; *9–15,* anisopolar specimens, AND/LPA, ×100; *LPA,* length of polar axis; *LED,* largest equatorial diameter; *AND,* distance from apical pole to LED (adapted from Peck & Morales, 1966, text-fig. 2).

(*Atopochara, Globator, Flabellochara, Sycidium*).

General shape and number of convolutions.—Gyrogonites that have similar morphological characters are placed into the same species. To define gyrogonite shapes mathematically, Horn af Rantzien (1956b) has provided a useful set of descriptive terms based on the relationships of the **polar axis** (LPA, length) to the **equatorial diameter** (LED, width) (Fig. 12). The **isopolarity index** (ISI) represents the value of (LPA/LED) ×100. The number of **convolutions** visible on lateral views of gyrogonites and to a lesser extent their thickness are useful characters for definitions of species. A relationship exists between the number of convolutions and the general shape. Peroblate to oblate sphe-

roidal gyrogonites of *Gyrogona* and *Maedleriella* have a low number (4 to 8) of relatively thick convolutions (Fig. 66,*2a,2g,* Systematics, herein p. 126), whereas *Chara* has generally a prolate to perprolate shape and numerous, thin convolutions, often more than 10 (Fig. 64,*1a–1b,* Systematics, herein p. 122).

Dimensions.—Gyrogonites generally range from 200 µm to 2 mm maximum diameter. The giant of the group is the Devonian *Sycidium xizangense* Z. Wang, whose utricles reach 3.2 mm in diameter. As the process leading to calcification commences only after fertilization of the oosphere, all the gyrogonites correspond to the same mature stage, and the differences in dimensions must reflect natural populational variation.

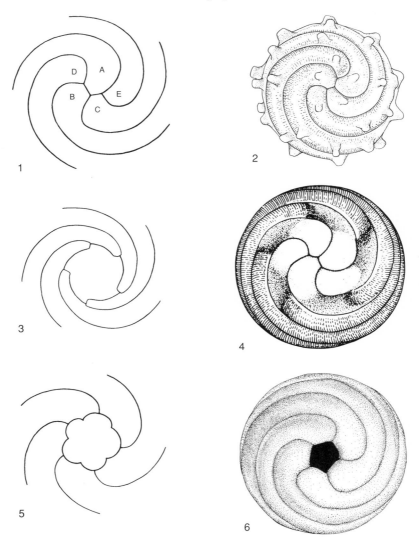

Fig. 13. *1,* Apical view showing junction line of spiral cells (Grambast, 1958, p. 34); *2, Maedleriella mangenoti* Grambast; apical view showing thin tubercles at ends of spiral cells, ×70 (Grambast, 1957, fig. 4); *3,* pore of dehiscence of a Characeae in shape of a toothed wheel (Grambast, 1958, p. 201, fig. c); *4, Gyrogona lemani capitata* Grambast; apical view showing rosette in center, ×50 (Grambast & Grambast-Fessard, 1981, fig. 5b); *5,* pore of dehiscence of a Raskyellaceae in shape of a rose (Grambast, 1958, fig. d); *6,* apical pore of a Porocharaceae, ×50 (new).

Within a population of a given species the variation of dimensions has a Gaussian distribution provided the sample is large enough (>100 specimens) and chosen randomly from a larger population. Sampled gyrogonites from one or a few specimens, as can be measured in modern species, are expressed by non-Gaussian histograms reflecting individual allometric variation (Soulié-Märsche, 1989).

Apex.—The characters of the gyrogonite summit have great importance for the systematics of fossil charophytes as well as for extant charophytes: the primary subdivision of the living Characeae is based on the number of coronula cells (Fig. 6.3). The coronula is not preserved generally in fossil forms, but other features allow the assignment of fossil characean genera to subfamilies. Characters of the apex have revealed also their usefulness for distinguishing taxa of various ranks (GRAMBAST, 1956a, 1958; HORN AF RANTZIEN, 1959b; FEIST & GRAMBAST-FESSARD, 1982).

Characeae.—**Junction line:** The spiral cells are contiguous at the gyrogonite apex. The junction consists of a broken line (Fig. 13.1) where one of the spiral cells (A) is in connection with the four others: two (B and C) are contiguous to three cells, and two (D and E) are adjacent to only two cells (GRAMBAST, 1958; MASLOV 1966). In some genera (e.g., *Nitellopsis* and *Gyrogona*) the junction line may be hidden by the voluminous nodules at the spiral apical ends, but it corresponds to the same basic pattern.

Periapical and apical differentiation: The periapical region corresponds to the dehiscence zone during germination. At this level the spiral cells generally become narrow or thinner. This differentiation delimits the so-called apical part. When convex, the apical part is called a **rose** or **rosette**. The apical ends of the spirals may bear more or less developed apical nodules that are either isolated or coalescent. For example, nodules are convex, massive, and jointed in *Gyrogona lemani capitata* GRAMBAST (Fig. 13.4), or thin and prominent, similar to those ornamenting the lateral parts of the spirals in *Maedleriella mangenoti* GRAMBAST (Fig. 13.2).

The characters of the apical part of the gyrogonite are useful to determine subdivisions in the family Characeae, which includes half the described charophyte genera (see Systematics section, herein p. 119).

Pore of dehiscence: In a characean population some specimens with an apical opening subsequent to germination are found together with closed gyrogonites. The breaking off of the apical part leaves an aperture in the shape of a regularly toothed wheel that is characteristic of the family (Fig. 13.3).

Coronula cells: Only a few coronula cells have been reported so far in fossil Characeae:

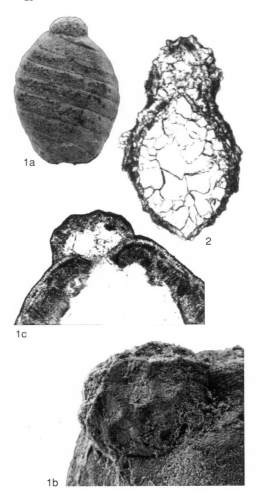

FIG. 14. Coronula cells; *1a–c, Feistiella* sp., El Koubbat, Morocco, Paleocene (new); *a,* specimen with coronula surmounting apex, ×35; *b,* detail showing 3 coronula cells, ×120; *c,* section of same specimen showing apical pore surmounted by coronula cells, ×75; *2, Microchara vestita* CASTEL; longitudinal section showing junction of spiral cells at apex, surmounted by coronula cells, lower Eocene, France, ×100 (Castel, 1969, fig. 5).

in *Chara* (e.g., *C. sausari* SAHNI & RAO; Fig. 10.7) and *Microchara* (e.g., *M. vestita* CASTEL; Fig. 14.2).

Raskellaceae.—In this family, the apex is closed by an operculum made of five supplementary apical cells that leaves, after it falls off, a dehiscence opening in the shape of a rosette with rounded lobes (GRAMBAST, 1957) (Fig. 13.5). In *Saportanella,* the apical opercular cells are in the prolongation of the spiral cells (Fig. 62,*1b,* Systematics, herein p. 118), but in *Raskyella* the two kinds of cells alternate (Fig. 13.5).

Forms with an apical pore always open.—In numerous fossil forms (Sycidiales, Moellerinales, and, among Charales, the Porocharaceae and Clavatoraceae) the calcified spiral cells are interrupted at the periphery of the apex, leaving an opening varying in shape and size according to different taxa. Its diameter is generally smaller than in the family Characeae. The pore of these ancient forms represents the dehiscence opening that, during life, must have been obstructed by an organic, uncalcified part that is generally not fossilized (CROFT, 1952). Gyrogonites with a flat summit generally have a relatively wide apical pore of various shapes: star shaped (e.g., *Stomochara moreyi,* Fig. 50,*1b,* Systematics, herein p. 102), rounded (e.g., *Feistiella bijuescencis* SCHUDACK, Fig. 50,*2b,* Systematics, herein p. 102) or rose shaped (e.g., *Porochara douzensis* (FEIST & GRAMBAST-FESSARD) SCHUDACK, Fig. 50,*3c,* Systematics, herein p. 102). The apical pore is smaller in the forms with an apical neck (e.g., *Leonardosia langei* SOMMER, Fig. 52,*3a,* Systematics, herein p. 105).

Coronula cells: *Karpinskya* (family Trochiliscaceae) has seven to ten coronula cells corresponding in number and position with the spiral cells that form an erect broad ring around the large apical pore (Fig. 46,*1b,* Systematics, herein p. 96). In only one instance has a coronula been found preserved in a member of the family Porocharaceae (Fig. 14.1).

Base.—**Basal pore:** Spiral cells are not joined at the base of the gyrogonite; their terminal ends delimit a pentagonal space, the basal pore, which is closed to the interior by the basal plate. The basal pore may be superficial at the same level as the external surface of the spirals (e.g., in *Peckisphaera verticillata* (PECK) GRAMBAST; Fig. 74,*1b,* Systematics, herein p. 138) or at the bottom of a funnel made of the truncation of the spirals (e.g., in *Amblyochara begudiana* GRAMBAST; Fig. 64,*2c,* Systematics, herein p. 122).

Basal plate.—In the fructification of living as well as fossil charophytes, the basal orifice is closed by a pentagonal piece termed the basal plate (Fig. 15). GRAMBAST (1956b) has shown that this element corresponded to the sister cell of the oosphere and that its morphology is useful in the characterization of genera and species. The basal plate is simple when comprising only one piece in the Characeae subfamily Charoideae, *Aclistochara* excepted; it is multipartite (Fig. 15.1) when comprising two or three pieces in the Characeae subfamily Nitelloideae, *Sphaerochara* excepted, as well as in such Porocharaceae as *Porochara, Latochara,* and some *Stellatochara* species. The multipartite basal plates are generally relatively thin (e.g., *Tolypella*), whereas the thickness varies considerably in the simple basal plates. When the calcification is limited to its upper face in contact with the oospore, the basal plate is very thin as in *Nitellopsis* and *Harrisichara* (Fig. 15.2); in contrast, the basal plate can be higher than wide (e.g., *Gyrogona lamarcki* GRAMBAST; Fig. 15.3*a*) or nearly as high as wide (e.g., *Gyrogona medicaginula* LAMARCK; Fig. 15.3*b*). In *Rhabdochara* (Fig. 15.6), the basal plate is conical with a hollow lower face. In *Chara* (Fig. 15.5), the height is typically greater than half the width. In *Sphaerochara,* the basal plate, in the form of a short column, has an upper face that is rounded and pentagonal; lateral faces are slightly concave, and the lower face is stellate and visible from the exterior (Fig. 15.4).

Enveloping cells.—**Orientation and number of spiral cells:** The orientation of the enveloping cells of the gyrogonite is the feature on which the subdivisions of higher rank are founded: they are dextrally spiralled in the order Moellerinales and sinistrally spiraled in the order Charales. Their number is significant for families; initially high (up to 13), it is reduced to 5 in the upper Carboniferous (see section on Evolutionary History, herein p. 60).

Calcification.—Except for ornamentation, which is unknown in modern species, the structure of the enveloping cells is quite comparable in extant and fossil forms. All types of calcification occur in fossils.

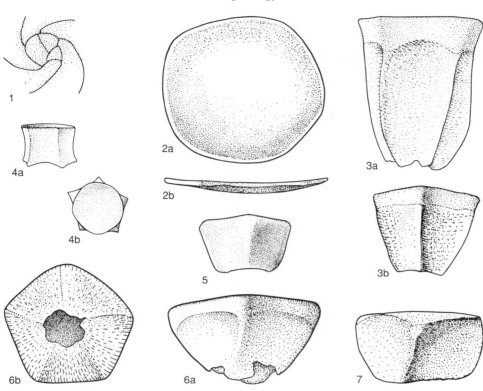

Fig. 15. Different types of basal plates; *1, Tolypella* sp., multipartite basal plate, upper side, ×280 (Grambast, 1956a, fig. 8); *2a–b, Harrisichara tuberculata* (LYELL) GRAMBAST, *a,* lower side, *b,* lateral side, ×250 (Grambast, 1957, fig. 2a–2b); *3a, Gyrogona lamarcki* GRAMBAST (*Brachychara archiaci*), lateral view, ×190 (Grambast, 1956a, fig. 5); *3b, Gyrogona (Brachychara) medicaginula* LAMARCK, lateral view, ×190 (Grambast, 1956a, fig. 4); *4a–b, Sphaerochara granulifera* (HEER) MÄDLER, lateral and lower sides, ×190 (Grambast, 1956a, fig. 6–7); *5, Chara hispida* L., lateral view, ×190 (Grambast, 1956a, fig. 2); *6a–b, Rhabdochara langeri* (ETTINGS) MÄDLER, hollow basal plate; *a,* lateral view, *b,* basal view, ×250 (Grambast, 1957, fig. 7a, 7c); *7, Feistiella (Porochara) globosa* (GRAMBAST & GUTIÉRREZ) SCHUDACK, lateral view, ×210 (Grambast & Gutiérrez, 1977, fig. 2a).

Calcification with parallel lamination (Fig. 16.3) is the most frequent. The Y-calcification (Fig. 16.2) is known in the halophilic genera *Lamprothamnium, Porochara,* and *Stellatochara.* The typical calcification of the extant Nitelloideae occurs in a more complete state in their fossil representatives. In *Sphaerochara ulmensis* (STRAUB) GRAMBAST, from the Oligocene of southern France (Fig. 16.1), the lamellar endocalcine is surmounted by a crest that must represent the ectocalcine. It is made of rows of crystals that are borne by thin lamellae diverging from points localized in the endocalcine. These crystals weather easily, giving a characteristic powdery aspect to the spiral surface.

According to the degree of calcification, which may vary within a population, the spiral cells may be concave, planar, or convex, providing gyrogonites of different outlines; but intermediate specimens allow one to recognize the homogeneity of a taxon. In such instances, the diagnostic criteria are those of the most calcified specimens.

Ornamentation.—Ornamentation consists of reticula, tubercles, punctuations, rods, and midcellular crests that are continuous or tend to split into individual nodules (Fig. 17). A specimen may be ornamented partly, usually at the upper part of the gyrogonite, as in *Nitellopsis (Tectochara) thaleri* (CASTEL & GRAMBAST) GRAMBAST &

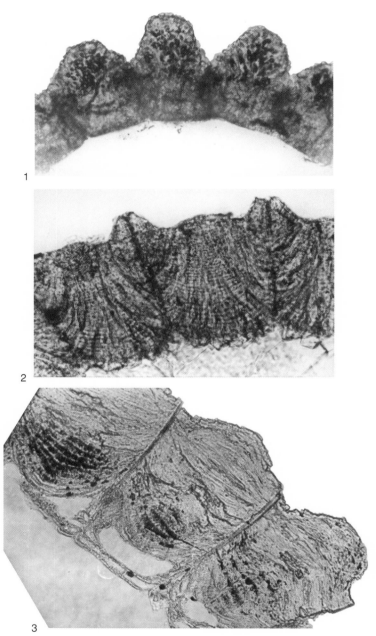

FIG. 16. Types of calcification in fossil gyrogonites in axial longitudinal sections; *1,* nitelloid type of calcification, *Sphaerochara ulmensis* (STRAUB) GRAMBAST, lower Oligocene, France, ×280; *2,* Y-calcification, *Porochara douzensis* (FEIST & GRAMBAST-FESSARD) SCHUDACK, Middle Jurassic, France, ×450; *3,* parallel lamination, *Nitellopsis (Tectochara) meriani* (L. & N. GRAMBAST) GRAMBAST & SOULIÉ-MÄRSCHE, upper Oligocene, France, ×310 (new).

SOULIÉ-MÄRSCHE, where this feature is one of the identifying criteria of the species. On the other hand, a species may include both typically ornamented and completely smooth specimens (e.g., *Rhabdochara praelangeri* CASTEL). Such examples have led GRAMBAST (1957) to recognize only a limited systematic value in the characters of the ornamentation.

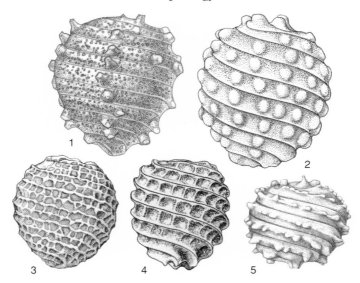

FIG. 17. Different types of ornamentation; *1, Harrisichara sparnacensis* GRAMBAST; small punctuations and tubercles, ×40 (adapted from Grambast, 1977a, pl. II,*3a*); *2, Sephanochara compta* GRAMBAST; tubercles, ×40 (Grambast, 1959b, fig. 3a); *3, Peckichara cancellata* GRAMBAST; reticulum, ×40 (Grambast, 1971, fig. 12a); *4, Rhabdochara praelangeri* CASTEL; rods, ×40 (new); *5, Maedleriella cristellata* GRAMBAST; midcellular crest tending to subdivide into tubercles, ×50 (Grambast, 1977a, fig. 11a).

We see below (in the section on Classification, herein p. 83) that opinions on this may have differed fundamentally in the past. In general, ornamentation is characteristic of species and more rarely of such genera as *Harrisichara* and *Maedleriella,* whose representatives nearly always have well-developed ornamentation. Among fossils, ornamentation has been reported only in the families Raskyellaceae and Characeae.

Oospore membrane.—Remains of oospores are relatively common in the fossil record, but preservation of the ornamentation of the sporostine is exceptional. Silicified rock (chert and flint) and gypsum are the most favorable for preservation of this organic membrane (Fig. 18). The sporostine appears as a translucent, brown or black layer lining the calcified (or secondarily silicified) gyrogonite wall. In noncalcified species, the oospores are isolated in the rock. Different types of ornamentation have been reported from fossil oospores. Among oospores inside gyrogonites, there is the granulate type in the Devonian *Trochiliscus podolicus* CROFT, where granules occur together with crateriform wounds (Fig. 18.4), and in the

Oligocene Characeae *Stephanochara ungeri (Chara escheri)* (CROFT, 1952); the vermiculate type in the Oligocene *Rhabdochara praelangeri* CASTEL (Fig. 18.1), in which the vermiculations look much more intricate than in the extant *Nitella syncarpa* that also has this type of ornamentation; and the tuberculate perforated type in an Oligocene *Chara* species similar to the extant *C. zeylanica* (SOULIÉ-MÄRSCHE, 1989) (Fig 18.2). Among oospores isolated in the sediments, the well-preserved oospores of the Jurassic *Nitellites,* occurring in chert, have a fine reticulate ornamentation very similar, if not identical, to that of the extant *Nitella tenuissima* (HORN AF RANTZIEN, 1957) (Fig. 18.3).

These few examples show that the ornamentation of fossil oospores is relatively diverse; however, the scarcity of well-preserved remains does not allow presently the use of this character in recognition of fossil species.

Utricle

The utricle is an envelope made of vegetative appendages investing the gyrogonite. The most complex structure occurs in the

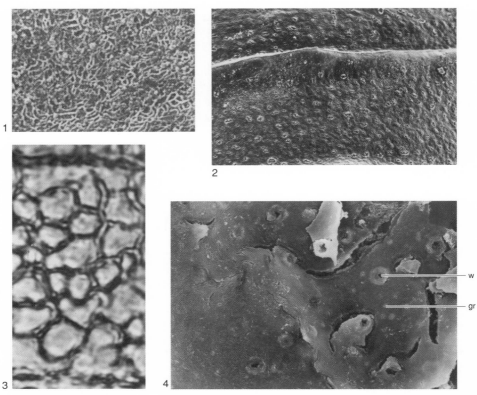

FIG. 18. Fossil oospore sculpturing; *1, Rhabdochara praelangeri* CASTEL; vermiculate sculpture, upper Oligocene, Marseille, southern France, ×600 (Feist & Grambast-Fessard, 1991, fig. 4ac); *2, Chara* sp. tuberculate perforated sculpture, upper Oligocene, Portel, southern France, ×800 (new); *3, Nitellites sahnnii* HORN AF RANTZIEN; reticulate sculpture; Middle Jurassic–Upper Jurassic, Rajmahal Hills, Bihar, India, ×2500 (Horn af Rantzien, 1957, pl. II, fig. 2); *4, Trochiliscus podolicus* CROFT; granulate sculpture, Lower Devonian, Ukraine, *gr,* granules, *w,* wounds, ×900 (new).

Clavatoraceae Clavatoroideae and in the Sycidiales where the utricle is composed of three layers: an internal layer, smooth or made of thick nodules; a middle layer, represented by a system of canals; and an external layer, constituted by whorls of branchlets. The internal nodulose layer may be represented alone, with possibly a whorl of leaflets in the basal region of the utricle; this structure exists in the oldest Clavatoraceae (*Nodosoclavator*) as well as in the incompletely calcified, more complex utricles that have been named nodosoclavatoroid utricles by SCHUDACK (1989). The canals of the middle layer, which correspond to the cavities of long cells, originate in a basal chamber; they could have been occupied by a gas, which lightened the fructifications and could thus benefit their dispersion (GRAMBAST, 1966b). In the Clavatoraceae Atopocharoideae and in the Pinnoputamenaceae, the utricle has only the external layer, and the internal layer is reduced to an amorphous surface covering the gyrogonite, sometimes visible between the external whorls. The structure of the utricles in most Sycidiales is at present still incompletely known, but they seem to have a complexity similar to that of the Clavatoraceae Clavatoroideae; two layers are visible in *Trochiliscus podolicus* CROFT (Fig. 46,2*h,* Systematics, herein p. 96), and a system of canals occurs in *Sycidium xizangense* Z. WANG (Fig. 45*k,* Systematics, herein p. 95).

Inside utricles, gyrogonites are preserved only rarely. The presence of gyrogonite cells may be recognizable in thin sections (Fig. 55,*2b,* Systematics, herein p. 109), but these do not provide information on gyrogonite morphology. The orientation and number of gyrogonite cells are detectable in casts on the internal utricular surface (Fig. 58,*2e,* Systematics, herein p. 114) or on the surface of the internal mold of the oospore and egg (MARTIN-CLOSAS, 1988, fig. 12). These observations were made in the Clavatoraceae. For the present, the exact gyrogonite morphology of the Sycidiales is still unknown.

The external layer of the utricle in the Clavatoraceae has undergone a high degree of diversification, which has been illustrated in particular by GRAMBAST (1974) and MARTIN-CLOSAS (1996).

The morphology of the utricle in Sycidiales and Clavatoraceae is relatively well documented. In contrast, very little about its nature and origin is known from the fossil record. Data from morphogenesis studies in extant species give some information on the process by which the utricles may have been formed in the geological past. After placing female buds of *Chara vulgaris* LINNAEUS in an artificial growth medium, DUCREUX (1975, p. 270, pl. VIII,*3*) observed that the oogonia have two whorls of spiral cells, the external being composed of loose cells and the internal forming the oogonial wall (see Fig. 63, Systematics herein, p. 120); the spirals eventually become ramified and bear antheridia. DUCREUX (1975) noticed that these modifications recall the Cretaceous *Perimneste-Atopochara* phylogenetic lineage (GRAMBAST, 1967), where the utricle cells of ancestral species are ramified and carry antheridia at the nodes of the ramifications. Supernumerary whorls and unusual features never appear during the normal development of living species; however, the occurrence of these features in culture suggests potentialities that are expressed only in special conditions. The laboratory experiments conducted by DUCREUX (1975) are evidence of the developmental remnants of utricular cells in Characeae. The morphology of *Lagynophora* STACHE and *Coenoclavator* WANG & LU may indicate that this family has already expressed the tendency to develop utricles. This observation might indicate that possible development of a utricle is a phenomenon inherent in Charophyta that could have developed at any time and could presumably also develop in the future.

Antheridia

Antheridia are not calcified, but antheridial casts of some genera have been recorded. These casts have internal features quite similar to those of the extant species (M. FEIST & R. FEIST, 1997). In *Pinnoputamen* sp. (Fig. 48*e,* Systematics, herein p. 99) and *Perimneste horrida* HARRIS (Fig. 60*b,* Systematics, herein p. 116), the antheridia lie on branches of the external layer of the utricle, whereas in *Diectochara andica* MUSACCHIO (Fig. 59,*2b,* Systematics, herein p. 115) they occur below the fructifications, as in many living forms.

Chiralization

Chirality, the pattern of spiraling of structures around vegetative axes, has been recognized in Charophyta as a fundamental feature, not only of oogonia and gyrogonites but also of thallus morphology and architecture in general. SOULIÉ-MÄRSCHE (1999) stated that the first-formed axillary buds of branchlets are arranged in a helical pattern toward the apex and around the axis. The divergence angle between two successive buds is 144°; the phyllotaxis index is thus 2/5th, the same as that often encountered in land plants. MARTIN-CLOSAS, BOSCH, and SERRA-KIEL (1999) modelled biomechanically the Early Cretaceous *Globator* species and concluded that spiralization tends to accentuate the globular shape of utricles by increasing the resistance of the calcified wall to internal pressure caused by the accumulation of reserves. They hypothesized that the resulting accumulation of storage material devoted to supplying young germlings has been a driving force in charophyte evolution.

MINERALIZATION

Monique Feist

[Université Montpellier II, France]

MINERAL COMPOSITION

Charophytes are aquatic and metabolize CO_2 dissolved in water by photosynthesis. Being fixed by rhizoids to the bottoms of lakes, they absorb HCO_3^- and minerals (mainly $CaCO_3$) from the substratum. Calcification of the oosporangium is initiated after fertilization by a process yet to be elucidated. Calcification starts at the internal surface of the spiral cells on the adaxial and lateral faces, sometimes at the surface of the ectosporostine (SOULIÉ-MÄRSCHE, 1989; LEITCH, 1989) and continues as long as the cell is living. Timing of maturation of the oosporangium is influenced by altitude and latitude and generally completed by middle to late summer. Calcite is the major constituent of the calcareous shell, although acid etching shows very thin organic lamellae (3 to 5 μm in thickness) between the layers of calcite. Chemical analysis of the whole organism (BATHURST, 1971; STRAUSS & LEPOINT, 1966) as well as microprobe and X-ray analysis of oosporangia have revealed traces of several additional elements, ions, and compounds: magnesium, strontium, silica, chloride, and barium. In some species that live in saline environments, the percentage of magnesium can reach one percent of the calcified oosporangia (SOULIÉ-MÄRSCHE, 1989). Diagenesis of the mineral composition of fossil forms has not yet been studied in detail and may be related broadly to the disappearance of the organic parts and to diagenetic processes at work in the surrounding rock.

ISOTOPIC COMPOSITION

JONES and others (1996) established that the composition of oxygen and possibly carbon isotopes of living characean gyrogonites are in equilibrium with the surrounding water; consequently, these shells can be used to reconstruct the geochemical properties of the ancient water bodies in which they grew. In isotopic analyses, however, account should be taken of the relationships to the substratum and the fact that gyrogonites calcify during the highest temperatures of the year (i.e., the time window of JONES & others, 1996).

There have been few investigations of the isotopic composition of fossil charophytes. BERGER (1990) and BECKER, PICOT, and BERGER (2002) analyzed the variations in stable isotopes of ^{13}C and ^{18}O in late Cenozoic charophytes of western Switzerland (Fig. 19). According to J.-P. BERGER (personal communication, January 2001), an isotope excursion lower than 2‰ is not significant for paleoecological or paleoclimatical interpretation; the general covariance between $\delta^{13}C$ and $\delta^{18}O$ excursions is typical for closed lakes, and the important excursions observed in the isotopic record are probably due to an increase of seasonality during the Cenozoic, the negative values indicating a more humid period. This seasonality could have resulted from different climatic, paleogeographic, and tectonic events occurring during this time. Also, the erosion of marine Mesozoic carbonate could produce more positive excursions in the $\delta^{13}C$. The isotopic curves for

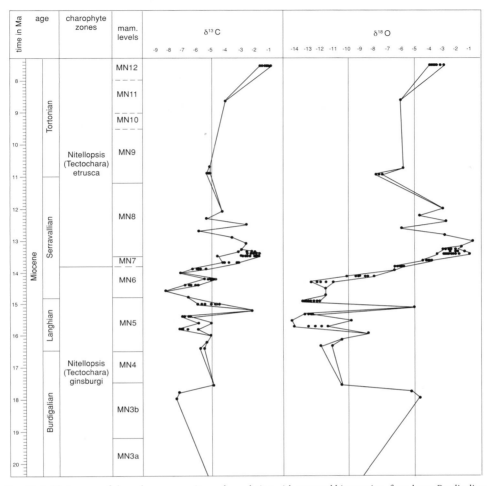

FIG. 19. Stable isotopes of charophyte gyrogonites and correlation with mammal biozonation, from lower Burdigalian to upper Tortonian; *mam. levels,* mammal standard levels, after Schmidt-Kittler, 1987 (adapted from Becker, Picot, & Berger, 2002).

the time interval between early Burdigalian and late Tortonian show several warming and cooling phases that are correlated on the whole with the variations observed in oceanic DSDP records (WOODRUFF, SAVIN, & DOUGLAS, 1981). In particular a cold phase occurred approximately 12 Ma, which is thought to be related to the formation of the Antarctic ice cap. The latter correlations do not include consideration of the new calibration of the inferred geological time scale (BERGGREN & others, 1995).

TECHNIQUES FOR PREPARATION AND STUDY OF FOSSIL CHAROPHYTA

MONIQUE FEIST

[Université Montpellier II, France]

The first step in studying fossil charophytes is to release the gyrogonites from the matrix. One to five kilograms of sediment are necessary to obtain a high enough number of specimens to allow the study of populations, to make oriented thin sections, and for photography. Nondetrital lacustrine or nonmarine brackish-water deposits are the most likely to yield charophytes. The specific methods used for the treatment of charophytes are much the same as those used for other small fossils, the ostracodes in particular (SOHN, 1961).

RELEASE FROM MATRIX

Depending on the lithology, two different methods can be used to release charophytes from the matrix. Washing and sieving are used to extract charophytes from such loose sediment as argillaceous or lignitic marls. Found with charophytes are such various small fossils as foraminifers, molluscs, ostracodes, dinosaur eggshell fragments, microscopic teeth of mammals, and, rarely, seeds, conodonts, and scolecodonts. For one kilogram of sediment, 50 g of sodium carbonate (Na_2CO_3) and one liter of 30-percent hydrogen peroxide are required. The dry sediment is poured into a plastic jar, mixed with sodium carbonate, and covered with water. Add the hydrogen peroxide and allow the mixture to react for 12 to 48 hours. Sieve with running water, pouring the mixture through a set of three sieves of meshes 2 mm, 500 μm, and 150 μm. The sieves can be air dried or placed in a drying cupboard.

Well-preserved gyrogonites may be extracted from more indurated sediments such as marls and marly limestones by using copper sulfate. For 100 g of rock, 100 g of anhydrous copper sulfate, 250 ml of acetic acid, and 500 ml of ammonium hydroxide are needed. In a fume hood, mix a solution of acetic acid and copper sulfate in a glass jar two hours before use. Into the solution, place the completely dry rocks, cut into pieces approximately 1 cm in size. Let the mixture react for 12 to 24 hours until most of the limestone pieces have been dissolved. Neutralize the remaining solution with ammonium hydroxide, then wash and sieve with water.

Extremely hard, recrystalized limestones can be studied only with thin sections. These provide information as to the microfacies, which, in turn, furnishes ecological information but generally few details of gyrogonite morphology.

CONCENTRATION OF FOSSILS

Once the sediment has been washed and sieved, the charophytes can be concentrated by using a number of methods.

Kerosene can be used to eliminate the argillaceous fraction of the sediment. The dry sediment is soaked in kerosene. Once it is thoroughly impregnated, it is mixed with water and left to soak for 4 to 12 hours, then washed and sieved again. Some people prefer to use gasoline instead of kerosene, but because of the highly volatile, inflammable, heavy vapor and the consequent danger of fire or explosion, such work should be done out of doors or in a fume hood with a strong exhaust fan.

Bromoform, with a specific gravity of 2.8, is appropriate to separate gyrogonites from other sediment matrix. This procedure is to be used only in open air or using a fume hood. The dry sediment is poured into a fine-meshed sieve inside a large container without any trace of water. Bromoform is added. Then pure ethyl alcohol is added gradually until flotation of gyrogonites occurs. Gyrogonites are removed from the top of the liquid with a fine wire mesh.

To facilitate the picking process, the dry sediment is subdivided into similarly sized fractions by using a column of six metallic sieves. Generally, these sieves are 10 cm in diameter and their meshes range from 65 μm to 1.25 mm.

To bring about mechanical separation on an inclined plane, thin lines of sediment are placed around the periphery of a rectangular, flat container with shallow edges. By inclining and agitating the container, gyrogonites will roll down to the bottom where they can be collected with a wet brush. This procedure, which relies on the broadly spherical shape of the gyrogonites, is not appropriate for the angular utricles of the Clavataraceae.

Gyrogonites may also be picked from the sediment with a fine wet brush (number 00 to 1) at powers 5× to 40×, depending on their size. Charophytes may be stored in small plastic boxes or in hollowed slides.

CLEANING

Boiling in water with addition of a detergent removes argillaceous dust from the spirals. For hardened incrustations, a more efficient method is immersion in EDTA (ethylenediaminetetraacetic acid) disodium salt dihydrate followed by use of an ultrasonic cleaner. A six-percent solution is used for well-calcified specimens; a three-percent solution is used for fragile material. Gyrogonites are immersed for five minutes in the EDTA disodium salt dihydrate solution; a slight release of bubbles from the disaggregation of the crust indicates that the process is complete. The gyrogonites are then rinsed with freshwater and placed into an ultrasonic cleaner for three minutes (power 50W, frequency 40 kHz).

COLORATION

Coloration can be applied to the gyrogonite to enhance definition when viewed with a binocular microscope. An al-

cohol solution of methyl green outlines the external structures without covering them. In contrast, volatile correcting fluid mixed with alcohol, acetone, and chrysoidine covers the specimens entirely. The process is simple but delicate: a gyrogonite or a utricle is placed into a watch glass and covered with a drop of coloring liquid and shifted rapidly until dry. The liquid covers the hollows evenly with an orange coating and underlines the relief in red. This coloration, which was used for optical photography during the 1960s, is still useful for showing complex structures of clavatoracean utricles. An apex of *Septorella brachycera* GRAMBAST (Fig. 56,*1b*, Systematics, herein p. 111) provides an example of this coloration.

PREPARING THIN SECTIONS OF GYROGONITES

Axial sections are used most often. They provide valuable information about the calcified wall and the basal plate; more rarely, when revealing the structure of the summit, sections allow a taxonomic assignment, generally at the family level (CASTEL, 1969). Axial sections also allow examination of the oospore wall, if the latter has been preserved.

The procedure involves embedding the specimen in plastic. It is then thinned on both sides by polishing in the selected orientation. The product used for the embedding is a clear epoxy resin. A mixture of resin and hardener is put into a container, preferably of cardboard, and stirred for two minutes on a hot plate. The specimen is fastened to the external side of a small plastic box whose borders are fringed with paraffin or wax from a candle; the specimen is then covered with a few drops of the mixture and left to polymerize.

To polish the specimen, first remove the wax fringe with a razor blade. The resin block including the specimen is abraded directly on the lapidary disk with 600-mesh grit, during which the process is carefully monitored using a binocular microscope. The abrasion should stop when the level of the axial plane of the gyrogonite is nearly reached. Then, a drop of the plastic mixture is applied to the ground surface of a glass slide, and another drop is applied to the worn side of the specimen. The specimen is then attached to the slide, and the solution is allowed to polymerize. Then the second side of the section is ground down and covered with Canada balsam or with the resin mixture.

OBSERVATION AND PHOTOGRAPHY
REFLECTED LIGHT

Charophytes are usually examined with a binocular microscope using reflected light at 20× to 100×. Gyrogonites are held in position on a glass slide smeared with an adhesive (rubber cement). The use of glue or gum tragacanth, which seeps inextricably into the spiral sutures, is not recommended.

The basal plate may be extracted by crushing the gyrogonite carefully between two glass slides. The basal plate is recognizable by its pentagonal shape among the fragments of spiral cells.

Photographs may be taken directly with the microscope at low magnification. Use of a camera with a tube and bellows between the objective and the camera provides higher magnifications. Three or four lamps or a neon ring provides adequate light.

TRANSMITTED LIGHT

Thin sections of rocks or of isolated gyrogonites may be examined with transmitted light at powers 50× to 500×.

SCANNING ELECTRON MICROSCOPY (SEM)

For charophytes, the SEM allows observations and photography of general views at magnifications from 30× to 200× and details of structure at up to about 20,000×. Specimens are glued to a stub, preferably with a metallic glue that holds the specimen in position and provides good electronic imaging. The metallic coating, whatever medium is used (gold, gold-palladium, platinum), must be thick enough (150 to 200 Å) to avoid the electronic charge inherent in the spherical shape of gyrogonites.

MEASUREMENTS

An ocular micrometer can be used with magnifications of 25×, 40×, or 50× to determine gyrogonite dimensions (see Fig. 12.1) as well as the number of spiral cells and the coefficient of spirality (DEMIN, 1967). Tests of the reliability of the methods of measurements (SOULIÉ-MÄRSCHE, 1989) show that variation due to observer error is lower than those due to the capabilities of the equipment. For example, a difference of five to six percent was observed in a test of four methods for a population of 100 specimens that were 530 µm in mean diameter. Dimensions are important but not of prime significance for distinguishing species, and a margin of error should be considered when comparing numerical data from different charophyte populations.

ECOLOGY AND PALEOECOLOGY

Monique Feist and Micheline Guerlesquin

[Université Montpellier II, France; and Université Catholique de l'Ouest, Angers, France]

The habitats of the Characeae are mainly freshwater, but some species successfully colonize brackish lagoons, and a few species inhabit the Baltic Sea. The species of the family Characeae are fundamentally aquatic: apart from the oospores and gyrogonites, which can survive desiccation, the only forms that survive as a whole organism when aerially exposed are those that develop on damp ground in special conditions. The thallus of *Nitella hyalina* (De Candolle) Agardh is enclosed in a mucilage that maintains sufficient moisture, and *"N. terrestris"* (a *Nitella* species whose taxonomic status is still unclear) grows in the very high atmospheric humidity of the equatorial part of India (Iyengar, 1958).

Characeae are pioneer species, colonizing environments lacking vegetation, whether new or reworked, before the development of higher plant communities. Subjected to competition from the phanerogams, most of them regress to refuges on open beaches or even disappear from a locality. The positively phototactic fertile tips of branches grow toward the water surface where the orange to red color of the mature gametangia is visually striking and may provide some protection from ultraviolet light.

Regarded as annual, the Characeae possess a vegetative thallus that may, under special conditions, persist during unfavorable seasons. Each individual produces a large number of oogonia and antheridia (often more than a hundred). After fertilization in water, the oospores mature, then break off and fall to the bottom, where they germinate after a period of dormancy. The germinating oospores give rise to a rather dense population, forming a carpet of benthic vegetation. Similarly, the gyrogonites of fossil species, which correspond to the calcified parts of the oogonia, are found in abundance in sediments, allowing statistical estimates of ancient populations.

The Characeae, which are fixed by very thin rhizoids, colonize preferentially quiet waters. In slow currents (5 to 6 m per minute), thalli develop into spindles, which are characterized by the elongation of the internodes and phylloids. Habitats where Characeae grow may be permanent or temporary but must be moist for at least a few months: lakes, salt ponds, rice fields, pisciculture ponds, lagoons, chotts, and water bodies of all sizes. The habitats must not be subject to drainage during the growing period of the protonemata or just before fertilization. The germination potential of some Characeae persists for several years [e.g., *Chara braunii* Gmelin, *Nitella syncarpa* (Thuiller) Chevallier, and *Lamprothamnium succinctum* (A. Braun) R. D. Wood], but dried soil with characean spores must not be subject to extensive mixing, which may bury the oospores too deeply for germination.

WATER QUALITY

Well-mixed waters with high levels of oxygen and carbon dioxide provide the best conditions for respiration and assimilation and thus increase development of the thallus. Moreover, the complex structure of the thallus favors the sedimentation of suspended particles, resulting in clarification of the water. Due to their large biomass, Characeae also contribute to the maintenance of water quality. Most species develop in low-nutrient waters that are oligotrophic, mesotrophic, or slightly eutrophic (Imahori, 1954).

SUBSTRATUM

Characeae prefer less dense soils (sand, silt, or mud) that rhizoids can penetrate

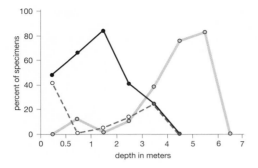

FIG. 20. Vertical range of *Chara globularis* var. *aspera* (DETHARDING *ex* WILLDENOW) R. D. WOOD (*solid line*), *Chara vulgaris* f. *contraria* (A. BRAUN *ex* KÜTZING) R. D. WOOD (*dashed line*), and *Nitellopsis obtusa* (DESVAUX in LOISELEUR-DESLONGCHAMPS) J. GROVES (*gray line*) in Nors Sø Lake, Denmark (adapted from Olsen, 1944, fig. 36).

more easily. They also root in interstices between stones or gravel or at the bottom of artificial basins covered with a thin film of silt. They do not grow on rocks.

DEPTH

Most Characeae grow in shallow water, between 0.1 and 10 m deep (Fig. 20), but some species are able to survive at greater depth, such as *Nitellopsis obtusa* (DESVAUX in LOISELEUR-DESLONGCHAMPS) J. GROVES, which ranges from 1 to 30 m (STROEDE, 1933). Deep-dwelling species often grow and form fructifications down to 10 meters depth late in the season. In deep zones, also carpeted by a few species of *Nitella,* individuals remain sterile and persist by vegetative multiplication, as occurs, for example, with *N. flexilis* (L.) AGARDH in Pavin Lake in France (HY, 1913).

LIGHT

Quality and quantity of light affect vegetative growth, especially internode length and phylloid development, and sexual reproduction (development of the gametangia). Light also affects the distribution of species according to depth, resulting in vertical and horizontal zonation of vegetation belts. Finally, in terms of fructification development,

species may be classified into short-day (vernal), long-day (estival), or indifferent species. Light largely controls photosynthesis and influences calcification, according to the reaction:

$$Ca^{++} + 2HCO_3^- \rightleftharpoons CaCO_3 + CO_2 + H_2O$$

(IMAHORI, 1954). The fact that light intensity is a function of latitude explains why most calcified species occur in temperate and subtropical climatic zones.

TEMPERATURE

Some species of Characeae are restricted in climatic zones and are evidently influenced by temperature. Temperature affects significantly both germination and development. Generally in temperate areas, Characeae occur in waters of about 12 °C to 26 °C, but in tropical areas they may survive in waters as warm as 30 °C. Three species grow and fructify in the cold waters (not more than 16 °C) of Grande Terre, the largest of the Kerguelen Islands (CORILLION, 1982). Thalli cannot withstand sudden temperature variations, although the species living on the fringes of lakes or ponds are exposed to nychthemeral variations, often over 10 °C in summer, or seasonal variations. Increased water temperature that results in evaporation yields an increased concentration of soluble substances, as well as a decrease in concentration of dissolved gases. As calcification is related to temperature, calcified species prefer biotopes in temperate zones. In contrast, uncalcified species, such as those from the Kerguelen Islands, can tolerate very cold water.

SALINITY

Salinity is thought to be the major factor governing distribution of charophytes (STROEDE, 1933). Characeae are mainly lacustrine, but some species tolerate continental brackish waters. In the Baltic Sea, Characeae occur in areas where the percentage of NaCl is not higher than 30 g Cl liter[-1] (Fig. 21), approximately 30 psu (practical salinity units; UNESCO, 1981).

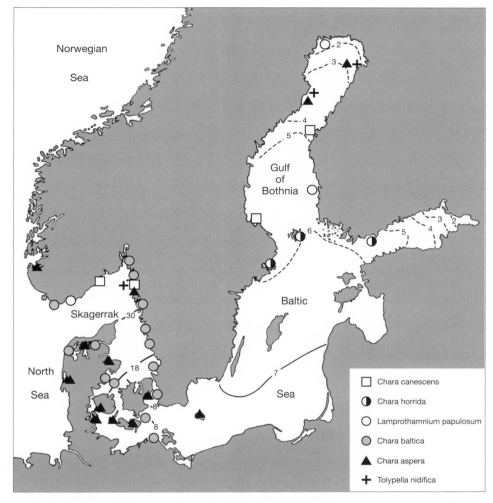

FIG. 21. Distribution of 6 Characeae species in littoral zones of Scandinavia, in function of salinity; *broken lines,* annual isohaline; *solid lines,* August isohalines; *numbers* refer to salinity in ‰ (adapted from Olsen, 1944; with data from Langangen, 1974, and Blindow & Langangen, 1995).

According to their salinity tolerance, the Characeae fall into four categories (WINTER, SOULIÉ-MÄRSCHE, & KIRST, 1996.

(1) Strict halophobes or obligatory fresh-water species. Salinity 0 to 0.5 psu. This group includes most *Nitella* and a few *Chara.*

(2) Freshwater to brackish-water tolerant species. Salinity 0.5 to 5 psu. Most Characeae occur in these waters: numerous *Chara,* rare *Nitella, Tolypella glomerata* (DESVAUX in LOISELEUR-DESLONGCHAMPS) R. D. WOOD, *Nitellopsis obtusa* (DESVAUX in

LOISELEUR-DESLONGCHAMPS) J. GROVES, and *Lychnothamnus barbatus* (MEYEN) LEON-HARDI.

(3) Brackish-water species. Salinity 5 to 16 psu. Some *Chara, Lamprothamnium papulosum* (WALLROTH) J. GROVES, *Tolypella nidifica* (MÜLLER) A. BRAUN, and oligo-brackish species that withstand brackish waters [*Nitella hyalina* (DE CANDOLLE) AGARDH].

(4) Strict halophilic species. Salinity 16 to 26 psu. *L. papulosum, L. papulosum* f.

macropogon (A. Braun) R. D. Wood, *Chara globularis* var. *aspera* f. *galioides* (De Candolle) R. D. Wood; tolerance of 69 psu has been reported for *Lamprothamnium,* which is the most halophilic extant genus; however, even if the charophyte can remain apparently healthy, photosynthesis and sexual reproduction are inhibited at such salinities (Burne, Bauld, & DeDecker, 1980).

The salinity tolerance of the Characeae has been related to a physiological mechanism that regulates turgor pressure (Winter & Kirst, 1991); there is evidence of a pumping mechanism involving diverse salts, including sodium and potassium chloride (Hutchinson, 1975; Winter, Soulié-Märsche, & Kirst, 1996).

ALKALINITY

Charophytes thrive in pH generally from 5.5 to more than 9. Acid waters with pH as low as 3 containing thriving populations of *Chara fibrosa* (de Candolle) Agardh and *Nitella hyalina,* however, have been reported from rehabilitated mining excavations in Western Australia (Melanie Ward, personal communication, 1996). According to their preferences, Characeae may be categorized into three groups.

Acidophilic: mainly *Nitella* and rare *Chara* species, in waters from pH 5 to 7.

Neutrophilic: mainly *Chara, Nitellopsis,* rare *Nitella.*

Alkaline: *Chara, Tolypella, Lamprothamnium.*

Some species tolerate wide ranges of pH, for example, from 5 to 9.5 for *Nitella translucens* (Persoon) Agardh in Denmark (Olsen, 1944).

CONTENT OF LIME IN WATER

The encrustation of the cell walls by calcium carbonate is related to the calcium concentration of the water. For example, *Chara* starts to develop between 15 to 60 mg/l CaO depending on the species and tolerates 200 mg/l CaO to 400 mg/l CaO. Beyond 2,000 mg/l CaO it stops developing. Quantitative analysis and use of X-rays show that the ions are found mainly as insoluble combinations, thus limiting their toxic effect (Walter-Lévy & Strauss, 1974). For uncalcified taxa, the optimal values of hardness are between 0 and 200 mg/l CaO.

MODES OF LIFE OF FOSSIL GENERA

Evidence from the fossil record shows that, like the modern species, fossil charophytes inhabited continental fresh- and brackish waters as well as possibly shallow, low-salinity, sheltered marine habitats. The earliest charophytes known from the upper Silurian and Lower Devonian of Laurentia already occupied different habitats. The Ludlowian Hamra Beds of Gotland, which have yielded *Moellerina laufeldi* Conkin, were deposited in shallow water at the end of the regressive Lau cycle (Jeppsson, 1998), whereas the slightly younger *Praesycidium,* which is associated with land plants in the Ludlowian of Podolia (T. A. Ishchenko & A. A. Ishchenko, 1982), seems to have occupied a freshwater habitat.

FOSSIL GENERA WITH EXTANT REPRESENTATIVES

On the whole, extant genera have modes of life similar to those of their fossil representatives. Fossil *Lamprothamnium,* which are generally found in Upper Cretaceous–Holocene brackish-water deposits, share the same ecological preferences as modern, congeneric species.

Among the Nitelloideae, *Tolypella* and *Sphaerochara* seem to have tolerated a wide range of salinities, like their living descendants. *Tolypella* occurs frequently in brackish-water deposits, such as the Maastrichtian Prince Creek Formation at Ocean Point, Alaska, which has yielded *T. grambasti arctica* (Feist & Brouwers, 1990). The Paleocene *Sphaerochara edda* Soulié-Märsche occurs in brackish and lacustrine facies (Riveline,

1986). The occurrence of *T. caudata* in the freshwater upper Eocene Limnäenmergel of the Rhine graben (BREUER & FEIST, 1986) is an exception.

Chara has been reported from a number of different biotopes. The ecological preferences of *Lychnothamnus* seem comparable for extant and fossil forms, as shown by the lacustrine upper Miocene locality at Asseiceira (Portugal) with *L. barbatus* var. *antiquus* (ANTUNES & others, 1992). Very little is known of the uncalcified *Nitella* as fossils; the exceptional Indian Jurassic locality with *N. sahnii* is thought to be a lake deposit (HORN AF RANTZIEN, 1957).

In the fossil record *Nitellopsis* differs from other genera by its clearly more diverse modes of life than the unique extant species *N. obtusa*, which is restricted to permanent, relatively deep, cold lakes (SOULIÉ-MÄRSCHE, 1991). Most fossil species of *Nitellopsis* occur in lacustrine deposits, such as the upper Oligocene Argile des Milles, with *N. (Tectochara) meriani* L. & N. GRAMBAST accompanied by the freshwater gastropods *Limnaea* and *Planorbis* (FEIST-CASTEL, 1977c). The genus also occurs in brackish-water deposits: for example, *N. (Tectochara) thaleri elongata* FEIST-CASTEL, in the lower Eocene Oyster beds of Corbières and Minervois (southern France), is associated with *Lamprothamnium priscum* CASTEL & GRAMBAST as well as with a brackish-water fauna of foraminifers and ostracodes (TAMBAREAU & others, 1989). In the extant *N. obtusa*, the ability to withstand a low concentration of salt in laboratory experiments (KATSUHARA & TAZAWA, 1986) may be related to the former tolerance of the genus to a higher salinity.

TOTALLY EXTINCT GENERA

Because comparison with living species is not possible, ecological data for extinct genera are based mainly on evidence provided by associated faunas, generally foraminifers, molluscs, ostracodes, echinoderms, and conodonts. SCHUDACK (1993a) evaluated the salinity tolerances of 13 charophyte genera on the basis of more than 500 associations from the Upper Jurassic and Lower Cretaceous of Europe (Fig. 22). We refer readers to this paper for examples from times apart from the Paleozoic Era, which has been the subject of controversy regarding the ecology of the charophytes.

PALEOECOLOGY OF PALEOZOIC CHAROPHYTES: WERE THEY MARINE?

The paleoecology of Paleozoic charophytes is far from being completely understood. The salinity preferences of only a few genera have been recognized: *Karpinskya* seems to be euryhaline, *Sycidium* and *Trochiliscus* are freshwater species but occasionally tolerant of brackish water (RACKI, 1982; LANGER, 1976), and *Gemmichara* and *Leonardosia* are strictly freshwater genera (LU & ZHANG, 1990).

The possibility of early charophytes occupying marine habitats has been discussed for a long time, as some of their localities include other kinds of fossils that are thought to have been marine. Major contributions on the subject have been analyzed by RACKI (1982). The main point of the debate bears on the possibility that early charophytes could have been adapted to a wider range of habitats than modern species.

Two hypotheses have been formulated. In the first the association of the two types of organisms is artificial: when gyrogonites are not well preserved and in low abundance, they may have been washed from fresh- or brackish-water swamps into a marine environment by passage through estuaries (HECKEL, 1972); transportation of gyrogonites as far as 80 km from the coast has been noted in the English Channel (MAGNIEZ, RAT, & TINTANT, 1960).

The second hypothesis erected to explain the apparently abnormal assemblages of charophytes and marine organisms requires acceptance that in the past charophytes could have had lifestyles different from those of living ones and might have tolerated

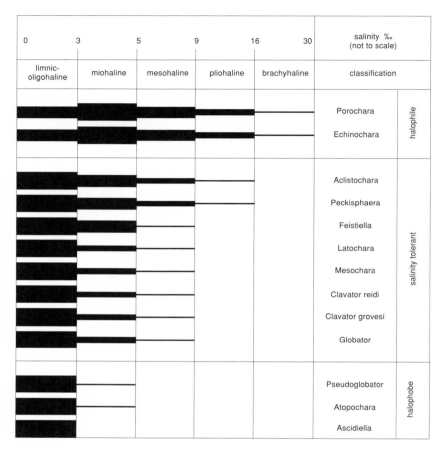

FIG. 22. Integrated interpretation of salinity tolerances of most important Late Jurassic–Early Cretaceous charophyte taxa (adapted from Schudack, 1993a, fig. 10).

open-marine conditions. Nothing in the fossil record except co-occurring marine species, however, suggests the existence of fundamental differences in the constitution of the extant and fossil forms. The thin rhizoids of the Devonian *Palaeonitella* (KIDSTON & LANG, 1921; EDWARDS & LYON, 1983) testify that, as in the modern forms, their ancestors were not floating algae but were fixed to the bottom. More recent work with *Palaeonitella* and the Rhynie Chert (TAYLOR, REMY, & HASS, 1992) indicates that deposition was in a freshwater oligotrophic peat swamp. We have noted earlier that depths between 0 and 10 m were optimal for light penetration, inducing both photosynthesis and reproduction. CROFT (1952) judged that the structure of the gyrogonite, being particularly resistant and able to withstand periods of desiccation, is indicative of adaptation to life in nonmarine environments.

This view is not in contradiction with the presence of several species of Characeae living in the Baltic Sea, which supports the idea that some Paleozoic species might have inhabited marine habitats. Moreover, Paleozoic seas are thought to have had a lower concentration of chlorides, as the Baltic Sea does now (RACKI, 1982). The Baltic Characeae live along the coast (Fig. 21) in shallow water where wave action is not strong (OLSEN, 1944). This mode of life compares well with some Devonian nearshore marine habitats and possibly also with some Paleozoic epeiric seas, such as the Devonian shallow, offshore deposits of the Holy Cross Mountains (Poland), which have yielded abundant populations of *Karpinskya* (RACKI, 1982).

Thus the biology of charophytes does not support the idea of an adaptation of their Paleozoic ancestors to fully marine environments implying tides and high waves, and the presence of abundant gyrogonites in marine sedimentary rocks is evidence of shallow water near the land.

BIOGEOGRAPHY

MICHELINE GUERLESQUIN and MONIQUE FEIST

[Université Catholique de l'Ouest, Angers, France; and Université Montpellier II, France]

INTRODUCTION

The extant charophytes are broadly distributed with respect both to latitude (from 80° N to 50° S) and to altitude (from 0 to more than 4,000 m in the Andes) in habitats where aquatic conditions are permanent or persist for at least a few months. Being aquatic, charophytes often have a rather wide distribution in relation to the relative uniformity of the aquatic environment. Probably their great power of propagation, due to their oospores being protected by resistant walls and characterized by a long viability, also plays a role in their broad distribution, which is effectively cosmopolitan.

CORILLION (1957), WOOD and IMAHORI (1959, 1965 in 1964–1965), and KHAN and SARMA (1984) gave an overview of the distribution of the species in the world. All the continents have been explored, but many areas have been insufficiently sampled, particularly central Africa, South America, central Asia, and many islands; consequently, the reported ranges are certainly smaller than in reality, and the number of endemic taxa has probably been overestimated.

CORILLION (1957) has reviewed the modes of dispersion of the Characeae. The oospores, bulbils, and nodes of the thallus are transported mainly by water currents or by animals. Species that grow along the banks of rivers and their estuaries are disseminated during floods. Animals can transport the organs of reproduction to considerable distances. The oogonia, protected by their resistant wall, can pass through the digestive canals of water birds without damage, or, together with vegetative fragments, can be present in mud adhering to their feet and wings, thus being distributed along migration routes (PROCTOR, 1962). KRASSAVINA (1971) has reported oogonia of *Nitellopsis obtusa* (DESVAUX in LOISELEUR-DESLONGCHAMPS) J. GROVES in the stomach of a duck. Oogonia and vegetative parts are also transported by frogs and toads and by large and small mammals. RIDLEY (1930) observed the occurrence of *Nitella furcata* subsp. *mucronata* var. *sieberi* f. *microcarpa* (A. BRAUN) R. D. WOOD in the footprints of a rhinoceros.

Human intervention also has its effects as a result of artificial habitats favorable to such species as *Lamprothamnium papulosum* (WALLROTH) J. GROVES, which has established itself on European coasts as a result of the formation of salt marshes in past centuries. Human activity can result also in the destruction of natural habitats through draining and management of especially sensitive aquatic environments (GUERLESQUIN, 1986), leading to the increasing rarity and finally the disappearance of species in some areas. To prevent this, species that are especially at risk have been accorded protected status, for example *L. papulosum* in Great Britain (MOORE, 1991) and *Lychnothamnus barbatus* (MEYEN) LEONARDI in Australia (CASANOVA, 1997). Other species are reported as rare or endangered in Sweden (BLINDOW, 1994) and in Germany (KRAUSE, 1984). Elsewhere, programs for the amelioration of water quality have recently allowed the return of species to some localities from which they had disappeared several years previously (SIMONS & others, 1994).

AREAS OF DISTRIBUTION

The concepts of areas of distribution and endemism can be interpreted in different ways. Thus endemism may perhaps be defined as the presence of a taxon either in a single very restricted area or, following KHAN and SARMA (1984), over all of a continent. Between these two extremes are other possibilities of grouping charophyte species in isolated geographic entities, such as the Indian subcontinent, Japan, and southern Africa.

TABLE 1. Number of microspecies known in the different genera by continent (*sensu* Wood & Imahori, 1965 in 1964–1965).

Continent	Chara	Nitella	Tolypella & Sphaerochara	Lamprothamnium	Nitellopsis	Lychnothamnus
Africa	53	48	4	3	0	0
North America	59	31	5	0	0	0
South America	50	38	4	2	1	0
Asia	77	105	6	3	1	1
Australia s.l.	21	39	3	3	0	1
Europe	46	21	9	2	1	1

The number of taxa known in each continent varies according to the size. Asia, by far the largest, has the greatest number, while Europe, being much smaller, has the fewest. The number of species in the genera varies among continents (Table 1). The proportion of endemics, highly variable, is least in Europe and highest in southern Africa and Japan (Table 2).

COSMOPOLITAN SPECIES

We have seen that the characteristics of charophytes allow their dispersion over great distances. The percentage of cosmopolitan species, i.e., occupying four or five continents, is nine percent among living species. These are generally species with great tolerance to variations in physicochemical factors as well as having long-lived oospores. This group comprises especially those species that populate regions that are isolated geographically such as Greenland, Iceland, Newfoundland, and some Pacific islands (Hawaii, Fiji, New Caledonia).

SUBCOSMOPOLITAN SPECIES

Containing 41 percent of species, this group of species, which are present on two or three continents, occupies an important place in the characean flora. These species are environmentally less tolerant or sometimes ancient species, the area of distribution of which has been reduced and broken up.

ENDEMIC SPECIES sensu lato

This group comprises 50 percent of the total number of species. These have ecological preferences that limit them to a single continent, to a broad area, or to a limited region with a highly variable landscape.

CLIMATICALLY CONTROLLED SPECIES

For some species, climate is the essential factor, as for *Chara zeylanica,* the tropical species par excellence (ZANEVELD, 1940), which occurs between 40° N and 30° S (Fig. 23). It is worth noting that in the complex *C. zeylanica,* the variety *diaphana* f. *diaphana* (MEYEN) R. D. WOOD has the broadest distribution; two other subspecies each occupy a more or less restricted climatic area. In other instances local ecological conditions allow species to flourish in climatic zones to which they are not adapted otherwise. In some, it is altitude, giving a cooler and more humid climate, that allows species from temperate zones to live in subtropical regions. Conversely, southern species may benefit from local shelter from the cold (PROCTOR, 1962). Thus *Chara canescens* DESVAUX & LOISELEUR-DESLONGCHAMPS is able to live in Spitzbergen (79° N) in hot springs (LANGANGEN, 1979).

DISTRIBUTIONS OF GENERA AND SPECIES

The distribution of the seven extant genera is unequal on the various continents and independent of their surface features. Africa and North America have four genera; South

TABLE 2. Percentages of endemic and worldwide species in the continents (new).

Continent	% endemics	% worldwide
Africa	20	6
North America	15	4
South America	24	4
Asia	23	13
Australia	13	2
Europe	7	2

FIG. 23. Repartition area of 3 microspecies (*sensu* WOOD & IMAHORI, 1965 in 1964–1965) of *Chara zeylanica; 1, Chara zeylanica* var. *diaphana* forma *diaphana* (MEYEN) R. D. WOOD; *2, Chara zeylanica* var. *diaphana* forma *oerstediana* (BRAUN) R. D. WOOD; *3, Chara zeylanica* var. *sejuncta* (BRAUN) R. D. WOOD (new).

America and Australasia have five. All seven genera are present in Europe and Asia (Table 1). *Chara* and *Nitella* have a global distribution, and these genera are also the richest in species. *Tolypella* is represented in different parts of the world but with gaps in its distribution. *Lamprothamnium,* confined to saline continental environments or exceptional instances in marine environments (e.g., the Baltic Sea), is unknown in North America and barely represented in Australia; it is absent from most of Africa. The reduction of areas of distribution in geologic time, most evident in *Nitellopsis* and *Lychnothamnus,* indicates genera on the decline.

Even in the widespread genera *Chara* and *Nitella,* several species have quite disjunct distributions. These are usually interpreted as corresponding to relict areas. Thus *Chara baueri* A. BRAUN occurs exclusively in Europe, Kazakhstan, and Australasia in regions that are always subject to similarly temperate climatic conditions. In other instances, for example such species as *Nitella tenuissima* f. *transilis* (T. F. ALLEN) R. D. WOOD, present in rare and sparse localities in India (Bihar) and the northeastern part of North America including Cuba, our present knowledge does not allow us to propose a satisfactory explanation.

To assess the affinities of regions to each other on the basis of their charophyte floras, we should examine geographically circumscribed regions (Table 3) with significantly large areas and with great floral richness. India, which harbors 40 percent of the total characean flora, seems to be a good example in this respect. Affinities are closest with other tropical regions, specifically neighboring regions of Asia and South America. Few species occur both in India and Africa, despite the geographic proximity of the two regions in former times. *Chara setosa* f. *pseudobrachypus* (J. GROVES & STEPHENS) R. D. WOOD, reported from both India (Maharastra) and southern Africa, is an example.

TABLE 3. Percentages of endemic and worldwide species in isolated regions (new).

Region	% endemics	% worldwide
India	14	6
Japan	30	6
New Zealand	11	1
Peri-Antarctic zone (Tierra del Fuego, Kerguelen Islands)	25	0.3
South Africa	31	5.5
Tasmania	20	2

STRATIGRAPHIC DISTRIBUTION AND PALEOBIOGEOGRAPHY

MONIQUE FEIST and NICOLE GRAMBAST-FESSARD

[Université Montpellier II, France]

Charophytes are essentially continental, living in freshwater or brackish water with land nearby. The changes induced by movement of the continents during the past 420 million years have certainly influenced the distribution of species and is thus accountable for some stages of their evolution, including periods of diversification or extinction.

The ecological factors that control the distribution of recent forms are mainly water clarity, temperature, pH, and percentage of dissolved salts; among these, the presence of calcium carbonate is the most important because it is essential for the calcified forms, which form most of the fossil record. At present, charophytes occur at nearly every altitude and at every latitude, polar regions excepted. Species and genera are widely distributed geographically. The greatest barriers to their dispersal are the deep oceans, deserts, and glaciers.

The information supplied by living forms is indispensable for the interpretation of the distribution of fossil forms; however, this information cannot be applied directly, as the factors that affect species distributions may have differed through geological time. Concerning charophyte dispersal, for example, birds did not exist during the Paleozoic and early Mesozoic. On the other hand, until the Late Cretaceous, charophytes were not competing with angiosperms in aquatic environments. The water chemistry may also have differed; as indicated in the Ecology chapter (herein, p. 34), a lower salinity of seawater might have allowed some Paleozoic forms to live in marine environments in coastal areas (RACKI, 1982). Moreover, the distribution of the continents, which was different in the past, induced the establishment of climatic conditions often more homogenous than at present, thus favoring cosmopolitan distribution. The distribution of

the continents, winds, and marine currents, which are important factors for the transportation of propagules, may have varied in direction and intensity in the geological past. Variations in sea level have certainly played a leading role in the distribution of fossils. The periods of transgression, such as the Early Jurassic and Coniacian, were unfavorable; conversely, times of emergence such as the late Silurian and Early Cretaceous must have allowed these pioneering species to establish themselves in newly emerged continental areas. Cosmic events have been proposed to explain times of mass extinction, such as at the Cretaceous-Tertiary boundary (ALVAREZ & others, 1980), but these are not treated herein. We do not comment about the hypothetical causes of extinction (cosmic events, volcanism, and so on). Phases of charophyte extinction and recovery are treated in Evolution of Charophyte Biodiversity in the chapter on Evolutionary History (herein, p. 74).

PALEOZOIC

SILURIAN

Charophytes are known with certainty in the upper Silurian. *Moellerina laufeldi,* the most ancient, comes from the Ludlowian Stage of Gotland (Sweden; CONKIN & CONKIN, 1992), and *Sycidium* (*Praesycidium*) is from the Ludlow Slasky Formation of Ukraine (ISHCHENKO & ISHCHENKO, 1982). *Primochara* is of Pridolian age (ISHCHENKO & SAIDAKOVSKY, 1975). In the paleogeographical reconstructions of SCOTESE (1997) all the charophytes from the upper Silurian come from the same paleogeographic province, Baltica. The presumed order Sycidiales from the lower Silurian (Llandovery-Wenlock boundary) of Quebec (MAMET & others, 1992), comes from Avalonia, located southwest of Baltica. If the affinity of this taxon to the charophytes were confirmed, the nearshore marine character of the Anticosti and Gotland deposits would indicate a migration toward Baltica by marine currents through the Rheic Ocean.

DEVONIAN

The charophytes diversified during the Devonian. The three orders of the group, Sycidiales, Moellerinales, and Charales, were represented as early as the Middle Devonian with seven widely distributed genera (Fig. 24). This phase of expansion went on until the Late Devonian.

In the Early Devonian, possibly from dispersal centers in the Silurian of Sweden (CONKIN & CONKIN, 1992) and Ukraine (ISHCHENKO & ISHCHENKO, 1982), the genera *Moellerina* and *Sycidium* extended onto the Euramerican continent (present USA, Canada, and Spitsbergen). The presence of *Moellerina* in the Early Devonian might be explained by migration in epeiric seas at the northern boundary of Gondwana. Similarly, the genera *Sycidium* and *Pinnoputamen* might have reached South China and, in the case of *Sycidium,* as far as Australia during the Late Devonian. Only a few deposits with charophytes are known from the Early Devonian, although their disjointed but wide distribution implies a much larger original area of distribution.

In the Middle Devonian the genera *Sycidium* and *Moellerina* are the best-documented examples of the number of species and localities. *Sycidium* is present in the Middle Devonian of South China, central and northern Europe, Iran, and Australia. It is missing from North America where it is noted only in the Lower Mississippian. The genus *Moellerina,* which occurs less frequently, had a much wider distribution: during the Middle Devonian it was present in South China, central Europe, east-central North America, and Australia.

According to the plate-tectonic reconstruction proposed by SCOTESE (1997) for the Devonian at 390 Ma, the two genera occupied Baltica and the northern margin of Gondwana and extended onto Laurentia.

These areas lay in the subtropical zone, suggesting a sufficiently warm climate to allow the calcification of the gyrogonites. Conversely, the deposits with Eocharaceae from the Upper Devonian of South Africa, at that time quite near the pole, have produced only impressions of thalli and fructifications (GESS & HILLER, 1995). This exceptional type of fossilization shows that the Eocharaceae included noncalcified species. This might explain the apparent highly disjunct areal distribution of the Eocharaceae as well as the long time gap that separated the different genera of this family. First described from the Middle Devonian of Canada (CHOQUETTE, 1956), the family has been reported since from the Upper Devonian of South Africa (GESS & HILLER, 1995), and its last occurrence was 100 million years later in the Triassic of central Europe (KISIELEVSKY, 1996).

EARLY CARBONIFEROUS

The early Carboniferous was a time of clear reduction of the number and occurrences of taxa. The area of distribution was reduced to North America (*Sycidium, Karpinskya;* PECK & MORALES, 1966) and South China (*Xinjiangochara, Gemmichara;* YANG & ZHOU, 1990; LU & ZHANG, 1990). Only *Moellerina* was common to the two areas (CONKIN & others, 1974; LU & LUO, 1990). In Europe, lacustrine sedimentary rock is rare and limited to the cratonic northern areas where the detrital formations contain rare carbonates but are often rich in organic matter; no charophytes are known from the lower Carboniferous rocks.

LATE CARBONIFEROUS

After the extinction of Trochiliscales and Sycidiales, a new order and two families originated, the Palaeocharaceae and Porocharaceae. Within this last family, a new morphological type appeared: gyrogonites with five sinistral spiral cells (Charinae), which persists to the present time.

Palaeochara is known from only two localities, one in Canada (BELL, 1922; PECK & EYER, 1963a), the other in northern China

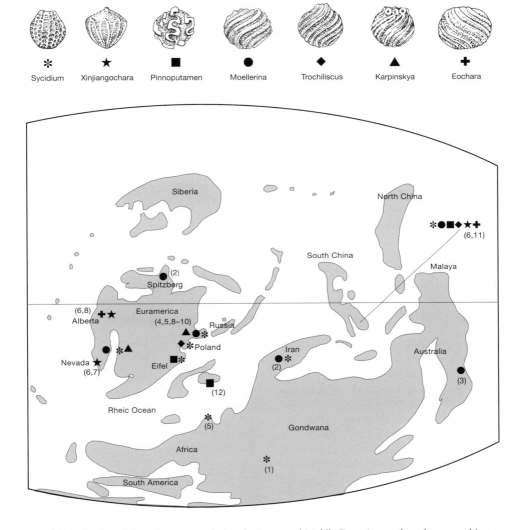

FIG. 24. Distribution of charophyte genera during the Lower and Middle Devonian on the paleogeographic map schematized after SCOTESE (1997); *1,* Choubert, 1932; *2,* Feist & Grambast-Fessard, 1985; *3,* Feist in Talent & others, 2000; *4,* Karpinsky, 1906; *5,* Langer, 1991; *6,* Lu, Soulié-Märsche, & Wang, 1996; *7,* Peck & Eyer, 1963a; *8,* Peck & Morales, 1966; *9,* Racki & Racka, 1981; *10,* Samoilova, 1961; *11,* Z. Wang & Lu, 1980; *12,* M. Feist & R. Feist, 1997 (new).

(LU & LUO, 1990). *Stomochara,* the first representative of the family Porocharaceae, was present in different localities of North America (PECK & EYER, 1963b) and Europe (SHAIKIN, 1966; KISIELEVSKY, 1980; GEBHARDT & SCHNEIDER, 1985; SAIDAKOVSKY, 1989). *Gemmichara,* which was present in the early Carboniferous and occurs in the

Permian (Z. WANG, 1984), must also have lived during the late Carboniferous, although it has not yet been discovered.

At the end of the early Carboniferous, the principal continents (Euramerica and Gondwana) were joined, and what would later constitute Europe was the site of the Variscan orogeny. Conditions prevailing within the paralic basins formed in this new continental configuration were certainly catastrophic for the charophytes, as evidenced by the scarcity of deposits with charophytes during this time. Charophytes must have entered into competition with higher plants that were then spreading profusely. In the rare instances when calcified structures might occur, they could seldom be preserved owing to the acidity of the entrophic lacustrine medium. It is noteworthy that during this crisis, which led to the extinction of two entire orders, new taxa appeared, characterized by a morphological change, the realization of the modern type of gyrogonite with five spiral cells, regarded as an innovation.

PERMIAN

In the Permian *Palaeochara, Gemmichara,* and *Stomochara* were extant from the previous periods, the last of them with a wide distribution in North America, Europe, and China. Other representatives of the Porocharaceae appeared. *Porochara* and *Leonardosia* were present in Europe and China; *Leonardosia* was also present in the upper Permian of Brazil, *L. langei* being the only charophyte representative known from the Paleozoic of South America. In the late Permian, from this same family, *Clavatorites* (synonym: *Cuneatochara*) and *Stellatochara* occurred in Europe (SAIDAKOVSKY, 1968; KOZUR, 1974; BILAN, 1988; KISIELEVSKY, 1993c). The Permian was thus a period of diversification.

The widespread distribution of genera in North and South America, Africa, and Europe was probably favored by the vast nonmarine areas of Pangaea. Connections with Asia may have occurred through present-day Russia where several Permian species have been described.

MESOZOIC

TRIASSIC

Following the close of the Permian, new occurrences of charophytes took place at the beginning of the Triassic, probably in relation with the regression at the beginning of this period. The well-calcified, large-sized Paleozoic genera were replaced by generally small genera, frequently with concave cells. This reduction of calcified structures may be related to the drop of temperatures resulting from the late Permian glaciations. The boundary between the Paleozoic and the Mesozoic thus seems relatively well marked in charophytes. The persistence of two-thirds of the Permian genera into the Triassic shows, however, that this break was not really abrupt. The same holds true with respect to terrestrial plants and freshwater fishes (KNOLL, 1984; BRIGGS, 1995) that similarly were not drastically affected by the end-Permian events.

Baltica and China seem to have been the dispersion centers of charophytes during the Triassic as they were during the late Permian. Apart from these regions, the sole records are from the North American Upper Triassic (PECK & EYER, 1963b).

During the Triassic, three families existed: the Porocharaceae, which were dominant both in number of taxa and localities; the Characeae, which had their earliest occurrence with *Aclistochara,* first reported from the Upper Triassic of South China (LIU & CHEN, 1992); and a unique representative of the ancient family Eocharaceae, last known from the Middle Devonian (CHOQUETTE, 1956) and having persisted in a refuge in Kazakhstan (KISIELEVSKY, 1996).

JURASSIC

During the Early Jurassic, the distribution of charophytes was restricted to a few localities in China, India, and Europe (FEIST & CUBAYNES, 1984; FEIST, BHATIA, & YADAGIRI, 1991; LU & YUAN, 1991; LIU & CHEN, 1992). The extinctions at the end of the Triassic led to an impoverishment that was not compensated by evolution of new forms during the Early Jurassic; the four genera recorded from this epoch were present already in the Early Triassic. The Early Jurassic was one of the most critical times in the evolution of the group, perhaps in relation to the disjunct distribution of landmasses that interrupted paths of migration.

The Middle Jurassic was marked by a renewal. Three new genera arose, and charophytes reached North America as well as Africa. A number of localities with *Porochara* species have been reported worldwide from the Bathonian; this coincided with an episode of regression (FEIST & GRAMBAST-FESSARD, 1984; CHARRIÈRE & others, 1994).

During the Late Jurassic, the expansion phase continued. Newly emerging lands in Laurasia (now North America, Europe, Central Asia, and China) as well as in northern Gondwana (Algeria, Tanzania) certainly favored the worldwide spread of charophytes (LU & LUO, 1990; FEIST, LAKE, & WOOD, 1995; SCHUDACK, TURNER, & PETERSON, 1998; SCHUDACK, 1999). A new family, the Clavatoraceae, evolved, initially with seven genera. The same number of new genera also evolved in the Characeae, while the Porocharaceae persisted from previous periods without renewal.

CRETACEOUS

During the Early Cretaceous, charophyte floras diversified on the lands that had emerged since the Late Jurassic (MARTIN-CLOSAS & SERRA-KIEL, 1991). Nine new genera of the Characeae evolved and eleven of the Clavatoraceae but none of the Porocharaceae. The Early Cretaceous was a time of vast geographical expansion. Some species, such as *Atopochara trivolvis* PECK and *Flabellochara harrisii* PECK, have a cosmopolitan distribution (SIRNA, 1968). Eighty-six percent of genera in the Clavatoraceae and 31 percent in the Characeae, however, went extinct during the Albian. This extinction phase may be attributed to the opening of the Atlantic Ocean, which must have interrupted migration routes and brought about climatic variations, disturbing the aquatic habitats where charophytes were growing. Another factor that may have contributed to the alteration of the charophyte

flora was the increasing development of the angiosperms during the Albian and Cenomanian. The Clavatoraceae, which favored calcareous environments owing to their multilayered utricles, were more sensitive than the Characeae to the eutrophication and acidification that resulted from accumulation of organic matter.

During the Late Cretaceous, the Characeae, taking advantage of vacant niches, radiated dramatically with the occurrences of 21 new genera in this family. Only two genera of Clavatoraceae lived during the Cenomanian: *Embergerella* and *Atopochara*. After the Coniacian to Santonian, where the fossil record of charophytes is nearly nonexistent, the family was represented again by only two genera, a new one, *Septorella* GRAMBAST, and *Atopochara* PECK, which persisted from the Early Cretaceous. No change occurred in the Porocharaceae, but the Raskyellaceae, which appeared during the Late Cretaceous, are thought to have evolved from members of this family, presumably the *Feistiella* group, which exhibits undivided basal plates.

Late Cretaceous genera are reported as showing provincial differentiation as a result of the fragmentation of Pangaea. As in other periods, however, the charophyte flora included subcosmopolitan genera that occurred on at least three continents. Among the Porocharaceae, both *Porochara* and *Feistiella* were widely distributed during the Cretaceous. The same was true for *Atopochara* (Clavatoraceae) until the Turonian and for the Characeae *Amblyochara, Chara, Charites, Lamprothamnium, Microchara, Peckisphaera, Platychara, Sphaerochara,* and *Strobilochara* as well as for the Raskyellaceae *Saportanella.*

During the Late Cretaceous, charophytes were distributed in four main zones.

Eurasia

With five genera recorded only from China and Mongolia (*Collichara, Mongolichara, Neochara, Pseudolatochara,* and *Zhejiangella*), this province has a high degree of endemism; Eurasia was also a refuge for the last representatives of *Latochara, Atopochara,* and *Aclistochara.*

Southern Europe

This area was a center of dispersion of *Dughiella* and *Nitellopsis;* southern Europe also yielded three endemic genera: *Embergerella, Septorella,* and *Bysmochara.*

North and South America

The fossil record is very poor in North America from the Turonian onward. According to the record of *Tolypella* (*sensu stricto*) from the Late Cretaceous of Argentina (ULIANA & MUSACCHIO, 1978) and Alaska (FEIST & BROUWERS, 1990), North America and South America seem to have been centers of dispersal of the genus, which is found only from the Eocene onward in other continents. *Nothochara* is endemic to South America.

India

Besides cosmopolitan genera (*Chara, Microchara*), India shares the genus *Nemegtichara* with China and Mongolia; *Peckichara* is common to Asia and Europe; and *Nodosochara* is common to Europe and South America. Thus, at the generic level charophytes do not provide clear indications on the position of the Indian subcontinent at the end of the Cretaceous.

BHATIA and RANA (1984) reported, however, an Upper Cretaceous–Eocene assemblage from intertrappean beds, including *Platychara perlata* (PECK & REKER) GRAMBAST, *Peckichara varians* GRAMBAST, and ostracodes. According to these authors, this assemblage has floral and faunal affinities with the northern Asian part of India, and thus its distribution is not in accordance with paleogeographic reconstructions where the Indian plate is isolated from other continuous landmasses.

CRETACEOUS-TERTIARY BOUNDARY

The end of the Cretaceous was a time of marked importance for the charophytes (see Stratigraphic Range Chart, herein p. 148).

The events triggering the K-T crisis must have been fatal to the last representatives of the Clavatoraceae, already severely impoverished by the extinctions during the early Late Cretaceous. In the sections calibrated by magnetostratigraphy (GALBRUN & others, 1993; WESTPHAL & DURAND, 1990) the last *Septorella* became extinct about two million years before the beginning of the Danian.

The episodes of cooling during the Maastrichtian pointed out by MÉDUS and others (1988) may have caused a decrease in the amount of calcium carbonate precipitation, thus inhibiting the development of calcified utricles.

The diversity of Porocharaceae had remained unchanged with the persistence of the same three genera, *Latochara, Porochara,* and *Feistella,* since the Early Cretaceous. The family crossed over the K-T boundary but was already very much impoverished and disappeared during the Eocene.

The K-T boundary is well marked in the Characeae, as 40 percent of the genera became extinct. In this family, the crisis did not result in a complete extinction and coincided with the family's major stage of expansion. This scenario is similar to that of the early Carboniferous when the expanding Porocharaceae allowed the survival of the charophytes.

It appears thus that the K-T boundary marks a break within the charophytes but not really a mass-extinction phenomenon. The most outstanding consequences occurred after the K-T crisis. Indeed, the extinctions at the end of the Cretaceous were not balanced by an equivalent number of newly appearing genera (see Fig. 40). This resulted in a drastic reduction in diversity during the Cenozoic. We suppose that the expansion of the aquatic angiosperms was a factor limiting the recovery of the charophytes.

CENOZOIC
PALEOCENE

After the extinctions at the end of the Cretaceous, the charophytes included 21 genera. The Paleocene assemblages, however, have an entirely distinct appearance due to the evolution of many new species in the Danian (FEIST & COLOMBO, 1983). At the generic level, only *Rhabdochara* originated in the late Paleocene (HAO & others, 1983). One genus, *Platychara,* disappeared at the end of the Danian, and the last occurrence of *Collichara* is in uppermost Paleocene rocks of the Jiangsu (China; LU, 1997). In addition, the Porocharaceae nearly became extinct before the Eocene; to date, a single occurrence of the family has been mentioned in the Eocene (SHAIKIN, 1977).

The provincial differentiation that started during the Late Cretaceous persisted throughout the Paleocene. Asia became a new center of endemism for several genera: *Collichara, Nemegtichara,* and *Neochara. Tolypella* was still restricted to North America (FEIST & BROUWERS, 1990); this is consistent with its American origin suggested by its occurrences in both North and South America during the Late Cretaceous. The Paleocene Epoch included also five widely distributed genera: *Feistiella, Harrisichara,* and *Dughiella,* as well as *Platychara* and *Peckichara,* both cosmopolitan.

EOCENE

After the extinction of most Porocharaceae, the charophyte flora included only two families: the Characeae, which was the most important in both the number of genera and localities, and the Raskyellaceae. In the earliest Eocene, 19 genera were in existence. *Raskyella* evolved in North Africa during the early to middle Eocene (MEBROUK & others, 1997); *Psilochara* evolved in Europe in the middle Eocene (FEIST-CASTEL, 1971); and *Linyechara, Lychnothamnus,* and *Shandongochara* evolved in China during the late Eocene. The last occurrence of *Peckichara, Maedleriella, Microchara, Nodosochara,* and *Raskyella* is in the upper Eocene.

The persistence of paleogeographic provinces is illustrated by Asiatic endemism. New migration routes resulting from continental collisions, however, must have favored the geographical dispersion of several genera. The most widely distributed were *Nitellopsis, Harrisichara, Maedleriella, Peckichara,* and *Stephanochara,* suggesting migration between Europe, China, India, and North Africa.

OLIGOCENE

As the extinctions at the end of the Eocene were not compensated by evolution of new taxa, the Oligocene was a time of impoverishment. This decline is shown moreover by the reduction of areas of distribution. The number of genera, initially 15, was reduced by the extinction of *Harrisichara* and *Shandongochara.* The genus *Gyrogona,* absent from Europe from the middle Oligocene onward, persisted in China until the late Miocene (LU & LUO, 1990). During the late Oligocene there was a renewal, marked by the evolution of new species within several genera (*Chara, Nemegtichara, Nitellopsis, Rhabdochara,* and *Sphaerochara*). Oligocene charophytes have been reported mostly from Europe and Asia.

MIOCENE

The diversification phase continued during the early Miocene: a new genus, *Rantzieniella,* evolved; and areas of distribution became more extended, especially of *Chara* and *Nitellopsis.* Reports of the last occurrence of *Grovesichara* at the end of the early Miocene (TANG & DI, 1991) as well as of *Gyrogona* and *Psilochara* before the end of the Miocene mark the end of this period of diversification, which was the last one for the charophytes.

PLIOCENE

The decline of the charophytes is underlined by the extinction during the Pliocene of *Amblyochara* and *Rantzieniella,* the last representative of the Raskyellaceae. *Nemegtichara, Stephanochara,* and *Rhabdochara* also became extinct before the end of the Pliocene. As during the Oligocene, areas of distribution were reduced and restricted mainly to Europe and Asia. Two cosmopolitan genera were an exception: *Chara* and *Lamprothamnium.* The latter of these, however, has not been reported so far from North America in rocks above the Lower Cretaceous.

PLEISTOCENE

The charophyte flora of the Pleistocene resembled that of the modern world. Only one genus reported from the Pleistocene, *Hornichara,* does not live at the present time. All the extant genera are represented but in some instances with a different distribution. *Lychnothamnus* has been reported from Africa (SOULIÉ-MÄRSCHE, 1981) where it is unknown today, and *Nitellopsis* was spread over a greater area than at present. *Chara* and *Sphaerochara* were cosmopolitan. The area of distribution of the halophilous genus *Lamprothamnium* was also very wide but localized in particular biotopes generally near the shoreline.

Genera with uncalcified fructifications are poorly represented. Thus a single locality in the middle Pleistocene of Russia has been reported for the genus *Nitella* (KRASSAVINA, 1966).

BIOZONATION

MONIQUE FEIST,[1] with contributions from LU HUINAN,[2] WANG QIFEI,[2] and ZHANG SHENZEN[2]

[[1]Université Montpellier II, France; and [2]Nanjing Institute of Geology and Palaentology, China]

INTRODUCTION

MONIQUE FEIST

Interest in the stratigraphy of the charophytes was revealed during the development of research on the group during the 1950s. MÄDLER (1952) established the sequence of some species for the upper Oligocene and Miocene in Germany and Switzerland, but for many of them the range appears too long. PECK (1957), in his studies of the Mesozoic charophytes of North America, insisted on their stratigraphic significance. Likewise, for the Eocene and Oligocene formations of the Paris basin studied by GRAMBAST (1958, 1962a), charophytes have been revealed as very accurate biostratigraphic indicators.

The distribution of charophyte floras in different European regions (France, Belgium, Great Britain) having shown that common species were present in correlative strata, the establishment of a biozonation appeared possible. Owing to the fact that the fossiliferous deposits were at first few and scattered, the first biozonations (CASTEL, 1968; GRAMBAST, 1972a) were named after local reference levels comparable to mammalian stages (THALER, 1965). They are assemblage zones, and their precise range is not defined.

Later, new biozonations were published: biochronological zones based on the succession of evolutionary stages within phylogenetic lineages (GRAMBAST, 1971, 1974; BABINOT & others, 1983) and interval zones (RIVELINE, 1986; RIVELINE & others, 1996). The latter, named after guide fossils, correspond theoretically to the interval between two succeeding first occurrences of guide fossils. In some cases the interval zone corresponds to the range of a species. The guide fossils present characters that facilitate easy identification and have short stratigraphic ranges, as well as a wide geographic distribution, such as *Atopochara trivolvis,* a cosmopolitan species of the upper Barremian and Aptian.

With the exception of some intervals, such as the Frasnian, the Rhetian–middle Oxfordian, and Coniacian–Turonian where data are too fragmentary, the charophyte biozonation constitutes a reliable biostratigraphical tool for dating and correlation in continental areas. Today this biozonation covers nearly all the fossil record of charophytes.

PALEOZOIC

LU HUINAN, ZHANG SHENZEN, and WANG QIFEI

The zonation of the Paleozoic has been established recently in China (WANG, YANG, & LU, 2003). Paleozoic charophytes have been reported from various levels in different areas of China. Due to their frequent occurrence in marginal-marine paleoenvironments, these charophyte floras are often associated with diverse organisms (spores, molluscs, conodonts) that are stratigraphically significant and ensure their correlation. Thus, the charophyte distribution, although relatively sporadic, has been taken into consideration for a preliminary biozonation of the Paleozoic. The following succession (Table 4) is based on the biozonation recently published by WANG, YANG, and LU (2003).

The charophyte assemblages comprise 11 different biozones. Three of them are not significant enough stratigraphically; nevertheless their occurrence furnishes clues for further research. The Paleozoic charophyte biozones are described below with the assemblages of their charophyte-yielding units. For the sake of brevity, locality information is given only at the level of county or province.

TABLE 4. Late Paleozoic charophyte biozonation of China (new).

Stage		Charophyte Assemblage
upper Permian	11	Stomochara kunlunshanensis–Porochara moyuensis–Leonardosia jinxiensis–L. jimsarensis–Gemmichara sinensis
upper Permian	10	Gemmichara pingdingshanensis–Leonardosia sp.
middle Permian	9	Leonardosia yongchengensis
lower Permian	8	Leonardosia sp.
Visean	7	Gemmichara hunanensis–Palaeochara sp.
Tournaisian	6	Ampulichara talimuica–Xinjiangochara rosulata–Palaeochara chinensis
Famennian	5	Karpinskya? sp.
Givetian	4	Sycidium lagenarium–Xinjiangochara burgessi
Eifelian	3	Trochiliscus ingricus–Pinnoputamen yunnanensis–Sycidium spinuliferum
upper Emsian	2	Sycidium sipaiense–Trochiliscus lipuensis–Xinjiangochara sp.
lower Emsian	1	Trochiliscus? sp.

The charophyte localities, more than 50 all together, are distributed differently through time: those referred to the Emsian and Eifelian (Biozones 1 to 3) have been found exclusively in South China, but for the Givetian (Biozone 4) they extend northward to central areas, and for the interval from Famennian to upper Permian (Biozones 6 to 11), the charophyte localities are all found in northern or north-central China. This change in distribution probably results from different paleogeographic conditions.

The oldest fossil charophyte is from the Lower Devonian of southwestern China. It is taken herewith as the beginning of the present list in decreasing age.

DEVONIAN

Lower Emsian

Trochiliscus? sp. biozone.—The only record of lower Emsian charophytes is the doubtful *Trochiliscus?* from the Ertang Formation of the Xiangzhou County in Guangxi. This record is, however, insufficient as a reliable criterion for the geological age of the fossil-bearing unit. It is based on brachiopod evidence that Biozone 1 has been referred to the lower Emsian (Z. WANG & others, 1980).

Upper Emsian

Sycidium sipaiense–Trochiliscus lipuensis biozone.—Charophytes occur in the Sipai Formation of Guangxi, which is more or less correlated with the Dacaozi Formation of

Yunnan. Both formations contain rich faunas of brachiopods, corals, ostracodes, and conodonts on which is based the assignment to the upper Emsian. The charophyte assemblage includes *S. sipaiense* (Z. WANG & LU) Z. WANG and others, *Trochiliscus lipuensis* Z. WANG, *Sycidium miniglobosum* Z. WANG and others, *S.* cf. *panderi* KARPINSKY, and *Xinjiangochara* sp. The two guide fossils have been recorded also from the correlative beds of Lipu County (J. ZHANG & others, 1978; Z. WANG & others, 1980; Z. WANG & LU, 1980); furthermore, the Dacaozi Formation has yielded *Xinjiangochara* sp. in Ninglang (Yunnan).

Eifelian

Trochiliscus ingricus–Pinnoputamen yunnanensis–Sycidium spinuliferum biozone.—This biozone (Table 5) is based on the assemblages from the Yingtang Formation of Guangxi and correlative beds of Yunnan and Hunan. On evidence of brachiopods and conodonts, the charophyte-

TABLE 5. Charophyte distribution in the Eifelian of China (new).

charophyte	Guangxi	Yunnan	Hunan
Trochiliscus ingricus	×	×	
Pinnoputamen yunnanensis		×	×
Sycidium spinuliferum	×		
Eochara changshanensis			×
Sycidium haikouensis		×	
Sycidium anhuaense			×

TABLE 6. Charophyte distribution in the Givetian of China (new).

charophyte	Guangxi	Yunnan	Guizhou	Hunan	Sichuan	Xizang
Sycidium lagenarium	×	××	×	×	×	×
Xinjiangochara burgessi		××				
Moellerina convoluta		×				
Sycidium anhuense				×	×	
Sycidium beiliuense	×			××		
Sycidium haikouensis		×××	×		××	
Sycidium xizangense	×				××	×
Trochiliscus zhanyiensis		×				
Trochiliscus sp.					×	

yielding beds have been attributed to the Eifelian (Z. WANG, 1976; J. ZHANG & others, 1978; ZENG & HU, 2001).

The charophyte assemblages are well diversified, with four genera and six species. The two most widely distributed species in South China are *Trochiliscus ingricus* KARPINSKY and, to a lesser extent, *Pinnoputamen yunnanensis* WANG & LU. *Sycidium spinuliferum* Z. WANG & LU, *Sycidium haikouensis* Z. WANG, *Sycidium anhuaense* Z. WANG, and *Eochara changshaensis* Z. L. ZHANG have each been reported from only one locality.

Among the mentioned species, *Trochiliscus ingricus* has been recorded also from the Givetian of Russia (KARPINSKY, 1906), Poland (RACKI & SOBON-PODGORSKA, 1992), and Iran (FEIST & GRAMBAST-FESSARD, 1985); and *Sycidium spinuliferum* resembles *Sycidium volborthi eifelicum* LANGER from the Eifelian Mountains in Germany (LANGER, 1976). These resemblances suggest easy communication between close paleogeographic landmasses (see chapter on Paleobiogeography, herein p. 39).

Givetian

Sycidium lagenarium–Xinjiangochara burgessi biozone.—Records of charophytes of Givetian age (Table 6) extend northward to the Guizhou and Sichuan Provinces as well as to the Xizang Zang Autonomous Region (Tibet). *Sycidium lagenarium* Z. WANG is the most widely distributed species, extending through the southern, central, and northwestern areas of China. *Xinjiangochara burgessi* (PECK & REKER) LU, SOULIÉ-MÄRSCHE, and Q. WANG has been reported from only two localities in Yunnan, from the lower part of the Xichong Formation in Zhanyi and Luquan as well from the Haikou Formation in Kunming, but this species is widespread in the Middle Devonian of North America (PECK & EYER, 1963a; PECK & MORALES, 1966). Another cosmopolitan species present in this assemblage is *Moellerina convoluta* (PECK) PECK, described from the Middle Devonian of Missouri (PECK, 1936; PECK & MORALES, 1966). The Givetian charophyte flora includes six other species, among which the most common are *Sycidium xizangense* WANG, *S. haikouensis* WANG, *S. anhuaense* WANG, and *S. beiliuense* WANG. *Trochiliscus zhanyiensis* Z. WANG & LU and *Trochiliscus* sp. have been reported from only a single locality each (WANG & CHANG, 1956; WANG, 1976; ZHANG & others, 1978; WANG & LU, 1980; CHEN & YANG, 1992; LU, 1997; ZENG & HU, 2001).

Frasnian

No charophytes have been reported from strata of this age in China.

Lower Famennian

Karpinskya? sp. biozone.—In China, the charophyte record of the Famennian is very poor. The single record is *Karpinskya*? sp. from a unit in Xinjiang questionably correlated with the Hongguleleng Formation of Hoboksar County, which is attributed to the lower Famennian on conodont evidence. The finding of Famennian charophytes has

TABLE 7. Charophyte distribution in the upper Permian of China (new).

charophyte	southern Xinjiang	northern Xinjiang	Gansu	Liaoning
Leonardosia jinxiensis			×	×
Leonardosia jimsarensis		×		
Gemmichara sinensis				×
Stomochara kunlunshanensis	×			
Stomochara sp. cf. moreyi	×			
Porochara moruensis	×			
Leonardosia bellatula		×		
Leonardosia bellatula f. longa		×		
Leonardosia elliptica		×		
Leonardosia gansuensis			×	
Leonardosia nanpiaoensis				×
Leonardosia turpanensis		×		
Leonardosia xinjiangensis		×		

been taken as a provisional reference for Zone 5; further investigations will be necessary to correlate the the Xinjiang sequences precisely.

CARBONIFEROUS

Tournaisian

Ampullichara talimuica–Xinjiangochara rosulata–Palaeochara chinensis biozone.—Tournaisian charophytes are known from northwestern China exclusively. *Xinjiangochara rosulata* YANG & ZHOU, *Ampullichara talimuica* YANG & ZHOU, and *Palaeochara chinensis* LU & LUO have been recorded from boreholes in a sequence ranging from the Bachu to the Kalasay Formations in the Tarim basin (Xinjiang) (YANG & ZHOU, 1990; GAO & others, 2002). The occurrence of *Xinjiangochara rosulata* YANG & ZHOU in the Tournaisian is confirmed by outcrop samples from the Qianheishan Formation of Zhongwei County in Ningxia (LU, SOULIÉ-MÄRSHE, & WANG, 1996).

Visean

Gemmichara hunanensis–Palaeochara sp. biozone.—In Hunan, *Gemmichara hunanensis* LU & ZHANG and *Palaeochara* sp. occur in the upper member of the Tseishui Formation of Lengshuijiang City (LU & S. ZHANG, 1990), which has been attributed to the Visean on palynological and floral evidence. This assemblage is also represented in the Yangjiazhangzi and Gaotai Formations of Liaoning (LIU & ZHANG, 1994).

PERMIAN

Lower Permian

Leonardosia sp. biozone.—*Leonardosia* sp. is the only charophyte record for the lower Permian. Only one gyrogonite has been obtained from the Kangkelin Formation of Kalping County in Xinjiang (LU & LUO, 1990). It is on faunal evidence (conodonts,

Triassic	stages	substages	charophyte zones (Polish Lowland) Bilan, 1988
Upper	Rhaetian	upper Rhaetic	not determined
	Norian	Sevatian	Auerbachichara rhaetica
		Alaunian	
		Lacian	
	Carnian	Tuvalian	Stellatochara thuringica
		Julian	
Middle	Ladinian	Longobardian	Stellatochara hoellvicensis
		Fassanian	
	Anisian	Illyrian	Stellatochara dnjeproviformis
		Pelsonian	
		Bithynian	
		Aegean	
Lower	Scythian	Spathian	Porochara triassica
		Nammalian	Porochara globosa
		Griesbachian	?

FIG. 25. Triassic charophyte biozonation (new, courtesy of W. Bilan).

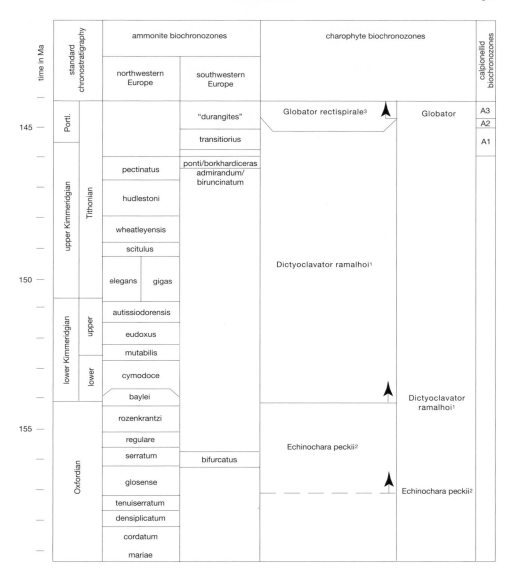

FIG. 26. Jurassic charophyte biochronozones, after cladistic nomenclature; *1, Dictyoclavator fieri ramalhoi; 2, Echinochara peckii; 3, Globator maillardii maillardii* (Martin-Closas & Schudack in Riveline & others, 1996; time, chronostratigraphy, ammonites, and calpionellid biochronozones, adapted from Hardenbol & others, 1998).

fusulinids) that the fossil-bearing unit has been referred to the Zisongian (lower Permian). Although this unique fossil is insufficient to characterize a biozone, we choose to mention the finding, given the poor record of lower Permian charophytes in general.

Middle Permian

Leonardosia yongchengensis biozone.— Outcrops of continental deposits of middle Permian age are exposed extensively in China. Charophytes are, however, known only from boreholes in Henan Province.

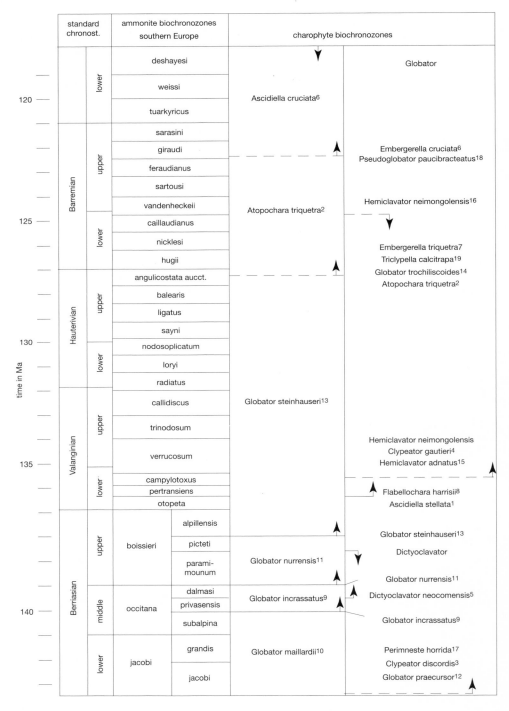

FIG. 27. *For explanation, see facing page.*

Leonardosia yongchengensis (Z. WANG & R. N. WANG) LU & ZHANG from Yongcheng County is the only taxon reported here (Z. WANG & R. N. WANG, 1986), with a stratigraphic range extending from the middle to the upper part of the Lower Shihhotse Formation (third and fourth coal formations, respectively). The two successive formations have been attributed to the Kuhfenginan ($P_2{}^3$) and Lengwuan respectively, according to floral data and magnetostratigraphy.

Lower Upper Permian ($P_3{}^1$)

Gemmichara pingdingshanensis–Leonardosia sp. biozone.—This assemblage has been described from the third member of the Upper Shihhotse Formation (sixth and seventh coal formations) of Henan, Anhui, and Jiangsu provinces.

In Henan, *Gemmichara pingdingshanensis* Z. WANG & R. N. WANG has been obtained from boreholes from the middle part of the Upper Shihhotse Formation of Xiangcheng County, and *Leonardosia?* sp. has been found in Pingdingshan and Yingshang. Remains of *Gemmichara* sp. occur in the correlated horizons in Huainan (Anhui), and *Leonardosia* sp. occurs in Feng County (Jiangsu). The assemblage is assigned to the Wuchiapingian ($P_3{}^1$) by floral data (Z. WANG & R. N. WANG, 1986).

Upper Upper Permian ($P_3{}^2$)

Leonardosia jinxiensis–L. jimsarensis–Gemmichara sinensis and *Stomochara kunlunshanensis–Porochara moyuensis* biozones.— Late Permian charophytes are well represented in northern China (Table 7). They have been reported from three provinces. In the Tarim basin in southern Xinjiang, the assemblage includes *Stomochara kunlunshanensis* LUO, which has been described from the Duwa Formation in Pishan and Hotan; *S.* cf. *moreyi* (PECK) GRAMBAST from Hotan only; and *Porochara moyuensis* LUO from Moyu County (LU & LUO, 1990). On evidence from ostracodes, the Duwa Formation is attributed to the Changhsingian ($P_3{}^2$). Data from fossil vertebrates and flora indicate the same age for the following occurrences.

In northern Xinjiang, *L. turpanensis* LU & ZHANG occurs in the lower part of the Guodikeng Formation of the Turpan basin (LU & ZHANG, 1990). In addition, *Leonardosia bellatula* (LU & LUO) LU & ZHANG, *L. bellatula* f. *longa* (LU & LUO) LU & ZHANG, *L. elliptica* (LU & LUO) LU & ZHANG, *L. jimsarensis* (LU & LUO) LU & ZHANG, and *L. xinjiangensis* (LU & LUO) LU & ZHANG have been described from the Guodikeng Formation of the Junggar basin (LU & LUO, 1984).

In Liaoning, *Gemmichara sinensis* Z. WANG, *Leonardosia jinxiensis* (Z. WANG) LU & ZHANG, and *Leonardosia nanpiaoensis* Z. WANG occur in the lower part of Hongla Formation of Jinxi County (Z. WANG, 1984).

In Gansu, *Leonardosia jinxiensis* (Z. WANG) LU and ZHANG and *Leonardosia gansuensis* (Z. WANG) LU and ZHANG have been recorded from the Sunan Formation of Sunan County (Z. WANG, 1984).

The distribution of charophyte species during the late Permian shows two distinct assemblages: in northern Xinjiang, Gansu, and Liaoning, the assemblage that is dominated by *Leonardosia* and includes the last representative of the Moellerinales, *Gemmichara*, has a typically Paleozoic aspect, while

FIG. 27. Cretaceous (Berriasian–lower Aptian) charophyte biochronozones, after cladistic nomenclature; *1, Ascidiella stellata; 2, Atopochara trivolvis triquetra; 3, Clypeator grovesii discordis; 4, C. grovesii gautieri; 5, Dictyoclavator fieri neocomensis; 6, Ascidiella cruciata; 7, Ascidiella triquetra; 8, Clavator harrisii; 9, Globator maillardii incrassatus; 10, G. maillardii maillardii; 11, G. maillardii nurrensis; 12, G. maillardii praecursor; 13, G. maillardii steinhauseri; 14, G. maillardii trochiliscoides; 15, Pseudoglobator adnatus; 16, Hemiclavator neimongolensis; 17, Atopochara trivolvis horrida; 18, Pseudoglobator paucibracteatus; 19, Clavator calcitrapus* (Martin-Closas & Schudack in Riveline & others, 1996; time, chronostratigraphy, ammonites, and biochronozones, adapted from Hardenbol & others, 1998).

in the Tarim basin (southern Xinziang), there occur only the newly evolved Porocharoideae. The two assemblages may suggest the existence of two paleobiogeographic provinces or a slight diachronism.

MESOZOIC–CENOZOIC

MONIQUE FEIST

A detailed account of the Mesozoic-Cenozoic biozonation was published by RIVELINE and others (1996). Herein only the main references are indicated as well as information on new zones introduced in the charophyte zonal scheme based on new data. At present, this biozonation is applicable only to Europe, but the general stratigraphic subdivisions can be recognized everywhere at the generic level. For example, *Auerbachichara* was common to Europe and China during the Triassic; most genera of the Clavatoraceae characterize the Cretaceous, and *Peckichara* as well as *Maedleriella* are universal markers of the Upper Cretaceous and Eocene. Exceptionally some stratigraphic markers allow the identification of stages, for example *Globator rectispirale*, which dates the Tithonian in two different continents, Europe and Africa (FEIST, LAKE, & WOOD, 1995).

TRIASSIC

The biozonation established by BILAN (1988) in the continental Triassic of Poland (Fig. 25) includes six partial range zones, each of which corresponds to the interval between the last occurrences of two guide species. The stratigraphic attributions are based on well-dated marine intercalations or on data on spores, molluscs, and ostracodes of continental origin present in levels with charophytes or intercalated between them. Most of the analyzed material comes from boreholes situated at the margin of the upper Silesian coal basin.

LOWER AND MIDDLE JURASSIC

No biozonation has yet been developed for the Rhaetian–middle Oxfordian interval, due to the rarity of charophytes, probably related to the scarcity of calcareous nonmarine deposits. Some well-dated occurrences of species, however, show that a potential exists for subdivision of this interval. The Planioles Limestone of the southwestern Massif Central (France), with *Latochara durand-delgai* FEIST, has been correlated with the lower Sinemurian *Arnioceras semicostatum* ammonite zone (FEIST & CUBAYNES, 1984). For the middle Bathonian, the Hampen Marly Formation of Oxfordshire (England), which has yielded *Porochara palmerii* (FEIST & GRAMBAST-FESSARD) SCHUDACK, is considered to be an equivalent of the *Procerites progracilis* ammonite zone (COPE & others, 1980; FEIST & GRAMBAST-FESSARD, 1984). *Porochara sublaevis* (PECK) GRAMBAST, which has been described from the Middle Jurassic Piper Formation of Montana (PECK, 1957) and is also present in the Comblanchien Limestone of Bourgogne (east-central France), referred to the lower to middle Bathonian (MOJON, 1989), could be viewed as a widely distributed guide fossil of the Middle Jurassic.

UPPER JURASSIC–UPPER PLIOCENE

The Meso-Cenozoic charophyte biozonation of RIVELINE and others (1996) is based on interval zones or range zones. The Jurassic and Cretaceous include 16 zones, the Paleogene 20, and the Neogene 4.

These zones have been established in different western European areas; their duration, variable according to periods, reduces in an ascending way. It varies from 4.3 Ma for the Upper Jurassic to 1.5 Ma for the Neogene. Correlations with marine stages are based on direct correlations, where charophytes are associated with marine markers at the same levels or on indirect correlations where charophytes and other markers occur in stratigraphically correlated layers. In some instances, correlations are deduced from the general biostratigraphic framework of a studied area. In addition, charophyte zones of the Upper Cretaceous have been related to the standard stages by direct correlation with the magnetostratigraphic scale (GALBRUN & others, 1993).

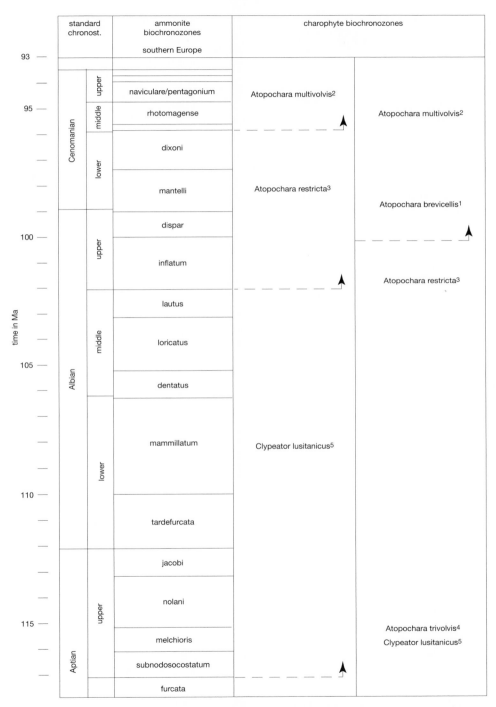

FIG. 28. Cretaceous (upper Aptian–Cenomanian) charophyte biochronozones. After cladistic nomenclature: *1, Atopochara trivolvis brevicellis; 2, A. trivolvis multivolvis; 3, A. trivolvis restricta; 4, A. trivolvis trivolvis; 5, Clypeator grovesii lusitanicus* (Martin-Closas & Schudack in Riveline & others, 1996; time, chronostratigraphy, ammonites, and biochronozones, adapted from Hardenbol & others, 1998).

Charophyta

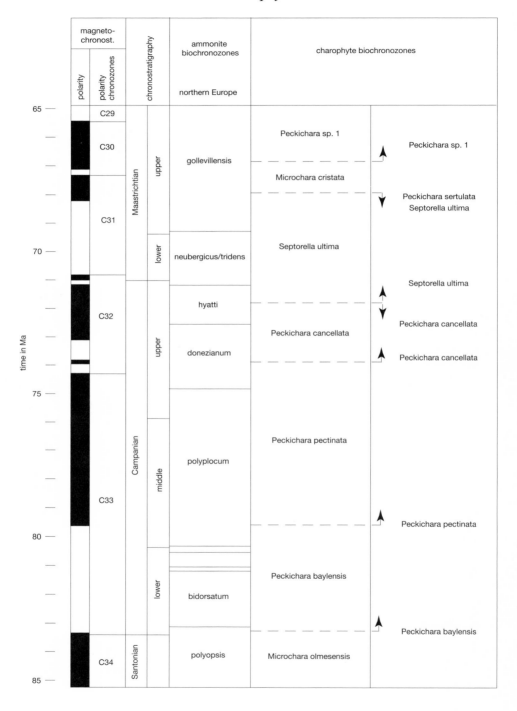

Fɪɢ. 29. Upper Cretaceous charophyte biochronozones (Feist in Riveline & others, 1996; magnetostratigraphy and chronostratigraphy adapted from Gradstein & others, 1994).

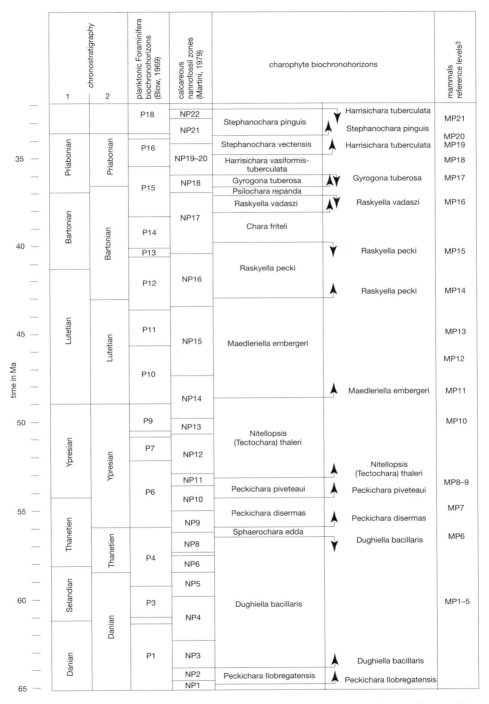

FIG. 30. Cenozoic (Paleogene: Danian–lower Rupelian) charophyte biochronozones (Riveline & others, 1996; time after Gradstein & others, 1994; chronostratigraphy: *1,* adapted from Gradstein & others, 1994; *2,* adapted from Cavelier & Pomerol, 1996; *3,* Schmidt-Kittler, 1987; Mein, 1989).

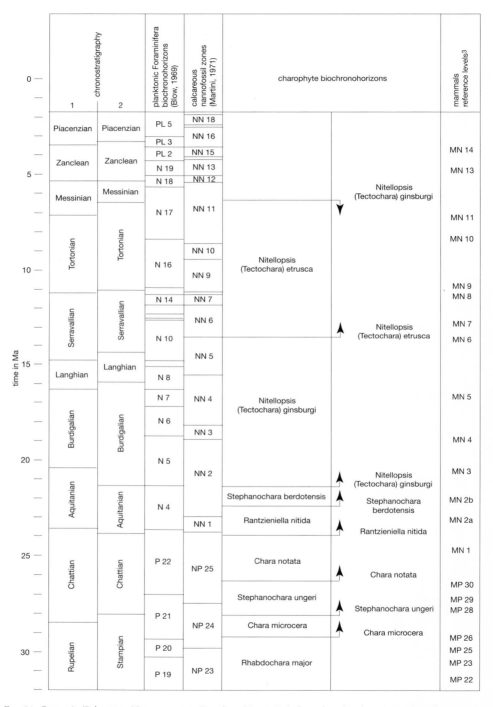

Fig. 31. Cenozoic (Paleogene–Neogene: upper Rupelian–Piacenzian) charophyte biochronozones (Riveline, Berger, & others in Riveline & others, 1996; time after Gradstein & others, 1994; chronostratigraphy: *1*, adapted from Gradstein & others, 1994; *2*, adapted from Cavelier & Pomerol, 1996; *3*, Schmidt-Kittler, 1987; Mein, 1989).

Upper Oxfordian–Upper Turonian

After the pioneering work of GRAMBAST (1974), MARTIN-CLOSAS and GRAMBAST-FESSARD (1986), SCHUDACK (1987), and DÉTRAZ and MOJON (1989), made important contributions to the biozonation of this interval. The scheme presented here is by MARTIN-CLOSAS and SCHUDACK (in RIVELINE & others, 1996), with addition of the *Globator rectispirale* Zone for the uppermost Jurassic (Fig. 26–28). The subdivisions of this interval are based on the Clavatoraceae, whose phylogenetic lineages are well suited for use in biozonation. Species have been named after the classification adopted in the charophyte *Treatise*. For the Upper Jurassic and Cretaceous, concordance with the cladistic nomenclature of the Clavatoraceae adopted by MARTIN-CLOSAS and SCHUDACK in RIVELINE and others (1996) is indicated in the captions of Figures 26–28.

JURASSIC-CRETACEOUS BOUNDARY

In charophyte biozonation, this limit has been established within the Broadoak Calcareous Member of southern England (FEIST, LAKE, & WOOD, 1995). The guide fossil of the terminal Jurassic, *Globator rectispirale* FEIST, is the only representative of the genus *Globator* with perfectly vertical cells. In addition to this characteristic morphology, the species has a wide distribution in northern Europe to northern Africa and until now has been the most precise marker for the end of the Jurassic. The Cretaceous begins with the first occurrence of spiral *Globator* species (FEIST & others, 1995).

Upper Turonian–Lower Santonian

Up to now, no charophyte localities have been published for this interval; thus no succession can be established.

Upper Santonian–Upper Maastrichtian

The biozonation of this interval (Fig. 29) was dealt with by FEIST in BABINOT and others (1983), FEIST and FREYTET (1983), and GALBRUN and others (1993), with an earlier account by GRAMBAST (1971). The succession was established in the south of France and northeastern Spain; it is calibrated with palynology and magnetostratigraphy.

PALEOCENE–PLIOCENE

The Cenozoic biozonation (Fig. 30–31) comprises 24 zones that have been correlated with the marine stages owing to correlations with the zones of nannoplankton (ANADÓN & others, 1983; RIVELINE, 1986); they have been correlated also with mammal zones (FEIST & RINGEADE, 1977; ANADÓN & FEIST, 1981; BERGER, 1986; RIVELINE, 1986; SCHWARZ & GRIESSEMER, 1992).

EVOLUTIONARY HISTORY

MONIQUE FEIST and NICOLE GRAMBAST-FESSARD

[Université Montpellier II, France]

The characters used to infer evolutionary trends in charophytes are primarily those of the fructification or postfertilization egg and associated cells and structures. Fossil fructifications comprise a gyrogonite (the enveloping cells, basal plate, and oospore membrane) and, in five families, a surrounding vegetative structure called a utricle. Details of gyrogonite and utricle structures are presented in the chapter on Morphology (herein, p. 1).

Characters useful in evolutionary reconstructions are both qualitative and quantitative. Qualitative characters include presence or absence of a utricle, shape and orientation of the enveloping cell (e.g., spiral or straight), apical-pore features, and basal-plate shape. Quantitative characters include size of the gyrogonite and utricle, number of enveloping cells, and number of basal-plate cells. The stratigraphic record of fossil charophytes provides a rationale for inferring primitive and derived character states (FEIST & GRAMBAST-FESSARD, 1991; MARTIN-CLOSAS & SCHUDACK, 1991; LU, SOULIÉ-MÄRSHE, & WANG, 1996). Based upon these inferences, a number of evolutionary trends are apparent and presented as hypotheses.

TRENDS IN CHARACTER EVOLUTION
ORIENTATION OF ENVELOPING CELLS

The direction of spiraling is visible from the base of the gyrogonites. In one of the oldest known charophyte species, the late Silurian *Moellerina laufeldi* CONKIN & CONKIN (Moellerinales), the gyrogonite is spiralled dextrally (clockwise spiralization; see *Pseudomoellerina*, Moellerinaceae, Fig. 44,*4b*, p. 93 herein). The sinistrally spiralled gyrogonites (Charales) appeared later during the Devonian in the Eocharaceae (counterclockwise spiralization; see *Rantzienella*, Raskeyellaceae, Fig. 62,*2c*, p. 118 herein).

Until recently, it was thought that the most primitive type of gyrogonite cell orientation was that of the vertical cells of the Sycidiales, but new data (see chapters herein on Classification, p. 83, and Systematic Descriptions, p. 92) show that these enveloping cells represent external layers of utricles, and the orientation and cell number of the enclosed gyrogonites are known incompletely. The utricular cells of the Sycidiales are vertical in the Sycidiaceae and most Chovanellaceae and dextrally coiled in the Trochiliscaceae. In *Ampullichara* YANG & ZHOU (Chovanellaceae) the utricular cells have a moderate dextral spiral.

NUMBER OF ENVELOPING CELLS

Paleozoic gyrogonites have a variable number of enveloping cells, five to twelve in the Moellerinales; a trend toward reduction in cell number is evident by the Late Devonian (*Pseudomoellerina* has five to seven cells).

High numbers of enveloping cells occur only in the utricles of *Sycidium* and *Trochiliscus;* in both genera, the number of cells varies little: 18 in *Trochiliscus* and most *Sycidium* species; in the latter, however, different numbers have been found: 12 to 14 in *S. karpinskyi* SAMOILOVA & SMIRNOVA from the Frasnian of the Moscow region (SAMOILOVA, 1955) and 16 in *S. clathratum* PECK from the Lower Mississippian of Missouri (PECK, 1934a; PECK & MORALES, 1966). A tendency toward reduction in number of utricular cells is well illustrated by the Chovanellaceae where *Xinjiangochara,* known from the Lower Devonian onward, possesses 9 to 14 cells; *Chovanella,* approximately 10 Ma younger, has 5 to 8; and the most recent, *Ampullichara,* has only 3 to 5.

The Charales also have a trend toward reduction of the number of enveloping gyrogonite cells in more recent taxa. The number is relatively high at first in the

Devonian Eocharaceae with 8 to 13 cells. The number is reduced to 6 or 7 in the Palaeocharaceae, also during the Devonian, and is finally fixed at 5 cells in the Porocharaceae and in all post-Paleozoic families, with the exception of an isolated record of an Eocharaceae in the Triassic (KISIELEVSKY, 1996).

APICAL PORE MORPHOLOGY

In the oldest charophyte fossils, the external cells of the fructification do not join at the apex, which leaves a small opening or pore that varies in size across taxa. An apical pore occurs in the Moellerinales, the Sycidiales, and the Palaeocharinae of the Charales. Among the Charinae, the Porocharaceae and Clavatoraceae also have an apical pore.

In the gyrogonites of the Raskyellaceae, the apex is closed by five small cells, which are missing in gyrogonites of germinated oospores. The complete closure of the apex, by junction of the enveloping cells, occurs in the Characeae, a condition that occurs first in *Aclistochara* from the Upper Triassic (LIU & CHEN, 1992).

GENERAL EVOLUTION

The general evolution of Charophyta from Silurian to Holocene is summarized in Figures 32 and 33. Recent findings on the nature of the fructification in Paleozoic forms bring a new understanding of the early stages of charophyte evolution.

THE OLDEST CHAROPHYTES: HYPOTHESES ON THE ORIGIN OF THE GROUP

The most ancient charophyte is the presumed ancestor of *Sycidium* from the uppermost lower Silurian (Llandovery-Wenlock boundary) of Anticosti Island (MAMET & others, 1992). Although the three-dimensional shape of the species cannot be established from the thin sections shown in illustrated specimens, the microstructure of the wall with concentric lamellae as well as the dark, inner part resembling an oospore membrane (MAMET & others, 1992, fig. 12–13) bear a close resemblance to Charophyta.

Two layers composing the wall, apparent in their figures 12 and 13, show the structure of a utricle; the high number (more than 30) of the sectioned enveloping cells suggests a spiral utricle similar to that in the Trochiliscaceae. *Primochara calvata* ISHCHENKO & SAIDAKOVSKY is referred tentatively to this family and, among the Sycidiaceae, *Pseudosycidium* HACQUAERT, 1932 and *Praesycidium* T. A. ISHCHENKO & A. A. ISHCHENKO, 1982 (now included in *Sycidium*), which were both reported from the upper Silurian, could be the immediate descendants of the Anticosti species.

To determine the identity of the possible ancestor of the Sycidiales, the first step is to find the type(s) of gyrogonite that are enclosed inside the utricles of the four families, Sycidiaceae, Trochiliscaceae, Chovanellaceae, and Pinnoputamenaceae. In these families, the fructifications are utricles, inside of which gyrogonites are generally uncalcified and not fossilized or, when preserved, do not have the characters that relate them to a defined group. The Moellerinales seem to be possible candidates, although they postdate by 2 to 3 Ma the hypothetical Anticosti species. Given the near absence of material from the lower Silurian, their existence in this period cannot be ruled out. Thus, new collections (M. FEIST) from the upper Silurian of Gotland show that *Moellerina laufeldi* CONKIN occurs earlier than the type level (J. E. CONKIN & B. M. CONKIN, 1992) in the Ludlow sequences. With their small size, the gyrogonites of *Moellerina* (especially those of *M. laufeldi,* whose diameter does not exceed 350 µm) might have been contained inside utricles. In fact, a gyrogonite of *Moellerina* type is enclosed in the utricle of the Chovanellaceae, but a different type of gyrogonite is suggested for *Sycidium* by the casts of undivided vertical cells that are visible at the internal face of a utricle of *S. xizangense* WANG (see Fig. 45*i*, Systematics, herein p. 95). These elongated cells, however, could be part of the inner utricle wall instead of gyrogonite components.

GRAMBAST (1974) speculated that the different Paleozoic forms may have independent origins from a primitive type in which the gyrogonite was not yet constituted, as the female organ (oosphere and egg) lacked sterile cells; the corresponding fructification would be a gametocyst rather than a gametangium. It seems probable that the gyrogonite first appeared by coalescence of unspecialized vegetative cells around a naked female cell; however, such a structure is unknown in charophytes.

The utricle of the Paleozoic families was probably elaborated progressively, as in the Clavatoraceae, and their origin is thus to be sought in former times. Molecular analyses of living charophytes suggest that they share a common ancestor with land plants (KAROL & others, 2001). Because fossil evidence for both charophytes and land plants is known from the Silurian (FEIST & GRAMBAST-FESSARD, 1991; KENRICK & CRANE, 1997), both groups diverged at some earlier time.

RELATIONSHIPS OF MODERN FORMS TO THEIR PALEOZOIC ANCESTORS

All post-Paleozoic taxa are grouped into the Charales; they have in common gyrogonites with sinistrally spiralled enveloping cells. The reversal of cell orientation that occurred first in the Eocharaceae may have arisen among the Moellerinaceae, which show a comparable gyrogonite cell number (8 to 13 in the former and 7 to 12 in the latter). Causes of this inversion remain enigmatic.

The oldest Charales, *Eochara wickendeni* CHOQUETTE (Eocharaceae) from the Middle Devonian of North America, has 8 to 13 cells. By reduction of the gyrogonite cell number, the Eocharaceae gave rise to the Palaeocharaceae and the latter to the Porocharaceae. The long time interval, ca. 40 Ma, between the first occurrences of Eocharaceae and Palaeocharaceae probably results from a gap in the fossil record, as a representative of the Eocharaceae has been found in the Middle Triassic (KISIELEVSKY, 1996).

EVOLUTIONARY TRENDS IN THE SYCIDIALES

Several evolutionary trends have developed in this group, mainly in the Devonian over a period of approximately 50 Ma.

Sycidium and Trochiliscus

The morphology of the basal pore, the long cells in comparably high number, and the cellular transverse ridges, which are common to *Sycidium* and *Trochiliscus,* suggest a close phylogenetic relationship between these genera (Z. WANG & LU, 1980; LU, SOULIÉ-MÄRSCHE, & WANG, 1996). *Trochiliscus,* which occurred first in the Early Devonian, was presumably derived from *Sycidium,* known possibly from the early Silurian but surely from the late Silurian onward, by spiral development of the long utricle cells.

Pinnoputamen

In the mid-Devonian *Pinnoputamen* WANG, the utricle presents two ramified, opposite branches (Z. WANG & LU, 1980) (see Fig. 48c, Systematics, herein p. 99) that in the Early Devonian *Pinnoputamen* sp. bear numerous antheridial casts (M. FEIST & R. FEIST, 1997) (see Fig. 48e, Systematics, herein p. 99). Although intermediate stages, probably including *Costacidium* LANGER, remain unclear, the evolution of the utricle, resulting in the coalescence of axes and in the reduction and loss of antheridia, is similar to the evolutionary trend in the Cretaceous *Perimneste-Atopochara* lineage.

Xinjiangochara-Chovanella-Ampullichara lineage

In these three genera, which comprise the Chovanellaceae, the utricle is composed of vertical long cells not reaching the apex. From the Early Devonian to the Mississippian, the cell number of the utricle reduces from 12 to 14 to 3 to 5. The utricle becomes spiral in the most recent of the three genera, *Ampullichara* from the Mississippian, which is the terminal member of the lineage.

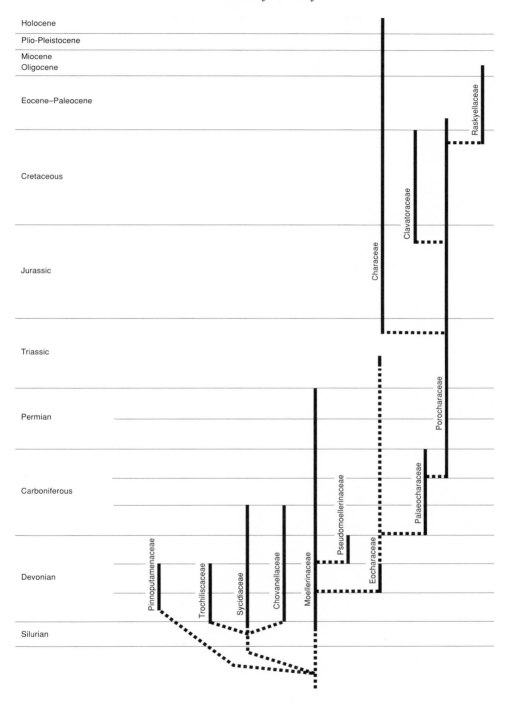

Fɪɢ. 32. Hypothesis of phylogenetic relationships between charophyte families (new).

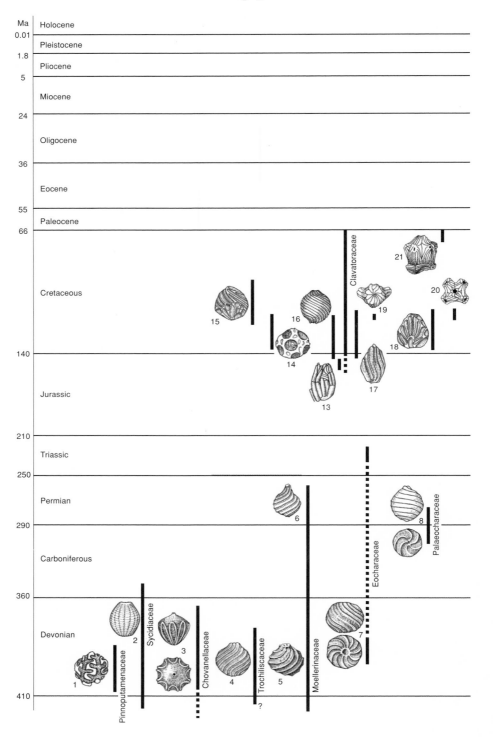

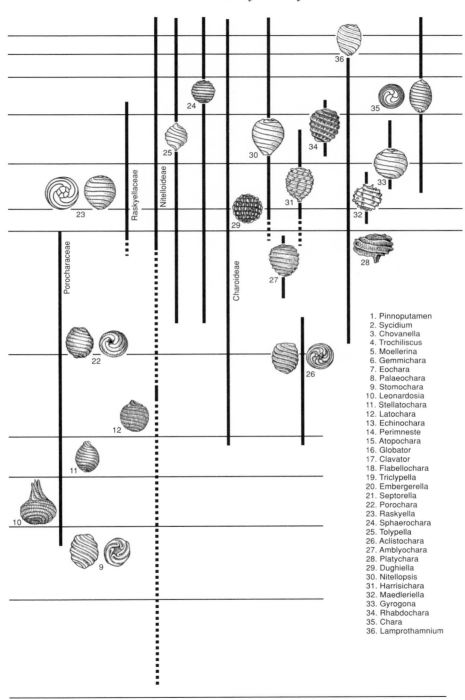

1. Pinnoputamen
2. Sycidium
3. Chovanella
4. Trochiliscus
5. Moellerina
6. Gemmichara
7. Eochara
8. Palaeochara
9. Stomochara
10. Leonardosia
11. Stellatochara
12. Latochara
13. Echinochara
14. Perimneste
15. Atopochara
16. Globator
17. Clavator
18. Flabellochara
19. Triclypella
20. Embergerella
21. Septorella
22. Porochara
23. Raskyella
24. Sphaerochara
25. Tolypella
26. Aclistochara
27. Amblyochara
28. Platychara
29. Dughiella
30. Nitellopsis
31. Harrisichara
32. Maedleriella
33. Gyrogona
34. Rhabdochara
35. Chara
36. Lamprothamnium

FIG. 33. Structural evolution of fructification in Charophyta (adapted from Grambast, 1974; Feist & Grambast-Fessard, 1991).

A. talimuica f. *crassa* YANG & ZHOU is the only specimen in which a gyrogonite can be observed in the utricle (see Fig. 47,*2e–f,* Systematics, herein p. 98). We may assume that the other members of this lineage also possessed a *Moellerina*-type gyrogonite within the utricle.

THE RADIATION OF THE POROCHARACEAE

After the extinction of Paleozoic families, the Porocharaceae constituted the core of the charophyte flora during the Triassic and the Jurassic. Porocharaceae often have small gyrogonites devoid of any ornamentation, but this family is of major phylogenetic importance (GRAMBAST, 1974). Porocharaceae are thought to have given rise to the three other post-Paleozoic families, based on the time of their appearance. The first lineage to diverge gave rise to the Characeae through closure of the apical pore by junction of the spiral cells at the apex. In the early representatives of this family, the Triassic *Aclistochara* species, the gyrogonite morphology is very similar to that of the Porocharaceae. In particular, the narrow apical zone (see Fig. 64,*3d,* Systematics, herein p. 122) resembles the small apical pore of the Porocharoideae (see Fig. 50,*2b,* Systematics, herein p. 102). The second group to diverge was the Clavatoraceae, in which the gyrogonite inside a utricle has an apex stretched into a neck and a persistent apical pore analogous to the Stellatocharoideae. Finally, the Raskyellaceae diverged by closure of the apical pore by an operculum of five apical cells.

The evolutionary tendencies inside the Porocharaceae themselves are twofold: toward the closure of the apical pore, in *Leonardosia* SOMMER and *Latochara* MÄDLER (Stellatocharoideae), and toward an increase of dimensions, culminating in the Late Cretaceous and Paleocene species of *Feistiella* SCHUDACK (Porocharoideae).

THE RADIATION OF THE CLAVATORACEAE

In this large family, the gyrogonite is enveloped in a utricle made of whorls of vegeta-
tive origin. Barely modified through early forms from the Upper Jurassic, this utricle appeared to undergo a fast and variegated morphological differentiation, mostly during the Early Cretaceous. This makes the group particularly well suited for precise phylogenetic studies. Stages linking distinct and apparently totally different extreme types are illustrated below.

Atopocharoideae PECK, 1938; emend., GRAMBAST, 1969

Members of this subfamily have a triradial symmetry, the utricle being composed of three similar units and characterized by a single-layered utricle wall (GRAMBAST, 1974).

The *Perimneste-Atopochara* phylogenetic lineage.—This lineage (Fig. 34) is the best documented and also has the longest duration, extending for perhaps 70 Ma, from the Berriasian to the Campanian. First described by GRAMBAST (1967, 1974), it was later completed by KYANSEP-ROMASCHKINA (1975), GRAMBAST-FESSARD (1980), FEIST (1981), and WANG and LU (1982). The successive evolutionary stages and species of the *Perimneste-Atopochara* lineage are reported here following FEIST and WANG (1995).

Perimneste horrida HARRIS (Fig. 34.1) is the oldest representative of the lineage and also the most primitive. It shows clearly the vegetative origin of the utricle. Dissolving the calcite with weak acetic acid shows the position of the utricle cells, which are grouped in three distinct clusters. Each cluster contains one basal cell bearing three branches, each of which is ramified into three cells except for the right branch, which is ramified into only two cells. Four to six superficial hollows with antheridial structures are borne by every secondary branch (see Fig. 60, Systematics, herein p. 116). The total cell number is 48, plus on average, 14 antheridia.

From the Berriasian to the Cenomanian, the three clusters condense progressively and the number of antheridial casts decreases. The separation of the two genera has been placed at the appearance of *Atopochara trivolvis,* when the central basal cell of each

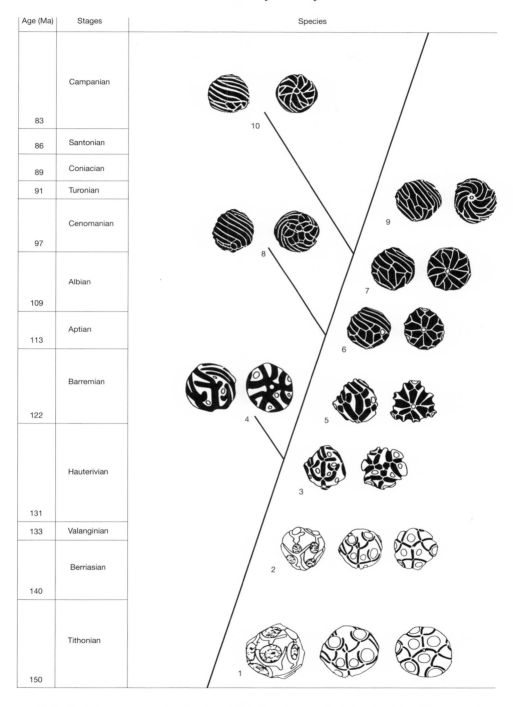

Fig. 34. Fossils of *Perimneste-Atopochara* lineage; *1, P. horrida; 2, P. micrandra; 3, P. ancora; 4, P. vidua; 5, A. triquetra; 6, A. trivolvis; 7, A. restricta; 8, A. brevicellis; 9, A. multivolvis; 10, A. ulanensis. 1–2,* left, surface of utricle with antheridia; center and right, lateral view, after etching of surface; *3–10,* left, lateral view; right, basal view (Feist & Wang, 1995, fig. 1).

cluster disappeared and the antheridial sites were reduced to one sterile cell (Fig. 34.6, and see Fig. 58,*1*, Systematics, herein p. 114). From the Barremian to the Cenomanian, the cells of antheridial origin disappeared altogether, and the upper cells are strongly spiral. The most derived condition of this evolutionary progression occurs in *A. multivolvis* PECK (Fig. 34.9) and *A. ulanensis* KYANSEP-ROMASCHKINA. This progressive series of structural modifications has been viewed as an illustration of the evolutionary species concept (MARTIN-CLOSAS & SERRA-KIEL, 1991; SCHUDACK, 1993b; MARTIN-CLOSAS & SCHUDACK, 1997). The succession of all representatives of the *Perimneste-Atopochara* lineage, however, shows that they are not disposed in a single series. Two of them present an assemblage of primitive and derived features. In *Perimneste vidua* GRAMBAST (Fig. 34.4), the large size recalls the oldest representative, *P. horrida;* the vegetative origin of the utricle is still visible; and the cell number (36) is the same as in *P. ancora* GRAMBAST. In contrast, the basal cells are shorter than in the latter species and thus comparable with those of the contemporaneous *Atopochara triquetra* FEIST.

In *Atopochara brevicellis* GRAMBAST-FESSARD (Fig. 34.8), the strong reduction of all lower cells and the correlative lengthening and spiralling of the upper cells, as well as the low cell number (30), indicate the most condensed structure of the lineage, but without subdivision of the upper cells, which occurs in *A. multivolvis* PECK. The existence of several evolutionary divergences is incompatible with monophyly as postulated under the evolutionary species concept. The combination of primitive and derived characters found in both taxa can be interpreted as the result of heterochronic development. Heterochronic processes, corresponding to changes in the timing and rate of ontogenetic development, may account for the simultaneous presence of ancestral and derived characters as in *Perimneste vidua* and *Atopochara brevicellis.*

Atopochara ulanensis (Fig. 34.10), which is the last representative of the *Perimneste-Atopochara* lineage, does not differ in its structure from *A. restricta.* In particular the lower cells of these taxa are triangular and relatively prominent. *A. ulanensis* has a lengthening and a spiralling of the upper cells that is comparable to that of *A. multivolvis,* although the upper cells are not divided in *A. ulanensis.* In Europe, *A. restricta* is succeeded by *A. multivolvis,* and the *Perimneste-Atopochara* lineage ends with the latter in the Turonian. In Asia (Mongolia and China) *A. restricta* subsequently gave rise to *A. ulanensis,* with dates ranging from Campanian to Maastrichtian. Allopatric speciation may explain the derivation of the two species from a common ancestor, *A. restricta,* during the Late Cretaceous.

The *Globator* lineage.—This series shows the evolution from the Tithonian *Globator rectispirale* FEIST to the Barremian and Aptian *G. trochiliscoides* GRAMBAST (Fig. 35). Initially reconstructed by GRAMBAST (1966a, 1974), this lineage was completed by the discovery of new stages and a reappraisal of the chronology (MARTIN-CLOSAS & GRAMBAST-FESSARD, 1986; MOJON & STRASSER, 1987; FEIST, LAKE, & WOOD, 1995; MARTIN-CLOSAS, 1996).

The utricle of *Globator rectispirale* is composed of three units of eight cells each: one basal cell bears three long upper cells and, on each side of the central units, a relatively long basal cell bears one upper cell. Altogether the 24 cells of a utricle have a vertical orientation. In *G. trochiliscoides,* only 15 strongly coiled long cells are present, and all the basal cells have disappeared. In successive localities of the Lower Cretaceous, intermediate species such as *Globator incrassatus* MARTIN-CLOSAS & GRAMBAST-FESSARD (upper Berriasian) and *G. mutabilis* MOJON (Barremian), show that the general trends of the succession are a progressive reduction of all the basal cells together with an increase in length and spiralling of the long cells.

Globator nurrensis PECORINI is separated from the main line by its utricle shape, which is elongated and fusiform and, above all, by the disposition of the basal part where only the central cell of each group is reduced.

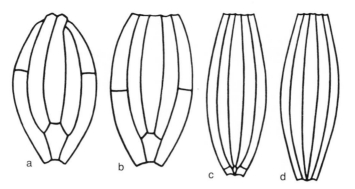

FIG. 35. Structure of utricular unit in *a, Globator maillardi* (SAPORTA) GRAMBAST; *b, G. incrassatus* MARTIN-CLOSAS & GRAMBAST-FESSARD; *c, G. trochiliscoides* var.; *d, G. trochiliscoides* GRAMBAST (Grambast, 1974, fig. 6).

GRAMBAST (1966a) interpreted this species as a side branch of the main line of the sequence.

Clavatoroideae PIA, 1927; emend., GRAMBAST, 1969

The Clavatoroideae are the Clavatoraceae with the longest range, from the Oxfordian with the genus *Clavator* REID and GROVES, to the uppermost Maastrichtian when the last *Septorella, S. ultima,* became extinct. This group has been interpreted as the result of extensive cladogenetic change, at least through the upper Barremian, and its members have the highest degree of specialization of the female reproductive structures in the Charophyta. Members of this subfamily have bilateral symmetry and are characterized by a bilayered utricle wall as well as by the presence of internal canals, representing small stems (stemlets) with a succession of nodes and internodes. Two examples illustrate the diversity displayed in this subfamily.

The *Clavator-Flabellochara-Clypeator* phylogenetic lineage.—GRAMBAST (1970, 1974) has established very precisely the successive stages of the *Flabellochara-Clypeator* lineage during the Early Cretaceous (Fig. 36). MARTIN-CLOSAS (1996) connected this lineage to its ancestral form from the Upper Jurassic, the genus *Clavator*. In this lineage the utricle is composed of two opposite lateral units separated by several cells in the ventral (adaxial) and dorsal (abaxial) sides.

Flabellochara grovesi (HARRIS) GRAMBAST presents a distinct bilateral symmetry; each of the two lateral fans includes a short median basal cell bearing six or more, often seven, radiating upper cells and two lower cells situated on each side of the median basal cell. As noted by HARRIS (1939) the utricles of this species are always laterally compressed. The first known occurrence of this species is in the lower Berriasian (FEIST, LAKE, & WOOD, 1995), although its putative descendant, *Clypeator discordis,* has been reported from the Upper Jurassic. Given the rarity of charophyte records for the Upper Jurassic, it is possible that *F. grovesi* may have evolved earlier.

Clypeator discordis SHAIKIN has a structure very similar to that of *Flabellochara grovesi,* but two or three additional cells are intercalated between the basal cell and the upper radiating cells of the still recognizable fans. Generally these cells are placed laterally, surrounding a lateral pore. In contrast to *F. grovesi,* the lateral sides are not flattened but curved, tending sometimes to have light, protruding expansions. The species has been reported from the Hauterivian to the lower Barremian (GRAMBAST, 1974; MARTIN-CLOSAS & GRAMBAST-FESSARD, 1986).

Clypeator gautieri GRAMBAST comprises the same essential elements as the preceeding type, but the intermediate cells between the lateral pore and the basal cell are better developed, becoming similar to the fan cells.

FIG. 36. Transition from lateral fan to shield structure in *Flabellochara-Clypeator* lineage; *a, Flabellochara grovesi* (HARRIS) GRAMBAST; *b, Clypeator discordis* SHAIKIN; *c, C. gautieri* GRAMBAST; *d, C. combei* GRAMBAST; *e, C. corrugatus* (PECK) GRAMBAST (Grambast, 1970, fig. a–e).

Moreover, the expansions bearing the lateral pores are here quite distinct. *C. gautieri* ranges from the Hauterivian to the upper Barremian (GRAMBAST, 1974; FEIST, LAKE, & WOOD, 1995).

Clypeator combei GRAMBAST is large, and the intermediate cells in contact with the basal cell tend to reach the same length as the upper cells. The disposition of the 10 to 11 cells radiating around the lateral pores that are borne by protruding expansions shows clearly the shield structure characteristic of the genus.

In *Clypeator corrugatus* (PECK) GRAMBAST, from the Aptian, the shields are made of 11 to 13 sinuous radiating cells among which the basal cells are not distinguishable from the upper ones.

In these five species, the adaxial side presents a rather constant disposition, resembling the opposing side, but two median lateral cells are present in *C. gautieri* and *C. combei*.

The *Ascidiella-Embergerella* phylogenetic lineage.—In this group, the utricle presents lateral expansions (horns) ending with central pores, which represent the protrusion of internal stemlets. Stemlets and horns are in equal numbers: only one in *Ascidiella,* three or four in *Embergerella.* The utricle was probably fixed at a node of a branchlet, as always occurs in the fructifications of the extant Characeae. The superficial layer of the utricle is made of cellular whorls, more or less imbricated one in another (Fig. 37). Every pore in the center of a whorl corresponds to the termination of internal long cells, which themselves originate from a stemlet connecting the basal pore to a lateral horn. Besides

the number of horns, the two genera differ in the morphology of the external whorls, which are single in the former and twofold in the latter.

MARTIN-CLOSAS (1996) proposed a quite different interpretation (Fig. 38). In *Embergerella,* he interpreted the stemlets as fixed at the base of the utricle on the branchlet (phylloid), but for *Ascidiella* it is the branchlet itself that is included in the utricle. Bracts were seen as ramifications leading to the external whorls. In this representation, the structure of the utricle appears different in these two genera.

The new approach of the Clavatoroideae by MARTIN-CLOSAS (1996), based mainly on cladistic analysis, allowed him to establish and connect together different lineages that were formerly isolated. Thus, *Lucernella* (*Clavator calcitrapus* and *C. ampullaceus*) and *Septorella* (*Clavator brachycerus* and *Clavator ultimus*) are related to the series *Clavator-Flabellochara-Clypeator* (genus *Clavator* emend. SCHUDACK, 1993b). *Pseudoglobator* and *Hemiclavator* were derived from *Nodosoclavator.*

THE DEVELOPMENT OF THE CHARACEAE

Origin

The oldest Characeae are the four *Aclistochara* species from the Upper Triassic of Sichuan Province (China; LIU & CHEN, 1992). These forms show the junction of the spiral cells at the summit of the gyrogonite that characterizes the family, but the features of the dehiscence pore, narrow and situated at the bottom of a depression (see Fig. 64,*3d,* Systematics, herein p. 122), support the view

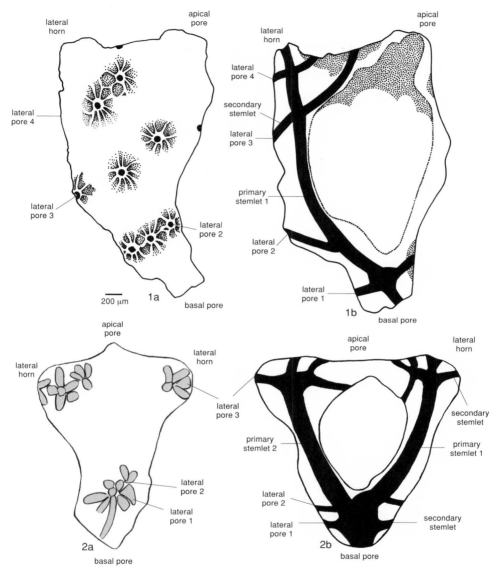

FIG. 37. Connections between external and internal structures of utricle; *1a–b, Ascidiella irregularis* GRAMBAST-FESSARD (Grambast-Fessard, 1986, fig. 1); *a,* external view, *b,* longitudinal section; *2a–b, Embergerella triquetra* GRAMBAST; *a,* external view, *b,* longitudinal section (new).

that the Characeae originated from the Porocharaceae.

Evolutionary Tendencies

During the Late Cretaceous, such larger gyrogonites as *Peckisphaera macrocarpa* (GRAMBAST) FEIST & GRAMBAST-FESSARD appeared, as well as gyrogonites with diverse types of ornamentation, such as *Peckichara pectinata* GRAMBAST and *Microchara punctata* FEIST. The Paleogene was the time of greatest diversification in the Characeae. The family has a great variety in the general shape, ornamentation, and apical features of the gyrogonites. From the Miocene onward, the family decreased in diversity and number

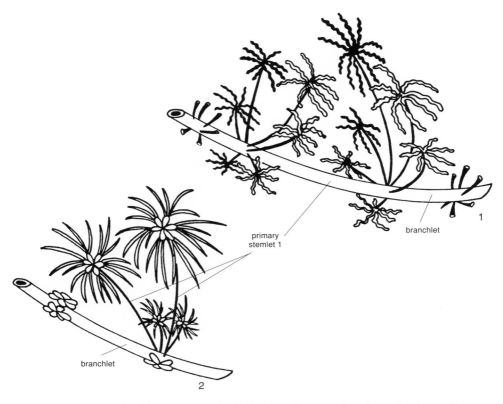

FIG. 38. Interpretation of utricle structure; *1, Ascidiella iberica* GRAMBAST; *2, Embergerella triquetra* GRAMBAST (*Ascidiella triquetra* in cladistic nomenclature) (Martin-Closas, 1996, fig. 13D, 13C).

of genera until the present day, when it is represented by seven unornamented genera including 80 species, according to WOOD and IMAHORI (1964–1965).

Special Cases of Evolution

Phylogenetic lineages as complex as in the Clavatoraceae are unknown in the Characeae. A simple succession connecting *Aclistochara* to *Lamprothamnium* has, however, been recognized. SOULIÉ-MÄRSCHE (1979) noted the affinities of the two genera, according to their apical structure, in which the apex of the gyrogonite, prominent in the center, is surrounded by a periapical furrow. She proposed the inclusion of *Aclistochara* in *Lamprothamnium*. Apical views of both genera (see Fig. 64,*3d* and 68,*1c,* Systematics, herein p. 122 and p. 129 respectively), however, show that the apical zone is much

smaller in the former, in which it resembles the porocharacean ancestors. The variation curves of the apical pore diameter (Fig. 39) confirm these morphological data: the curve corresponding to *Aclistochara* is distinct from *Lamprothamnium* and closer to *Porochara*. The two genera are also distinguished by the general shape of their gyrogonites and by their basal plates: multipartite in *Aclistochara* and simple in *Lamprothamnium* (LU & LUO, 1990). The significance of the basal plate character is discussed in the chapter on Molecular Phylogeny, herein p. 81.

Interspecific Relationships

An example of progressive evolution between species has beeen reported in the genus *Harrisichara* (FEIST-CASTEL, 1977a). *H. vasiformis* (REID & GROVES) GRAMBAST (see Fig. 67,*1a,* Systematics, herein p. 128) and

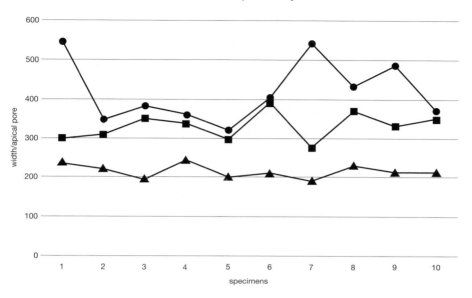

FIG. 39. Variation of apical pore in three species: curves for ratio of equatorial diameter of gyrogonite to diameter of apical pore; *Porochara douzensis* (FEIST & GRAMBAST-FESSARD) SCHUDACK, *circles; Aclistochara* aff. *jonesi* PECK, *squares; Lamprothamnium papulosum* GROVES, *triangles* (Feist, Bhatia, & Yadagiri, 1991, fig. 2).

H. tuberculata (LYELL) GRAMBAST (see Fig. 67,*1b,* Systematics, herein p. 128) are two distinct and easily recognizable species. In the Isle of Wight (Hampshire, England) from the Lower Headon Beds upward and mainly in the series occurring between these and the Bembridge Beds, specimens of *Harrisichara* occur that are morphologically intermediate between the two species. Besides England, *H. vasiformis-tuberculata* is also relatively common in northern and southern Europe. Due to its wide geographical distribution and short vertical extension, this form is of great stratigraphical value; it is one of the guide fossils of the upper Eocene in the Paleogene biozonation (RIVELINE & others, 1996; and Biozonation, herein, Fig. 31, p. 58).

PHYLOGENY OF THE RASKYELLACEAE

The Raskyellaceae are a small group, characterized by the pecular apical structure of the gyrogonite. In the three genera composing the family, the closure of the apex is brought about by a deciduous opercule of five cells, which upon falling out of the pore leaves a rose-shaped opening (GRAMBAST, 1957). The shape and relative narrowness of this pore of dehiscence are similar in some Porocharaceae (see Fig. 50,*3c,* Systematics, herein p. 102). These similarities suggest relationships between the families. The basal plate, which is simple in all the Raskyellaceae, suggests an origin in *Feistiella* SCHUDACK, which was, moreover, contemporaneous with the early genus *Saportanella* GRAMBAST during the Late Cretaceous.

The internal intercellular folds are another peculiar character common to *Raskyella* L. & N. GRAMBAST and *Rantzienella* GRAMBAST but not restricted to the Raskyellaceae. In both genera, the sutures between the spiral cells are strongly crenulated; such sutures also occur at the periphery of the apex between the tips of the spiral cells and the opercular cells. The internal folds are always visible at the internal face of the opercule (see Fig. 61*g,* Systematics, herein p. 117) but only rarely from the exterior, as in *Rantzieniella nitida* GRAMBAST (FEIST & GRAMBAST-FESSARD, 1984, fig. 3C).

The fossil record of the Raskyellaceae is relatively discontinuous: Upper Cretaceous (Campanian–Maastrichtian: *Saportanella*), Eocene (*Raskyella*), and Miocene (Aquitanian: *Rantzieniella*). According to NÖTZOLD (1965), Z. WANG (1978a), and SOULIÉ-MÄRSCHE (1989) the apical cells of the Raskyellaceae correspond to a thickening of the apical tips of the spiral cells and could have been derived in different periods from ancestors belonging to the Characeae. The individuality of the apical cells, however, cannot be questioned since the crenellated sutures differ from a straight dehiscence line or to a line of demarcation between differently calcified zones (ANADÓN & FEIST, 1981). Moreover, during the last two decades some gaps in the fossil record have been filled; for example, recent findings have contributed to completing the Eocene fossil record for the genus *Raskyella* (MARTIN-CLOSAS & others, 1999). The Raskyellaceae are thus deemed a valid family.

The characters used to detect affinities within the Raskyellaceae are the apex features, as well as the presence or absence of an ornamentation and of internal cellular folds. In *Saportanella* and *Rantzieniella,* the opercular cells occur as extensions of the spiral cells, and both genera are unornamented. In *Raskyella,* the opercular cells often alternate with the tips of the spiral cells; the genus is ornamented and shares with *Rantzieniella* the internal cellular folds. *Saportanella,* which is the oldest and has the most simple morphology, could be considered as the ancestor of *Saportanella* and *Raskyella.* The last occurrence of the Raskyellaceae is that of *Rantzieniella nitida* during the Aquitanian.

CONCLUDING REMARKS

The evolution of the fructification in Charophyta (Fig. 33) shows that the greatest morphological diversity occurred mainly in the Sycidiales and Clavatoraceae, groups that possess a utricle. A tendency to separation of sexes appears in two different lineages separated by nearly 300 Ma, the Devonian *Pinnoputamen* and the Cretaceous *Perimneste-Atopochara* evolutionary lineages. It is surprising that analogous trends occur in both thalloid haplobiontic charalean algae and in vascular plants. In the latter dioecy tends to replace hermaphroditism, which may lead to self-sterility (MAYNARD SMITH, 1990).

Several general features also appear in charophyte evolution: the tendency toward becoming spiral and reduction of cell number, as well as improvements in enclosing and protecting the egg. This took place in one of two different ways, either by the closure of the apical pore of the gyrogonite in the Characeae and Raskyellaceae or by the acquisition of a supplementary cover (utricle) around the gyrogonite that occurred independently in the Sycidiales and in the Clavatoraceae.

EVOLUTION OF CHAROPHYTE BIODIVERSITY

The 420-million-year charophyte fossil record is well documented but varies in completeness according to periods and regions (see chapter on Paleobiogeography, herein p. 39). Charophytes from the Paleozoic have been reported mainly from North America and China and to lesser extent from Europe and some other parts of the world, whereas they occurred worldwide during the Mesozoic. During the Cenozoic, charophytes were most abundant in Europe and Asia (mainly China and India) and less common in North and South America. The fossil record of charophytes from Australia is still nearly nonexistent.

The succession of most genera (see Fig. 33, p. 65 herein) and a table of the range of families (see Stratigraphic Range Chart, herein p. 148) show that there were several phases of diversification and extinction.

PHASES OF DIVERSIFICATION

The oldest certain representatives of charophytes have been reported from upper Silurian Ludlow deposits of Europe:

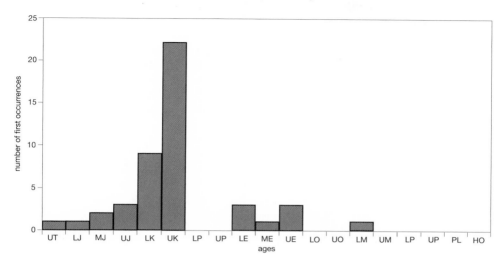

FIG. 40. First occurrences of charophyte genera, from Upper Triassic to Holocene (new).

Moellerina laufeldi CONKIN and *Praesycidium siluricum* T. and A. ISHCHENKO, now regarded as a species of *Sycidium*. The form from Anticosti (Canada) figured in a section evoking a sycidiaceaen gyrogonite (in MAMET & others, 1992), however, suggests that the group may have appeared as early as the early Silurian (Wenlockian-Ludlowian transition). These occurrences coincide with the first records of land plants during the Silurian (KENRICK & CRANE, 1997). The Devonian, when six charophyte families were in existence, was the period of greatest diversity.

The second phase of major diversification corresponds to the appearance and development of the Clavatoraceae during the Late Jurassic and Early Cretaceous, whereas the Late Cretaceous was a time of the initial diversification phase of the Characeae (Fig. 40).

After numerous charophyte extinctions at the end of the Cretaceous, a new phase of diversification occurred during the Eocene, but it is detectable only at the generic and specific levels.

The last new charophyte genus to appear was *Rantzieniella* GRAMBAST (Raskyellaceae), the only Miocene origination.

PHASES OF EXTINCTION AND RECOVERY

Pennsylvanian Extinction

After the extinction at the end of the Devonian of two or three families (as the Eocharaceae are unknown between Late Devonian and Middle Triassic) and the drastic reduction in number of species in the Moellerinaceae, charophytes as a group would probably have become extinct if a new and important family, the Porocharaceae, had not evolved during the Pennsylvanian. The small family Palaeocharaceae, which appeared simultaneously, were extinct before the Triassic. The Porocharaceae represent the major part of the fossil record of the Triassic and Lower Jurassic. This family survived until the Paleocene.

Cretaceous-Tertiary Boundary

The Cretaceous-Tertiary boundary represents a key period in charophyte history (Fig. 40). It marks the passage from the Cretaceous forms, dominated by the Porocharaceae and Clavatoraceae, to those of the Tertiary in which the radiation of the Characeae occurred. The small family Raskyellaceae apparently descended from the

Porocharaceae during the Late Cretaceous and persisted until the early Miocene.

If one compares the floras below and above the Cretaceous-Tertiary boundary, there is a sharp break between the Mesozoic and Cenozoic floras when approximately half of all charophyte species became extinct (FEIST, 1979). But this drastic decline in biodiversity did not cause the extinction of the group, most likely because it occurred during a diversificaton phase of one family, the Characeae. Thus the Cretaceous-Tertiary boundary marks a sharp decline within the charophytes, but not really a mass extinction. The most outstanding changes occurred after the K-T crisis. Indeed, the extinctions at the end of the Cretaceous were not balanced by an equivalent number of new genera. The result was a drastic reduction in diversity during the Cenozoic. The expansion of aquatic angiosperms may also have limited charophyte recovery.

PRESENT STATE AND PROSPECTS

Charophytes have shown remarkable resilience over the 420 million years of their existence. Their periods of greatest diversity and abundance occurred 300 to 400 million years ago. As shown by Figures 33 and 40, the present corresponds to a period of impoverishment of the Characeae, without any recent originations. Charophytes are cer-tainly outcompeted by angiosperms in many habitats, but a kind of equilibrium appears in the biotopes where the two groups coexist. In spring, charophyte growth precedes that of aquatic angiosperms after which the vegetative parts of charophytes regress. Charophyte populations persist by means of fertilized oosporangia in the sediments of the water body until the next spring, when they germinate and give rise to a new vegetative thallus.

Probably most dangerous to the existence of charophytes are the various transformations that often eliminate bodies of water and, at the same time, the biotopes of Characeae. Chemical pollution, generally of agricultural or industrial origin, is responsible for the disappearance of species from some regions.

Protective measures, however, such as those applied to *Lamprothamnium* in Great Britain (MOORE, 1991) and *Lychnothamnus* (CASANOVA, 1997; MCCOURT & others, 1999) in Australia as well as lake rehabilitation, for example in the Netherlands (SIMONS & others, 1994), have allowed the persistence of threatened species or the recovery of some species that had disappeared from their habitats. Such protective measures should be encouraged to preserve these interesting and scientifically important organisms.

MOLECULAR PHYLOGENY

R. M. McCourt,[1] K. G. Karol,[2] and Monique Feist[3]

[[1]The Academy of Natural Sciences, Philadelpia, USA; [2]University of Washington, Seattle, USA; and [3]Université Montpellier II, France]

INTRODUCTION

Molecular phylogeny provides a test of the homology of morphological characters used in construction of evolutionary hypotheses for fossil and extant taxa. Even though molecular data are not directly available for fossils, gene-sequence data for those taxa within a group such the charophytes with an ancient fossil record can tie together branches that include fossil and living taxa. Moreover, relating charophytes, a group with such distinctive morphology, to extant sister taxa with little in the way of shared morphology is very difficult. But doing so may be possible with molecular data, and this approach has yielded significant insights into phylogenetic relationships of charophytes, land plants, and other green algae (McCourt, Karol, & others, 1996; McCourt, Meiers, & others, 1996; McCourt & others, 1999; Chapman & others, 1998; Karol & others, 2001; Sanders, Karol, & McCourt, 2003).

For the charophytes, molecular research has used data from several different genes or nonprotein-coding DNA (reviewed by McCourt, Meiers, & others, 1996). Phylogenetic hypotheses for extant charophyte genera and species have been tested against phylogenies based on the morphology of gyrogonites for the Characeae and related families. These comparisons have provided information that has been considered critical to understanding charophyte evolution, i.e., convergent evolution of some characters. This chapter describes the methods used to obtain molecular data from living charophyte genera also reported as fossils and methods of analysis of these data.

METHODS OF MOLECULAR PHYLOGENETIC STUDIES

COLLECTION OF MATERIAL

Molecular samples must be free of contaminating epiphytes or endophytes to avoid spurious amplification and sequencing of genes from other than those of the target taxa (e.g., Sluiman & Guihal, 1999; Cimino, Karol, & Delwiche, 2000). Because charophytes are often collected in association with other green algae, careful examination of thalli prior to extraction is essential. Even when no epiphytes are evident, endophytes may exist within charophyte cells (Jost, 1895; Cimino & Delwiche, 2002). This source of possible contamination is all the more problematic when the endophyte is a species of *Coleochaete,* such as *C. nitellarum,* which is related relatively closely to charophytes and may be similar enough genetically to confound phylogenetic analysis. The diversity of such endophytes may be greater than previously thought (Cimino & Delwiche, 2002).

Culturing of material in soil water medium (microcosms of ponds, in glass jars of water over a sterilized soil and sand mixture, Hoshaw & Rosowski, 1973) can yield fresh growing tips that are often the best material for DNA sampling. Fresh or flash-frozen material (using liquid nitrogen) is best for sampling, and as little as 0.1 g of material is sufficient, using slightly modified CTAB (Cetyltrimethylammonium Bromide) methods (McCourt, Karol, & others, 1996; McCourt & others, 1999) for extraction.

GENES USED FOR STUDY

Early phylogenetic research on many algal groups employed sequences of the small subunit ribosomal DNA present in all eukaryotes (SSU rDNA, also called 18S rDNA) (Hillis, Moritz, & Mable, 1996). This nuclear gene has been used in a wide variety of organisms and has been sampled in the Characeae as well (Kranz & Huss, 1996). The relatively large size (~1,800 bp) and slow rate of change make it more suitable for studies of deep branching within the

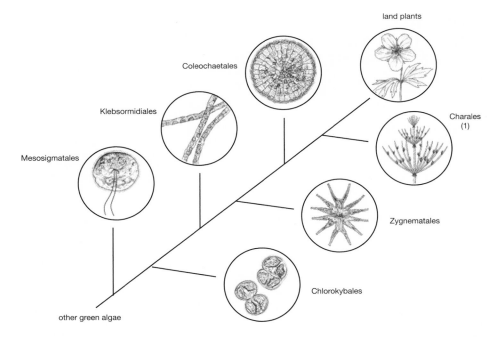

FIG. 41. Phylogeny of green algae and land plants based on four-gene analysis of Karol and others (2001); thumbnail sketches showing morphology of major groups of algae and one flowering plant in lineage including land plants or embryophytes (*i.e.,* liverworts, mosses, vascular plants, seed plants, and angiosperms); see Karol and others (2001) and Judd and others (2002); *1,* Charales, that is, Charophyta *s.s.* (adapted from Karol & others, 2001).

phylogeny of algae and green plants, although even at this relatively ancient level SSU sequences by themselves have been misleading (KRANZ & HUSS, 1996) or provided only weak resolution of phylogeny (KAROL & others, 2001). Internally transcribed spacer regions of DNA (ITS 1 and ITS 2) are transcribed but nontranslated regions located between the small subunit (SSU or 18S), 5.8S, and large subunit (LSU or 28S) of rDNA. The highly variable ITS regions are effective in studies of angiosperm species (BALDWIN & others, 1995), but they are apparently too variable to be equally informative in studies of more anciently diverged lineages in the Characeae (R. McCOURT & K. KAROL, personal observation, 2002).

Sequences from other genomic compartments have also been sampled. The large subunit of Rubisco (see Glossary, herein p. 90) from the chloroplast *rbcL* is a protein-coding gene that exhibits greater sequence

divergence than SSU sequences and is effective in deciphering sectional and generic relationships in the Characeae (McCOURT, KAROL, & others, 1996). While informative at the interspecific level, *rbcL* alone did not resolve fully the relationships among species. The four-gene analysis of KAROL and others (2001) provided additional support for the *rbcL* results (see below). The finding of *matK* in the plastid of characean taxa (SANDERS, KAROL, & McCOURT, 2003) provided an additional gene with more informative characters than other plastid genes normally sampled (MOHR, PERLMAN, & LAMBOWITZ, 1993; JOHNSON & SOLTIS, 1994, 1995; STEELE & VILGALYS, 1994; OOI & others, 1995; LIERE & LINK, 1995; GADEK, WILSON, & QUINN, 1996). This gene (~1,500 bp) resides within a group II intron of the *trnK* tRNA gene, which encodes the lysine tRNA. The level of divergence in *matK* holds promise for further species-level studies.

MOLECULAR PHYLOGENY AND IMPLICATIONS FOR FOSSIL CHAROPHYTES

RELATIONSHIP OF CHARACEAE TO OTHER GREEN ALGAE AND LAND PLANTS

The morphological complexity of charophytes compared to most other green algae has led workers to classify them in a distinct group, usually at the division (=phylum) level (i.e., Charophyta) or as a distinct class within the green algae in the broader sense (i.e., Charophyceae within the Chlorophyta) (SMITH, 1950; BOLD & WYNNE, 1985). SMITH (1950) preferred assigning the Characeae to the class Charophyceae because of the their distinctly different vegetative and reproductive features, such as verticillate branching and sheathing cells surrounding the reproductive structures. MATTOX and STEWART (1984) expanded the taxon Charophyceae to include the Charales plus an assemblage of other green algae (listed below) that share a number of traits with land plants. These characters included features of cell division, structure of the flagella, and other features that indicated this assemblage of green algae, including the Charales and fossil relatives, is on the line of evolution leading to land plants (embryophytes; i.e., liverworts, bryophytes, and nonvascular and vascular plants). Moreover, the Charophyceae or at least one of its member groups shared a more recent common ancestor with land plants than with other green algae. Thus, charophycean algae plus land plants constituted one of two major lineages, and the other comprised the rest of what we commonly call green algae (MISHLER & CHURCHILL, 1985; McCOURT, 1995). BREMER (1985) proposed to call the monophyletic group of charophycean green algae plus land plants the Streptophyta or streptophytes.

The hypothesis of MATTOX and STEWART (1984), based primarily on ultrastructural morphology, has been verified by molecular studies in the past decade (McCOURT, 1995;

CHAPMAN & others, 1998; KAROL & others, 2001; CHAPMAN & WATERS, 2002). The Charophyceae of MATTOX and STEWART (1984), however, included several groups in addition to charophytes *sensu stricto,* and the identity of the sister taxon of the land plants has proven elusive (GRAHAM, 1993; McCOURT, 1995; CHAPMAN & others, 1998). These other groups of the Charophyceae *sensu* MATTOX and STEWART include the Klebsormidiales (filamentous green algae), Chlorokybales (unicells arranged in packets), Zygnematales (conjugating green algae), and Coleochaetales (discoid or filamentous algae with sheathed hairs).

It is important to note that the advent of molecular data did not answer immediately the question of which group is the sister taxon of land plants. These new data from gene sequences occur not in a vacuum but in an arena of competing hypotheses on the relationships of green algae and land plants (see GRAHAM, 1993; CHAPMAN & others, 1998 for reviews). Analyses of the nuclear SSU gene suggested that the Charales were the earliest branch from the streptophyte lineage, with less complex filamentous forms (e.g., Klebsormidiales, Zygnematales, Coleochaetales, and Chlorokybales) forming an unresolved sister group of the land plants (KRANZ & HUSS, 1996). In contrast, data from the plastid gene *rbcL,* the large subunit of the photosynthetic enzyme Rubisco suggests that the Charales, the Coleochaetales, or a clade of both groups formed the sister taxon of the land plants (McCOURT, KAROL, & others, 1996; CHAPMAN & others, 1998). The reason for this conflict between analyses based on two genes is not clear but is likely due to inadequate taxon sampling and insufficient sequence data.

A recent four-gene study of a broad range of algal and plant groups using sequence data from chloroplast (*rbcL, atpB*), nuclear (SSU rDNA), and mitochondrial (*nad5*) genes suggested that the Charales (and presumably extinct charophytes) form an exclusive group that is the sister taxon of land plants (Fig. 41) (KAROL & others, 2001). The analysis and

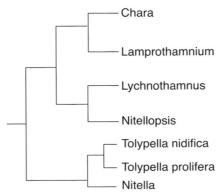

FIG. 42. Phylogenetic relationships of extant genera of Characeae based on analysis of four genes; sequences of four genes included 2 plastid genes (*rbcL, atpB*), 1 mitochondrial gene (*nad5*), and 1 nuclear-encoded gene (small subunit, or 18S, rDNA); an aligned dataset of 5,147 base pairs was subjected to Bayesian inference; same tree resulted from an analysis using maximum parsimony and minimum evolution. This tree represents a portion of phylogeny for green algae and land plants from Karol and others (2001), where more details may be found.

thorough taxon sampling of the latter study provides the strongest support to date of a sister-taxon relationship between charophytes and land plants. In other words, the Charales and their extinct relatives are descended from a unique, green-algal ancestor that was related to other streptophytes but distinct from them. These results are consistent with later analyses of *rbcL* in a large study of the Coleochaetales (DELWICHE & others, 2002) and SSU and LSU plastid rDNA in a broad survey of streptophytes *sensu* BREMER, 1985 (TURMEL & others, 2002).

The findings of KAROL and others (2001) raise intriguing questions regarding fossil charophytes, which were more diverse and abundant than their extant relatives. The oldest gyrogonites (order Sycidiales) are approximately the same age as the earliest-known fossils of land plants (GRAHAM, 1993; GENSEL & EDWARDS, 2001). Despite the diversity of fossil charophytes relative to living forms, charophytes never approached the ecological and evolutionary success of land

plants. The reason for this disparity of success is not clear. Since charophytes are so different from land plants and other charophycean algae *sensu* MATTOX and STEWART, it is unlikely that the common ancestor of charophytes and land plants closely resembled either group. Some traits are shared by charophytes and the primitive land plants, however: a filamentous germling stage, gross sperm morphology, many discoidal chloroplasts per cell, absence of zoospores, and envelopment of fertilized oogonia by sterile cells (KAROL & others, 2001). In addition, this common ancestor no doubt possessed ancestral forms of the many genes common to charophytes and land plants. Further studies of the functional genomics of these groups may shed light on the changes that occurred in these derived green algae that led to the successful colonization of land.

RELATIONSHIPS WITHIN THE CHARACEAE BASED ON MOLECULAR AND FOSSIL STUDIES

The first molecular study of genera in the Characeae was that of MCCOURT, KAROL, and others (1996), who used *rbcL* sequences and morphology to construct phylogenetic hypotheses of the group. The phylogenetic relationships of genera in the Characeae conformed generally with the traditional view that the family is divided into two subfamilies, the Charoideae and Nitelloideae, although support for the monophyly of the latter group was weak. This study supported the monophyly of the Characeae relative to green plants and resolved some relationships within the family. The topology based on *rbcL* sequences alone was strongly supported by the analysis of KAROL and others (2001) using three additional genes (Fig. 42). This larger data set also supports the monophyly of both subfamilies.

Perhaps most interesting about the phylogeny derived from these molecular studies is the very strong support of the monophyly of the two sections of *Tolypella* (*sensu* WOOD

& IMAHORI, 1964–1965). Previous studies had suggested that the genus might be paraphyletic because one section exhibits a multipartite basal plate, as found in *Nitella*, and another section in the genus has a simple, one-piece basal plate, as found in *Chara* (SOULIÉ-MÄRSCHE, 1989; FEIST & GRAMBAST-FESSARD, 1991). Clearly, either this character evolved more than once in *Tolypella,* or the genus should be split, and taxa with a simple basal plate should be put into a new genus in the Charoideae. The *rbcL* data clearly support the former hypothesis, that *Tolypella* is monophyletic and that a multipartite basal plate evolved twice within the Characeae. A further implication is that a multipartite basal plate is not necessarily a synapomorphy in other fossil taxa. A multipartite basal plate may have evolved twice in the Porocharaceae and in the *Aclistochara-Lamprothamnium* lineage. Still, basal plate features may be synapomorphies for some groups.

MEIERS and others (1997) and MEIERS, PROCTOR, and CHAPMAN (1999) used SSU sequence data to determine phylogenetic relationships within the Characeae. Their findings were generally congruent with those based on *rbcL* data; however, the taxon sampling and slower rate of evolution of the SSU gene relative to *rbcL* make comparison difficult. For example, MEIERS, PROCTOR, and CHAPMAN's (1999) finding that *Lamprothamnium* may be a member of *Chara* is contradicted by *rbcL* data for a larger sample of *Chara* and *Lamprothamnium*. The relationships of genera of Characeae based on *rbcL* were supported by the four-gene analysis of KAROL and others (2001).

MCCOURT and others (1999) sampled a wider range of species in the Characeae, in particular species of *Chara* and *Nitella*. Genera of the family Characeae are strongly supported as monophyletic. Within *Chara* the traditional grouping of species into sections by WOOD and IMAHORI (1965 in 1964–1965) is very strongly refuted, although some of the subsections within these sections

are monophyletic. WOOD's practice of combining monoecious and dioecious microspecies as forms of more inclusive, broader species is not supported, although monoecious and dioecious taxa believed to be closely related are supported as such by the *rbcL* data. Thus, sequence data in general support the monophyly of species (i.e., microspecies of WOOD & IMAHORI, 1965 in 1964–1965) and genera recognized on morphological grounds.

Branch length asymmetry between genera in the Characeae and Nitelleae of WOOD and IMAHORI (1965 in 1964–1965) was noted in the *rbcL* studies of MCCOURT, KAROL, and others (1996) and MCCOURT and others (1999). Branches in *Nitella* and *Tolypella* are much longer than those in *Chara* and the other genera of the family. The reasons for this asymmetry are difficult to discern because of the lack of a good fossil record for the noncalcifying *Nitella* and *Tolypella* (GRAMBAST, 1974). One explanation could be that sequence change is faster in the latter genera for some unknown reason. Alternatively, the rate of sequence change could be roughly equal in all genera of the family, but species lineages in *Nitella* and *Tolypella* may be more ancient, and branch length would be proportional to time since divergence. In other words, extant *Chara* species may be descended from a more recent common ancestor. One of the oldest fossils of Characeae is a *Nitella*-like thallus from the Lower Devonian (TAYLOR, REMY, & HASS, 1992). If *Nitella* or *Tolypella* are indeed the descendants of more ancient divergences and can be reliably dated in the fossil record, it will provide a paleontological test of a hypothesis derived from molecular data.

SUMMARY

Molecular and morphological data are complementary and may be mutually illuminating in studies of charophytes. Hypotheses derived from studies of fossil or extant taxa hold the promise of providing reciprocal tests that can further our understanding of charophyte evolution. Data from fossils provide evidence of much greater diversity of charophytes in the past, but many taxa have become extinct. Molecular data are valuable for revealing relationships of charophytes to the rest of the green algae and plants.

NOMENCLATURAL NOTE

The terms charophyte and Charophyta have traditionally been applied to living and fossil members of the monophyletic group of green algae in the Charales, Moellerinales, and Sycidiales (see p. 88). We have continued this usage herein. MATTOX and STEWART (1984), however, employed the root charo- for their class Charophyceae, including the traditional Charophyta MIGULA plus several other orders (Chlorokybales, Klebsor-midiales, Zygnematales, and Coleochae-tales). Because the latter group is paraphyletic without the inclusion of embryophytes, BREMER (1985) proposed the name of Streptophyta for the group (from the Greek *strepto,* for twisted, i.e., the morphology of the sperm of some members). Given the historical use of the term Charophyceae (SMITH, 1950), KAROL and others (2001) implied that the larger, more inclusive group of Charophyceae plus land plants be termed the Charophyta (see also DELWICHE & others, 2002). The Charales and fossil relatives would thus be relegated to the subdivision rank of Charophytina. This modified use of the division Charophyta, while controversial, would recognize the monophyly of a major clade of green algae and plants.

CLASSIFICATION OF CHAROPHYTA

MONIQUE FEIST and NICOLE GRAMBAST-FESSARD

[Université Montpellier II, France]

EARLY WORKS IN THE HISTORY OF CHAROPHYTE CLASSIFICATION

The first step toward classifying the Charophyta dates to 1719 when VAILLANT grouped several extant forms under the generic name *Chara,* taken from the memoir by DALECHAMPS (1587) and later validated by LINNAEUS in 1753. This name is thought to be derived from the Greek, meaning joy of water. AGARDH (1824) proposed the Characeae, based on the presence of verticillate branches bearing capsules (female) and globules (male) and including two genera, *Chara* and *Nitella;* the name Characeae had been previously mentioned by KUNTH (1815), who attributed it to L. Cl. RICHARD.

Fossil forms were discovered in the second half of the 18th century. SCHREBER (1759) was the first to describe and illustrate thalli and gyrogonites as well as oospores from around Halle (Germany) but without recognizing their true nature. Until the first half of the 19th century, charophyte remains were attributed to different groups of animals such as worms (SCHREBER, 1759) and corals (SANDBERGER, 1849), and the first fossil charophyte species, *Gyrogonites medicaginula,* was described by LAMARCK (1801, 1804) as a miliolid foraminifer.

LEMAN (1812) recognized the relationship between the fossil gyrogonite and the living genus *Chara.* LEMAN's viewpoint was generally accepted, and newly discovered fossil remains were attributed to *Chara* (BRONGNIART, 1822; LYELL, 1826; PREVOST, 1826). The first subdivisions of the fossil forms were introduced by STACHE (1889), who described several genera and erected two tribes, keeping them apart from the extant Chareae and Nitelleae: the Lagynophoreae for bottle-shaped gyrogonites and the Kosmogyrae for ornamented ones. GROVES (1933) and

GRAMBAST (1957) have expressed doubts as to the reconstitutions proposed by STACHE, and his pioneering classification has now been abandoned.

DEVELOPMENT OF CHAROPHYTE CLASSIFICATION

The first structured classification was established by PIA (1927), who added to STACHE's subdivisions two new families, the Palaeocharaceae and the Clavatoraceae. The Kosmogyrae STACHE that PIA considered as artificial were not included in this system.

CLASSIFICATION (PIA, 1927)
Class Charophyta
  Unquestioned Charophyta
    Family Characeae
      Subfamily Nitelleae
      Subfamily Chareae
      Subfamily Lagynophoreae
    Family Palaeocharaceae, based on the Devonian *Palaeochara* BELL, 1922
    Family Clavatoraceae, based on the Mesozoic *Clavator* REID & GROVES, 1916
  Doubtful Charophyta remains
    Genus *Palaeonitella* KIDSTON & LANG
    Genus *Trochiliscus* PANDER
    Genus *Sycidium* SANDBERGER

According to the bibliography of his paper, PIA (1927) was not aware of the monograph by KARPINSKY (1906), who had shown that *Trochiliscus* and *Sycidium* were distinct Paleozoic branches of the Charophyta that he placed into two new subdivisions, the Trochiliscidae and the Sycididae. These were renamed later by PECK (1934a) as Trochiliscaceae and Sycidiaceae KARPINSKY. KARPINSKY (1906) attributed *Trochiliscus* to PANDER (1856), but as noted by Peck (1934a), PANDER designated a group of species also including *Sycidium* under the name Trochilisken. Thus the attribution of the authorship of *Trochiliscus* to PANDER should not be maintained.

In 1938, PECK erected the Atopochara-ceae, but this family could not be maintained after the inclusion of *Atopochara* within the Clavatoraceae (HARRIS, 1939).

MÄDLER (1952) summed up the knowledge acquired to that date and erected new subdivisions at the ordinal level as well as the new subfamily Characeae Aclistocharae, defined later (MÄDLER, 1955). The Aclistocharae are characterized by a more or less distinct periapical dehiscence furrow. They include the genus *Porochara,* in which the apex is always open, and genera in which the apex is closed by the swollen terminal ends of the spirals, constituting a convex rosette. For MÄDLER (1955) this rosette was comparable to the opercule that falls during germination in the living forms.

CLASSIFICATION (MÄDLER, 1952)

Class Charophyta
  Order Sycidiales *nov. ord.*
    Family Sycidiaceae (KARPINSKY, 1906) PECK, 1934a
  Order Trochiliscales *nov. ord.*
    Family Trochiliscaceae (KARPINSKY, 1906) PECK, 1934a
  Order Charales *nov. ord.*
    Family Palaeocharaceae BELL, 1922
    Family Clavatoraceae REID & GROVES, 1916
    Family Lagynophoraceae STACHE, 1880
    Family Characeae RICHARD in KUNTH, 1815
      Subfamily Aclistocharae *nov. subf.*
      Subfamily Kosmogyreae STACHE, 1889
      Subfamily Nitelleae VON LEONHARDI, 1863
      Subfamily Chareae VON LEONHARDI, 1863

The classification proposed by GRAMBAST (1962b) includes four more families and three more subfamilies than that of MÄDLER, 1952. Within the Sycidiales, the Chovanellaceae were erected for gyrogonites with numerous, vertical cells that are undivided or subdivided only at their apical ends.

Within the Charales, the Eocharaceae GRAMBAST, 1959a include gyrogonites with numerous sinistrally spiralled cells. The Raskyellaceae are based on the presence of five apical cells closing the apex. Within the Characeae, the Gyrogonae (=Brachycharae) bring together gyrogonites in which the apex, bearing convex nodules, is surrounded by a clear periapical furrow (GRAMBAST, 1956c). Two subfamilies are not retained: the

Kosmogyrae STACHE and the Aclistocharae MÄDLER. GRAMBAST (1957) has shown that the ornamentation that characterizes the Kosmogyrae is not a feature of great taxonomic value and may not be constant within a species, such as in *Peckichara varians* GRAMBAST. Even a single specimen may be only partially ornamented, as in *Nitellopsis* (*Tectochara*) *thaleri* (CASTEL & GRAMBAST) GRAMBAST & SOULIÉ-MÄRSCHE. For GRAMBAST (1961) the subfamily Aclistocharae, which is composed of two distinct groups, is artificial. He erected the Porocharaceae for species with an apical pore always open, with the apical region either truncated (Porocharoideae) or drawn into a neck (Stellatocharoideae).

CLASSIFICATION (GRAMBAST, 1962b)

Order Sycidiales MÄDLER, 1952
  Family Sycidiaceae PECK, 1934a
  Family Chovanellaceae *nov. fam.*
Order Trochiliscales MÄDLER, 1952
  Family Trochiliscaceae PECK, 1934a
Order Charales
  Family Eocharaceae GRAMBAST, 1959a
  Family Palaeocharaceae PIA, 1927
  Family Porocharaceae *nov. fam.*
    Subfamily Porocharoideae GRAMBAST, 1961
    Subfamily Stellatocharoideae *nov. subfam.*
  Family Clavatoraceae PIA, 1927
  Family Lagynophoraceae STACHE, 1889
  Family Raskyellaceae GRAMBAST, 1957
  Family Characeae RICHARD in KUNTH, 1815
    Subfamily Charoideae BRAUN in MIGULA, 1897
      Tribe Gyrogoneae GRAMBAST, 1956b
      Tribe Chareae VON LEONHARDI, 1863
    Subfamily Nitelloideae BRAUN in MIGULA, 1897

WANG Zhen (1978a) proposed two subfamilies: Cuneatocharoideae, which includes gyrogonites of Porocharaceae with a conical outline in their upper part, and Gyrogonoideae for gyrogonites of Characeae with a depression or a breaking line around the apical zone. The Gyrogonoideae include two tribes: Gyrogoneae and Raskyelleae. For WANG Zhen, the apex structure of the Raskyellaceae corresponds to a Gyrogonoidae in which the reduction of width and thickness of the spiral cells around the apex reaches a point where it breaks, so the apical cells are separated from the spirals by a fracture and not by a true wall.

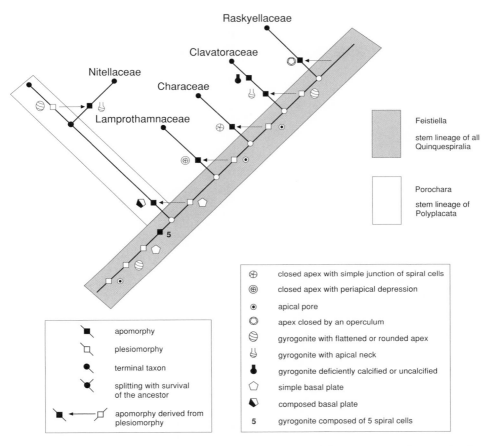

FIG. 43. Phylogenetic diagram of Quinquespiralia, with single-celled basal plate representing plesiomorphic character state (Martin-Closas & Schudack, 1991, fig. 2, hypothesis 2).

CLASSIFICATION (WANG, 1978a)
Family Porocharaceae GRAMBAST, 1962b
  Subfamily Stellatocharoideae GRAMBAST, 1962b
  Subfamily Porocharoideae GRAMBAST, 1961; *emend.*
  Subfamily Cuneatocharoideae *subfam. nov.*
Family Characeae RICHARD in KUNTH, 1815
  Subfamily Gyrogonoideae *subfam. nov.*
    Tribe Gyrogoneae GRAMBAST, 1956b
    Tribe Raskyelleae (L. & N. GRAMBAST) *comb. nov.*
  Subfamily Charoideae VON LEONHARDHI, 1863
  Subfamily Nitelloideae BRAUN in MIGULA, 1897
  Subfamily Aclistocharoideae MÄDLER, 1952

Additional families have been proposed, isolating one genus at a higher systematic level, without a new diagnosis. Thus the Nitellopsidaceae KRASSAVINA, 1971, the Primocharaceae ISHCHENKO and SAIDA-

KOVSKY, 1975, the Tectocharaceae MÄDLER and STAESCHE, 1979 and the Aclistocharaceae ZHOU, 1983 (in HAO & others, 1983) have not been retained in the classification adopted in the *Treatise.*

WANG Zhen and LU (1980) erected two new Paleozoic families. The Pinnoputamenaceae of the Sycidiales include gyrogonites with vertical ramified cells. The Trochiliscales are twofold, comprising the Trochiliscaceae emended, including gyrogonites with spiral cells segmented transversely and a basal pore with bilateral symmetry, and the Karspinskyaceae, for Trochiliscales devoid of these characters.

CLASSIFICATION (Wang & Lu, 1980)
Class Charophyta
  Order Sycidiales Mädler, 1952
    Family Sycidiaceae Peck, 1934a
      Genus *Sycidium* Sandberger, 1849
    Family Chovanellaceae Grambast, 1962b
      Genus *Chovanella* Reitlinger & Jarweza, 1958
    Family Pinnoputamenaceae *fam. nov.*
      Genus *Pinnoputamen gen. nov.*
  Order Trochiliscales Mädler, 1952; *emend.*
    Family Trochiliscaceae Peck, 1934a; *emend.*
      Genus *Trochiliscus* (Pander, 1856) Karpinsky, 1906; *emend.*
    Family Karpinskyaceae *fam. nov.*
      Genus *Karpinskya gen. nov.*
      Genus *Moellerina* Ulrich, 1886

Martin-Closas and Schudack (1991) proposed a new classification of the mainly post-Paleozoic charophytes based on cladistic analysis. In that system, the chief character is the morphology of the basal plate (simple or multipartite), and the hypothesis of an ancestral position for a simple basal plate is preferred (Fig. 43). In this analysis, the genera *Porochara* and *Feistiella* are interpreted as paraphyletic taxa and written with quotation marks.

1. Quinquespiralia *nov. subord.* (apomorphy: five spiral cells), stem lineage formed by *"Feistiella"* and other traditional "Porocharoideae."

1.1. Family: Polyplacata *nov. fam.* (apomorphy: composed basal plate), stem lineage formed by *"Porochara."*

1.1.1. Subfamily: Nitellaceae *emend.* (apomorphy: apical neck), stem lineage formed by traditional "Stellatocharoideae" Grambast; *emend.,* Breuer, recent terminals formed by *Nitella* and *Tolypella* (section *Tolypella*).

Genus: *"Porochara"*: stem lineage of Polyplacata and primitive sister-group of Nitellaceae.

1.2. Family: Lamprothamnaceae *nov. fam.* (apomorphy: closed apex with periapical depression), *Lamprothamnium* and traditional synonyms (*Aclistochara,* etc.).

1.3. Family: Characeae *emend.* (apomorphy: closed apex with simple junction of the spiral cells), traditional Charoideae, except for *Lamprothamnium* and synonyms,

but adding *Sphaerochara* (=*Tolypella* section *Rothia*).

1.4. Family: Clavatoraceae (apomorphy: apical neck, deficiently calcified gyrogonite) traditional Clavatoraceae.

1.5. Family: Raskyellaceae (apomorphy: apical operculum calcified), traditional *Saportanella, Raskyella,* (?) *Rantzienella.*

Genus: *"Feistiella"*: stem lineage of Quinquespiralia and primitive sister group of taxa 1.2 to 1.5 (Martin-Closas & Schudack, 1991, p. 69–70).

In their classification of the Paleozoic forms, Lu, Soulié-Märsche, and Q. Wang (1996) considered the subdivision of the gyrogonite cells by transverse ridges as the most important character.

CLASSIFICATION
(Lu, Soulié-Märsche, & Wang, 1996)
Class Sycidiphyceae Langer, 1976
  Order Sycidiales Mädler, 1952
    Family Sycidiaceae Peck, 1934a
      Genus *Sycidium* Sandberger, 1849
    Family Trochiliscaceae Karpinsky, 1906; *emend.,* Wang & Lu, 1980
      Genus *Trochiliscus* (Pander, 1856) Karpinsky, 1906
Class Charophyceae Smith, 1938
  Order Chovanellales Conkin & Conkin, 1977
    Family Chovanellaceae (Grambast, 1962b); *emend.*
      Genus *Chovanella* Reitliger & Jarzewa, 1958; *emend.*
    Family Xinjiangocharaceae *fam. nov.*
      Genus *Xinjiangochara* Yang & Zhou, 1990
  Order Moellerinales *ord. nov.*
    Family Moellerinaceae Feist & Grambast-Fessard, 1991; *emend.*
      Genus *Moellerina* Ulrich, 1886; *emend.,* Wang, 1984
    Family Pseudomoellerinaceae Wang, 1984
      Genus *Pseudomoellerina* Wang, 1984
  Order Charales Lindley, 1836
    Family Eocharaceae Grambast, 1959a
      Genus *Eochara* Choquette, 1956
    Family Palaeocharaceae Pia, 1927
      Genus *Palaeochara* Bell, 1922
    Family Porocharaceae Grambast, 1962b
      Genus *Porochara* Mädler, 1955
    Family Pinnoputamenaceae Wang & Lu, 1980
      Genus *Pinnoputamen* Wang & Lu, 1980

For Lu, Soulié-Märsche, and Wang (1996), whether the Pinnoputamennaceae Z. Wang & Lu, 1980, are charophytes is questionable.

CLASSIFICATION ADOPTED IN THE *TREATISE*

The classification adopted in the *Treatise* follows FEIST and GRAMBAST-FESSARD (1991) for the subdivisions of the Charales, but a new finding, the discovery of a utricle in most Paleozoic genera, led us to reconsider the concept of the Paleozoic orders and families.

As in previous classifications, Moellerinales and Charales are distinguished by the orientation of the gyrogonite cells, but for the Sycidiales, which contain all Paleozoic taxa with a utricle, this character cannot be used because the orientation of the gyrogonite cells is not preserved generally inside this organ. In the rare instances where gyrogonite cells are visible in thin section, their number is rather high, much greater than five. All other morphological evidence shows that it is not possible to classify the Sycidiales families together with the Clavatoraceae (Charales), which also present utricles but whose gyrogonites possess five sinistrally spiralled cells. Thus, it appears that the character of the utricle evolved independently in two groups of charophytes. The types of gyrogonites that may be inside the utricles of the Sycidiales are very likely to be found among the Moellerinales, the only charophytes devoid of a utricle that were in existence when the Sycidiales appeared during the late Silurian and Early Devonian. In our present state of knowledge, we keep the Sycidiales provisionally as a group apart but with close affinities to the Moellerinales.

The Sycidiales comprise four families, the Sycidiaceae, Trochiliscaceae, Chovanellaceae, and Pinnoputamenaceae, distinguished by the utricular characters. WANG and LU (1980) had already observed the similarities between Sycidiaceae and Trochiliscaceae, although they differ in cell orientation. The Chovanellaceae constitute a homogeneous group, characterized by utricles showing vertical undivided cells tending to spiral; the distinction of the Xinjiangocharaceae, which

differ only by the cell number of what has been shown to be a utricle, has been abandoned. The attribution of the Pinnoputamenaceae to charophytes has been confirmed by the discovery of antheridia at the surface of the utricle of *Pinnoputamen* sp. (Fig. 48*e*, Systematics, herein p. 99) (FEIST & FEIST, 1997). In this family, the utricles are bilateral, and they bear ramified branches as in *Sycidium.*

In the Moellerinales, which do not present utricles, gyrogonites are spiralled dextrally. Within this group, a new name has been proposed for the Karpinskyaceae WANG & LU, the Moellerinaceae. The Moellerinaceae are based on the earliest genus *Moellerina* ULRICH, which also exhibits the most typical characters of the family (FEIST & GRAMBAST-FESSARD, 1991; LU, SOULIÉ-MÄRSCHE, & WANG, 1996). The two families Moellerinaceae and Pseudomoellerinaceae are distinguished by different numbers of gyronite cells.

Within the Charales two new suborders have been introduced in order to separate the families with more than five gyrogonite cells (Palaeocharinae) from the ones with five sinistrally spiralled cells (Charinae) (FEIST & GRAMBAST-FESSARD, 1991).

The Raskyellaceae is deemed a valid family after new observations with scanning electron microscopy that have confirmed the individuality of the apical cells (ANADON & FEIST, 1981). The Lagynophoraceae STACHE, which do not differ from the Characeae regarding the apex morphology (BIGNOT & GRAMBAST, 1969), have not been maintained. The apical neck typical of this family represents an external encrustation of coronula cells (CASTEL, 1969). The subdivision of the Charoideae into Chareae and Gyrogonae, which GRAMBAST (1962b, p. 76) thought already quite difficult to apply, was abandoned subsequently when further observations displayed the possible relationships between genera placed in the two different subfamilies, such as *Rhabdochara* and *Stephanochara,* as well as *Tolypella* and *Sphaerochara.*

During the past twenty years, new paleontological and biological data have shed a different light on the problem of the classification inside the Characeae family. The oldest representative of the Charoideae, *Aclistochara,* possesses a multipartite basal plate, whereas in the extant forms this character is present only in the Nitelloideae. The attribution of *Aclistochara* to the Charoideae is based on its clear resemblance with *Lamprothamnium* concerning the morphology of the apex (SOULIÉ-MÄRSCHE, 1989). MARTIN-CLOSAS and SCHUDACK (1991) even considered both genera as synonyms. On the other hand, according to molecular data (MCCOURT, KAROL, & others, 1996), the two sections of *Tolypella,* including section *Rothia* (=*Sphaerochara*) with a simple basal plate and the section *Tolypella* with a divided (multicellular) basal plate, are included in the same clade. This suggests that the character is not a synapomorphy distinguishing groups at the family and subfamily level (SOULIÉ-MÄRSCHE, 1989; FEIST & GRAMBAST-FESSARD, 1991; MARTIN-CLOSAS & SCHUDACK, 1991). The basal plate character is valuable, but it can be applied only to the generic or subgeneric levels, and high-level taxa based only on it, such as the Monoplacata and Polyplacata MARTIN-CLOSAS & SCHUDACK (1991), are no longer justified.

In this classification, the criteria for the distinction of the different categories of taxa are as follows.

ORDERS

Distinction at the order level is based on the orientation of the gyrogonite cells, whether dextrally spiralled (Moellerinales) or sinistrally spiralled (Charales); and presence of a utricle and a high number of gyrogonite cells for the Sycidiales.

FAMILIES

Distinction at the family level is based on the number of spiral cells, the apical structure of the gyrogonite, or the presence of a special character such as the utricle of the Clavatoraceae and of the four Sycidiales families; the characters of the apical zone of the gyrogonite predominate also in the separation of the subfamilies. The classification of the extant forms, which are all included in the family Characeae, comprises two tribes, Chareae and Nitelleae. In the systematics of the fossil forms adopted in the *Treatise,* however, families are divided into subfamilies; and we do the same for the Characeae, which have been subdivided into Charoideae and Nitelloideae.

GENERA

Genera are distinguished on the basis of particular characters of the gyrogonite apex, the basal plate, and the general outline of the gyrogonite.

SPECIES

Distinction of species is based on special characters of gyrogonite shape, ornamentation, and dimensions; in the Sycidiales and Clavatoraceae characters of the utricle are also taken into account.

Thallus remains, which are not connected to gyrogonites, are not included in this classification; they are treated separately (see Morphology, herein p. 12).

In the *Treatise* charophyte volume, only the generic attributes in accord with this classification have been considered for determining the ranges and distributions of genera. Descriptions of genera are presented not as diagnoses but as brief decriptions that emphasize comparative characteristics.

CLASSIFICATION
(FEIST & GRAMBAST-FESSARD, herein)
Phylum Charophyta MIGULA, 1897
  Class Charophyceae SMITH, 1938
    Order Moellerinales LU, SOULIÉ-MÄRSCHE, & WANG, 1996
        Family Moellerinaceae FEIST & GRAMBAST-FESSARD, 1991; *emend.,* LU, SOULIÉ-MÄRSCHE, & WANG, 1996
        Family Pseudomoellerinaceae WANG, 1984
    Order Sycidiales MÄDLER, 1952; *emend.,* herein
        Family Sycidiaceae KARPINSKY, 1906; *emend.,* herein
        Family Trochiliscaceae KARPINSKY, 1906; *emend.,* herein
        Family Chovanellaceae GRAMBAST, 1962b; *emend.,* herein
        Family Pinnoputamenaceae WANG & LU, 1980; *emend.,* herein
    Order Charales LINDLEY, 1836
      Suborder Palaeocharineae FEIST & GRAMBAST-FESSARD, 1991
        Family Eocharaceae GRAMBAST, 1959a
        Family Palaeocharaceae PIA, 1927
      Suborder Charineae FEIST & GRAMBAST-FESSARD, 1991
        Family Porocharaceae GRAMBAST, 1962b
          Subfamily Porocharoideae GRAMBAST, 1961; *emend.,* WANG & HUANG, 1978
          Subfamily Clavatoritoideae KOZUR, 1974
          Subfamily Stellatocharoideae GRAMBAST, 1962b
        Family Clavatoraceae PIA, 1927
          Subfamily Clavatoroideae PIA, 1927; *emend.,* GRAMBAST, 1969
          Subfamily Atopocharoideae PECK, 1938; *emend.,* GRAMBAST, 1969
        Family Raskyellaceae L. & N. GRAMBAST, 1955
        Family Characeae AGARDH, 1824
          Subfamily Charoideae BRAUN in MIGULA, 1897
          Subfamily Nitelloideae BRAUN in MIGULA, 1897

GLOSSARY

Monique Feist and Micheline Guerlesquin

[Université Montpellier II, France; and Université Catholique de l'Ouest, Angers, France]

This glossary explains special terms used in this volume. Some of these definitions follow Corillion (1975) and Moore (1986).

AND. Distance from apex to widest portion of gyrogonite (LED), as measured along polar axis.

antheridium (pl., antheridia). Male reproductive organ producing motile spermatozoids; does not secrete calcium carbonate, therefore seldom preserved.

apex (=summit). Distal end of gyrogonite, opposite pole of attachment to thallus.

apical neck. Protruding ends of spiral cells on apex, which form elongated, constricted neck.

apical pore (=apical opening). Opening in apical end of gyrogonite.

axial nodes. Short nodes of main axis and branches of unlimited growth.

basal depression. At basal pole, when distal opening of basal pore is of smaller diameter than proximal opening; a crater-shaped depression present when viewed externally.

basal opening. See basal pore.

basal plate (=basal plug). Plate at distal end of basal pore, formed as a result of calcification of sterile sister cell of oosphere.

basal pore (=basal opening). Opening.

bract cells. Single-celled processes growing out from peripheral cells of branchlet nodes (Chareae).

bracteoles. Pair of single-celled processes (similar to bract cells) originating from basal node below oogonium, one growing on each side of oogonium (Chareae).

bractlet. Single-celled process subtending oogonium in females of dioecious species of *Chara* replacing the antheridium.

branchlets (=phylloids). Laterals of limited growth produced in whorls at stem (axial) nodes.

bulbils. Agglomerations of starch-containing cells developing on rhizoids and at stem nodes of some charophytes.

capitula. Small cells within antheridium from which filaments develop that produce spermatozoids.

calcine. Calcium carbonate deposited in enveloping cells.

cellular ridges. Ridges down center of spirals.

cladom. In phycology, designates an axis issued from unlimited activity of an initial apical cell that generates alternating nodes and internodes. The pluricellular nodes produce phylloids in turn (=branchlets) having structure similar to main axis, but of definite growth; one or more connected cladoms constitutes thallus.

conjoined. Having antheridium and oogonium adjacent at same branchlet node.

coronula. Small, crownlike structure at apex of oogonium in one row of five cells (recent Chareae) or two rows of five cells each (recent Nitelleae), at tops of spiral cells.

cortex. Outer covering of longitudinally arranged cells, giving thallus axes a striped or ridged appearance.

corticate. Thallus having a cortex.

corticulation. See cortex.

dichotomous branching. Typical of *Nitella;* phylloid (=branchlet) subdivided into two identical parts, which further subdivide themselves in two and so on; process results in formation of rays of 1st, 2nd, 3rd orders.

dioecious. Having male and female gametangia produced on separate male and female individuals of species.

diplostephanous. Having a double ring of stipulodes at base of each whorl of branchlets.

diplostichous. Having cortex arranged in alternate primary and secondary rows, there being two cortical rows corresponding to each branchlet, e.g., *Chara vulgaris.*

ecorticate. Lacking a cortex.

enveloping cells. External cells of gyrogonite or utricle.

equator. Widest portion of gyrogonite.

equatorial angle. Acute angle made between equatorial line (LED) and suture of spiral cell.

eutrophic. Water that is nutrient rich, thus supporting a large plankton population so transparency may be reduced.

eutrophication. Process of artificial enrichment, particularly by excessive level of phosphates from domestic and agricultural sources.

furcate. Forked.

gametangia. Gamete-producing sexual reproductive organs.

gymnophyllous. Having naked branchlets, i.e., branchlets without a cortex in species of *Chara* where main axes are corticate, as in *Chara gymnophylla* (recent).

gyrogonite. Fossil calcified oogonium.

haplostephanous. Having single ring of stipulodes at base of each whorl of branchlets.

haplostichous. Having cortex of primary cells only, i.e., one cortical row corresponding to each branchlet, as in *Chara canescens* (recent).

intercellular suture. Line marking junction between enveloping cells.

internode. Elongated portion of specimen stem between nodes consisting of single, elongated central cell.

ISI. Isopolarity index (LPA/LED), ×100.

LED. Largest equatorial diameter of gyrogonite.

LPA. Longest polar axis of gyrogonite.

manubria. Stalklike cells within antheridium that support capitula cells.

monoecious. Male and female gametangia produced on same individual of a species.

monogenetic (life cycle). In the Characeae, life cycle includes only one generation (haplobiontic); individuals generated by an oospore are haploid gametophytes, and meiosis occurs at germination of zygote (=fertilized egg).

monopodial. Having a main axis not supplanted by any lateral branch.

nodules. Swollen apical ends of spiral cells at center of apex.

oligotrophic. Water that is nutrient poor, does not support a large plankton population, and is therefore transparent.

oogamy. Female gamete (oosphere, egg) differentiated from large central cell of oogonium; motile sperm produced on cells of antheridium.

oogonium (=oosporangium). Female reproductive organ that encloses egg cell.

oosporangium. See oogonium.

oosphere. Female cell differentiated from large central cell of oogonium.

oospore. Fertilized egg cell (zygote).

parthenogenetic. Producing viable oospores without fertilization by male gametes: *Chara canescens* (recent).

phylloids. See branchlets.

proembryo. See protonema.

protonema. Small, rudimentary cladom issued directly from germination of oospore; gives rise to secondary erect cladom from which thallus develops.

ray. Internode of branchlet in Nitelloideae.

rhizoids. Colorless, hairlike filaments growing from charophyte base into substrate, with dual function of absorption and attachment.

rosette. Central apical swellings of ends of spirals on specimens with well-developed peripheral grooves.

Rubisco: Abbreviation of ribulose bisphosphate carboxylase/oxygenase, which is the critical enzyme in photosynthesis that takes carbon dioxide from the atmosphere and incorporates it into sucrose.

sejoined. Having antheridium and oogonium produced at separate branchlet nodes of same individual.

shield cells. Eight platelike cells that make up outer, protective layer of antheridium (8 shield cells = octoscutate; 4 = tetrascutate in some microspecies of recent *Chara zeylanica*).

sister cell of oosphere. See basal plate.

spine cells. Single-celled processes growing out from primary cortical cells.

spiral cells. Enveloping cells of gyrogonites; 5 in Charales, may be up to 12 in some Paleozoic genera.

sporostine. Two inner, suberized layers of oospore.

stipulodes. Single or double ring of single-celled processes growing out from base of branchlet whorls.

summit. See apex.

sympodial. Having branches that supplant and seemingly continue their parent branches so there is no one main axis.

taxon. Recognizable entity that may be separated from related entities at any level of classificatory hierarchy.

thallus. Vegetative system without stem and true leaves.

triplostichous. Cortex having two secondary rows alternating with each primary row, with three cortical rows corresponding to each branchlet, as in *Chara globularis* (recent).

tubercles. Rounded, obtuse, or acute protuberances distributed either at random or regularly over spiral cells of gyrogonites.

utricle. Outer covering of gyrogonite, made up of calcified segments of thallus.

SYSTEMATIC DESCRIPTIONS

Monique Feist and Nicole Grambast-Fessard

[Université Montpellier II, France]

Phylum CHAROPHYTA
Migula, 1897

[Charophyta MIGULA, 1897, p. 94] [=order Charales MATTOX & STEWART, 1984, p. 50]

Oogamous chlorophyte algal group with gametangia surrounded by a multicellular cover and verticillate thallus made of alternating giant coenocytic cells and short uninucleate nodal cells where whorls of branchlets originate. Main part found as fossils is female fructification (gyrogonite), representing oogonium that contained egg; resistant oospore (zygote) membrane made of sporopollenin and more or less calcified enveloping tube cells and basal plate. Antheridia, preserved as casts, rarely represented, and remains of thallus generally fragmentary and not taxonomically significant. Classification based mainly on gyrogonite. *Silurian (?Llandovery–?Wenlock, Ludlow)–Holocene.*

Class CHAROPHYCEAE
Smith, 1938

[Charophyceae SMITH, 1938, p. 127] [=Charophycophyta PAPENFUSS, 1946, p. 218]

Description as for phylum. *Silurian (?Llandovery–?Wenlock, Ludlow)–Holocene.*

Order MOELLERINALES
Lu, Soulié-Märsche, & Wang, 1996

[Moellerinales LU, SOULIÉ-MÄRSCHE, & WANG, 1996, p. 8]

Gyrogonites with 5 to 12 dextrally spiralled cells without transverse ridges. *upper Silurian (Ludlow)–Permian.*

Family MOELLERINACEAE
Feist & Grambast-Fessard, 1991

[Moellerinaceae FEIST & GRAMBAST-FESSARD, 1991, p. 198; *emend.*, LU, SOULIÉ-MÄRSCHE, & WANG, 1996, p. 8] [=Karpinskyaceae Z. WANG & LU, 1980, p. 196, *partim*]

Gyrogonites with 7 to 12 dextrally spiralled cells, without transverse ridges; equatorial angle of the spiral cells above 20°. *upper Silurian (Ludlow)–Permian.*

Moellerina ULRICH, 1886, p. 34, *non* SCHELLWIEN, 1898 [*M. greenei* ULRICH, 1886, p. 34, pl. 3,*8;* OD] [=*Calcisphaera* WILLIAMSON, 1880, p. 521, *partim* (type, *C. robusta,* OD); *Saccammina* DAWSON, 1883, p. 5 (type, *S. eriana* DAWSON, 1883, p. 5, fig. 3, OD), *non* SARS in CARPENTER, 1869; *Trochiliscus* KARPINSKY, 1906, p. 123 (type, *T. ingricus* KARPINSKY, 1906, p. 112), *partim; Trochiliscus* subgenus *Eutrochiliscus* CROFT, 1952, p. 209 (type, *Trochiliscus ingricus* KARPINSKY, 1906, p. 123), *partim; Weikkoella* SUMMERSON, 1958, p. 548 (type, *W. sphaerica* SUMMERSON, 1958, p. 548, pl. 81,*1–2,* OD)]. Gyrogonites with 8 to 12 dextrally spiralled cells, with no coronula cells; shape subglobular, apical area rounded, pointed, or elongated to form a neck. Apical pore small. Spirals not divided by transverse ridges; basal area rounded, apical pore larger than basal pore. [Nomenclatural history of *Moellerina* was given by PECK and MORALES, 1966. To date, *M. laufeldi* CONKIN & CONKIN, 1992 is the oldest charophyte species.] *upper Silurian (Ludlow)–Upper Devonian (Frasnian):* Ukraine, Sweden, China, USA, Australia.——FIG. 44,*1a–e.* *M. greenei* ULRICH, Middle Devonian, USA, neotype; *a,* lateral view; *b,* basal view, ×35 (Grambast-Fessard, Feist, & Wang, 1989, fig. 2, 1); *c,* lateral view, CF.2915-3/3, ×45; *d,* apical view, ×45; *e,* longitudinal section, CF.2915-3/4, ×50 (new).——FIG. 44,*1f.* *M. laufeldi* CONKIN & CONKIN, Ludlow, Gotland, Sweden; lateral view, CF.3012-1, ×120 (new).

Gemmichara Z. WANG, 1984, p. 55 [*G. sinensis* Z. WANG, 1984, p. 55, pl. I,*1–7;* OD]. Gyrogonites with 8 to 9 dextrally spiralled cells and no coronula cells. Shape bulbiform. Apical area drawn into an elongated neck; apical pore small or closed. Basal area rounded, basal pore large. [*Gemmichara* is the youngest known Moellerinales. WANG regarded this genus as the final step in a lineage starting in the Devonian with *Moellerina*. The lineage is defined by both the decrease in cell number and the closure of the apical pore. The latter feature seems to be linked to the tightness of the spiral cells, which are strongly stretched at the apex. A space (possibly a pore) between the apical ends of the spiral cells is visible on an internal mold of *G. sinensis* (Z. WANG, 1984, pl. I,*3*)]. *Carboniferous (Mississippian)–upper Permian:* China.——FIG. 44,*2a–c.* *G. sinensis* WANG, upper Permian; *a,* holotype, lateral view, NIGP PB11279, ×50; *b,* apical view, ×60; *c,* basal view, ×50 (Z. Wang, 1984, pl. I,*2,1,5*).

Primochara ISHCHENKO & SAIDAKOVSKY, 1975, p. 42 [*P. calvata* ISHCHENKO & SAIDAKOVSKY, 1975, p. 43, pl. I–III; OD]. Gyrogonites pear shaped, with dex-

1a
1c
1d

1b
Moellerina
1e
1f

2a
2b
Gemmichara
2c

3
Primochara
4a
4b
Pseudomoellerina

FIG. 44. Moellerinaceae and Pseudomoellerinaceae (p. 92–94).

trally spiralled cells. Cell number unknown. Size very large, up to 3 mm. [Tentatively attributed to the Moellerinaceae due to the incomplete state of preservation.] This genus is one of the oldest known charophytes. Gyrogonites of *P. calvata* sometimes occur on well-preserved vegetative parts. *Silurian (Pridoli):* Ukraine.——FIG. 44,*3*. **P. calvata* ISHCHENKO & SAIDAKOVSKY; lateral view, ×25 (Shaikin, 1987, pl. XXIII,*4*).

Family PSEUDOMOELLERINACEAE
Z. Wang, 1984

[*nom. transl.* FEIST & GRAMBAST-FESSARD, herein, *ex* Pseudomoellerinoideae Z. WANG, 1984, p. 54 (59)]

Gyrogonites with 5 to 7 dextrally spiralled cells, equatorial angle of spirals less than 20°. *Upper Devonian.*

Pseudomoellerina Z. Wang, 1984, p. 54 [*Trochiliscus maslovi* Samoilova, 1955, p. 911, fig. 3; OD]. Gyrogonites with 5 to 7 spiral cells, with no coronula cells, shape oblate or subglobular, apical and basal areas rounded to flat, apical pore smaller than basal pore. *Upper Devonian:* Russia.——Fig. 44,4a–b. *P. maslovi* (Samoilova) Z. Wang, holotype; *a,* lateral view; *b,* apical view, ×60 (Samoilova, 1955, fig. 3a–b).

Order SYCIDIALES Mädler, 1952

[Sycidiales Mädler, 1952, p. 13; *emend.,* Feist & Grambast-Fessard, herein] [=Chovanellales Conkin & Conkin, 1977, p. 178, *partim*]

Gyrogonites incompletely known. Presence of a utricle, composed of vertical or dextrally spiralled cells, or ramified branches. *Silurian (?Llandovery–?Wenlock, Ludlow)– Carboniferous (Mississippian).*

Family SYCIDIACEAE Karpinsky, 1906

[*nom. transl.* Peck, 1934a, p. 116, *ex* Sycididae Karpinsky, 1906, p. 83; *emend.,* Feist & Grambast-Fessard, herein] [=class Sycidiphyceae Langer, 1976, p. 217]

Utricle made of numerous long cells that may be vertical or dextrally spiralled and are divided or not by numerous horizontal ridges creating polygonal pits. *Silurian (?Llandovery–?Wenlock, Ludlow)–Carboniferous (Mississippian).*

Sycidium Sandberger, 1849, p. 671; *emend.,* Feist & Grambast-Fessard, herein [*S. reticulatum* Sandberger, 1849, p. 672, pl. VIIIB,*a–d;* OD] [=*Pseudosycidium* Karpinsky in Hacquaert, 1932, p. 10, fig. 5, 7, *nom. nud.; Praesycidium* T. A. Ishchenko & A. A. Ishchenko, 1982, p. 24 (type, *P. siluricum* T. A. Ishchenko & A. A. Ishchenko, 1982, p. 26, pl. V–VI, OD)]. Utricles bilaterally symmetrical, with 12 to 22 vertical cells divided into small polygonal pits by transverse ridges; division of vertical units around base follow determinate pattern. General shape subglobular to ovoid, apical pore large. Small pores representing apertures of internal canals present at utricle surface. [Langer (1991) established two subgenera according to the position of the pore canals: *S. (Sycidium),* with pore canals in the angles of the polygonal units, and *S. (Centroporus),* with pore canals in the center of the polygonal units; the distribution of *Sycidium* species within these subgenera has not been established. *Pseudosycidium,* which is one of the oldest charophytes, is known only from thin sections; Hacquaert (1932) noted that the laminate wall structure and the numerous outer polygonal units are typical of *Sycidium* and suggested assignment to that genus. The precise stratigraphic locality of the upper Silurian Turkestanian locality is unknown.

Maslov (1961, 1963b) suggested that forms referred to this family may be utricles. The specimens from the lower Silurian of Anticosti Island (Quebec, Canada), consisting of thin sections, are attributed with doubt to *Sycidium;* and they may not be charophytes (Mamet & others, 1992).] *Silurian (?Llandovery–?Wenlock, Ludlow)–Carboniferous (Mississippian):* Russia, Ukraine, Germany, China, Turkestan, Iran, Zaire, USA, Canada, Australia.——Fig. 45a. *S. reticulatum* Sandberger, Eifelian, Middle Devonian, Germany; lateral view, ×33 (Sandberger, 1849, pl. 8a).——Fig. 45b–d. *S. foveatum* Peck, basal Mississippian, USA, topotypes; *b,* lateral view, C.1237-1, ×50; *c,* apical view, C.1237-2, ×40; *d,* longitudinal section, C.1237-3, ×30 (new).——Fig. 45e–k. *S. xizangense* f. *turbineum* Z. Wang, Middle Devonian, China; *e,* topotype, lateral view, CF.2985-1; *f,* topotype, basal view, CF.2985-1, ×15; *g,* internal basal view of utricle with four branches, external layers removed, CF.3057-1, ×39 (new); *h,* longitudinal axial section with two-layered utricle wall, CF.3056-2, ×15 (new); *i,* internal view of utricle with casts of presumed vertical and undivided long cells of gyrogonite, ×40 (new); *j,* basal view with symmetrical disposition of utricular cells around basal pore (adapted from Wang, 1976, pl. 2,*7*); *k,* schematic reconstruction of utricular system of ramifications; *A–C* and *D–F,* basal cells of ending ramifications; *a1–f3,* basal cells of vertical calcified rows of polygons; *G–J,* basal cells of internal branches (new).

Family TROCHILISCACEAE Karpinsky, 1906

[*nom. transl.* Peck, 1934a, p. 104, *pro* Trochiliscidae Karpinsky, 1906, p. 83; *emend.,* Feist & Grambast-Fessard, herein]

Utricle with numerous, often 18, dextrally spiralled cells that are simple or subdivided by numerous transverse ridges; apical pore usually open. *Lower Devonian (Emsian)– Carboniferous (Mississippian).*

Trochiliscus Karpinsky, 1906, p. 112; *emend.,* Feist & Grambast-Fessard, herein [*T. ingricus* Karpinsky, 1906, p. 112, pl. II,*23–28;* OD; lectotype, pl. II,*23–24,* designated Feist & Grambast-Fessard herein] [=*Trochiliscus* Karpinsky, 1906, p. 123, obj., *partim* (including *Miliola panderi* Ehrenberg, 1858, p. 311, *partim*); *Trochiliscus* subgenus *Eutrochiliscus* Croft, 1952, p. 209 (type, *Trochiliscus ingricus* Karpinsky, 1906, p. 112, *partim*)]. Utricles with 18 dextrally spiralled cells, with no coronula cells; spirals occasionally divided by transverse ridges, shape subglobular to oblate, apical region flattened or depressed, apical pore larger than basal; basal pore sometimes surrounded by 2 bisymmetrical, lip-shaped protuberances. [The most important characters are the number of spiral cells (18) as well as the occasional transverse ridges, which recall *Sycidium.*] *Lower Devonian (Emsian)–*

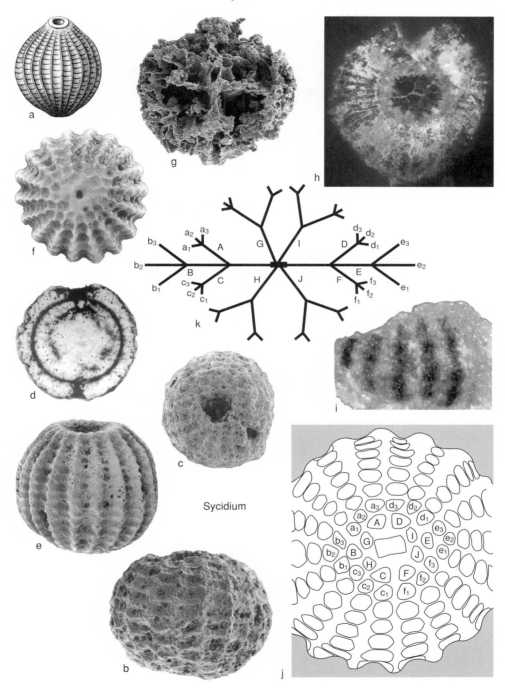

Sycidium

1a

1c

Karpinskya

1b

2g

2e

2h

2a

2c

2f

2b

Trochiliscus

2d

FIG. 46. Trochiliscaceae (p. 94–97).

Middle Devonian, ?Upper Devonian: United Kingdom, Poland, Ukraine, Russia, China, Iran.——FIG. 46,*2a–d.* **T. ingricus* KARPINSKY, ?Devonian, Russia; *a–b,* lectotype, lateral, apical views, ×60 (Karpinsky, 1906, pl. II,*23–24*); *c–d,* lateral, basal views, ×70 (Grambast-Fessard, Feist, & Z. Wang, 1989, fig. 4, *3*).——FIG. 46,*2e. T.* sp. cf. *ingricus,* Middle Devonian, Iran; lateral view, ×60 (Feist & Grambast-Fessard, 1985, fig. 8).——FIG. 46,*2f. T.* sp., Emsian, Wales; thin rock section with two-layered utricle wall, CF.2770, ×48 (new).——FIG. 46,*2g–h. T. podolicus* CROFT, Emsian, Ukraine, topotypes; *g,* lateral view, ×60 (Feist & Grambast-Fessard, 1985, pl. I,*4*); *h,* transverse section with two-layered utricle wall and black oospore membrane, CF.2717-5, ×66 (new).

Karpinskya (CROFT) GRAMBAST, 1962b, p. 65; *emend.,* FEIST & GRAMBAST-FESSARD, herein [**Trochiliscus laticostatus* PECK, 1934a, p. 109, pl. 11,*1–23;* OD] [=*Trochiliscus* KARPINSKY, 1906, p. 123, *partim* (type, *T. ingricus* KARPINSKY, 1906, p. 112); *Trochiliscus* subgenus *Karpinskya* CROFT, 1952, p. 209, obj.]. Utricles with 7 to 10 dextrally spiralled cells and an equal number of calcified coronula cells. Multilayered wall of utricle visible in thin sections. General shape globular, coronula units forming erect, parapet-like ring around large summit opening. *Middle Devonian–Carboniferous (Mississippian):* Poland, Russia, USA.——FIG. 46,*1a.* **K. laticostata* (PECK) GRAMBAST, Mississippian, USA; topotype, lateral view, C1237-2, ×30 (new).——FIG. 46,*1b–c. K. bilineata* (PECK) PECK & MORALES,

Upper Devonian, USA; *b,* apical view, CF.2915-3/1; *c,* basal view, CF.2915-3/2, ×50 (new).

Family CHOVANELLACEAE
Grambast, 1962

[Chovanellaceae GRAMBAST, 1962b, p. 64; *emend.,* FEIST & GRAMBAST-FESSARD, herein] [=Xinjiangocharaceae LU, SOULIÉ-MÄRSCHE, & WANG, 1996, p. 8]

Utricles with 3 to 14 vertical units that are simple or divided only at apical end. *Lower Devonian–Carboniferous (Mississippian).*

Chovanella REITLINGER & JARZEWA, 1958, p. 1,114; *emend.,* FEIST & GRAMBAST-FESSARD herein [**C. kovalevii;* OD; lectotype, REITLINGER & JARZEWA, 1958, p. 1,114, pl. 1,*1–3,* designated FEIST & GRAMBAST-FESSARD herein]. Utricles with 5 to 8 long vertical units, basal pore closed by discoid plate; summit opening occasionally surrounded and extended by short neck composed of separate apical cells equal in number to vertical cells. Apical cells occasionally missing. Long vertical units bifurcating into 2 secondary parts. *Upper Devonian:* Russia.——FIG. 47,*1a–c.*C. kovalevii* REITLINGER & JARZEWA, Famennian, lectotype; lateral, basal, apical views, ×60 (Reitlinger & Jarzewa, 1958, pl. I,*1–3*).

Ampullichara YANG & ZHOU, 1990, p. 272; *emend.,* FEIST & GRAMBAST-FESSARD, herein [**A. talimuica* YANG & ZHOU, 1990, p. 272, pl. II,*1–14;* OD]. Utricles with 3 to 4, long and thick, slightly dextrally spiralled units, not reaching apex; apical pore large, basal pore closed by discoid plate. Gyrogonites visible from exterior, at summit and laterally, between utricle units. Gyrogonites of *Moellerina* type with 10 to 12 dextrally spiralled cells and no coronula cells. Gyrogonite pyriform or bottle shaped, with basal and apical areas truncated. *Carboniferous (Mississippian):* China.——FIG. 47,*2a–d.* **A. talimuica* YANG & ZHOU, gyrogonites; *a–c,* holotype, lateral, apical, basal views, BPNWC XC-015; *d,* specimen with elongated neck, lateral view, ×180 (Yang & Zhou, 1990, pl. II, *4b,4a,4c,1b*).——FIG. 47,*2e–f. A. talimuica* forma *crassa* YANG & ZHOU, utricles; *e,* lateral view; *f,* apical view with 12 gyrogonite cells, ×70 (Yang & Zhou, 1990, pl. II,*15b,15a*).

Xinjiangochara YANG & ZHOU, 1990, p. 270; *emend.,* FEIST & GRAMBAST-FESSARD herein [**X. rosulata* YANG & ZHOU, 1990, p. 271, pl. I,*1–7;* OD] [=*Nucella* YANG & ZHOU, 1990, p. 271 (type, *N. bella* YANG & ZHOU, 1990, p. 272, pl. I,*14–15,* OD)].Vertical units, simple or bifurcating, up to 9 to 14 in number, going up to apical pore without intermediate apical cells. Basal plate rounded, slightly projecting. [Differs from *Chovanella* in having a higher cell number and by the apex, which is truncated instead of prominent. *Nucella,* which dif-

fers only in its more elongated utricle shape, is a synonym of *Xinjiangochara* (YANG Guodong, personal communication, 1996).] *Lower Devonian–Carboniferous (Mississippian):* USA, Canada, China.——FIG. 47,*3a–c.* **X. rosulata* YANG & ZHOU, Mississippian, China; *a,* holotype, lateral view; *b,* apical view; *c,* basal view, ×60 (Yang & Zhou, 1990, pl. I,*1b,1a,1c*).——FIG. 47,*3d–f. X. burgessi* (PECK & EYER) LU, SOULIÉ-MÄRSCHE, & Q. F. WANG, Middle Devonian; *d,* holotype, lateral view with coronula cells, western Canada, ×58 (Peck & Eyer, 1963a, pl. I,*7*); *e,* basal view with external basal plate, C.1238-1, Cooper Quarry, Missouri, USA, ×60 (new); *f,* longitudinal section with two-layered utricle, C.1386-1, Richfield, western Canada, ×60 (new).——FIG. 47,*3g. X. complanior* YANG & ZHOU; longitudinal section, ×60 (Yang & Zhou, 1990, pl. I,*13*).——FIG. 47,*3h. X. (Nucella) bella* YANG & ZHOU; lateral view, ×60 (Yang & Zhou, 1990, pl. I,*14b*).

Family PINNOPUTAMENACEAE
Z. Wang & Lu, 1980

[Pinnoputamenaceae Z. WANG & LU, 1980, p. 197; *emend.,* FEIST & GRAMBAST-FESSARD, herein]

Utricles with vertical units arranged in a symmetrical branching sequence. *Lower Devonian–Middle Devonian.*

Pinnoputamen Z. WANG & LU, 1980, p. 197 [**P. yunnanensis* Z. WANG & LU, 1980, p. 198, pl. 1,*1–6;* OD; lectotype, NIGP PB8680, WANG & LU, 1980, pl. 1,*1a–c;* designed FEIST & GRAMBAST-FESSARD herein]. Utricles bilaterally symmetrical; each face bearing one group of long vertical furrows and four branching short furrows obliquely directed upward; adjacent branching furrows overlapping each other and forming sawtooth ridges at their junction. [The species from the Emsian of southern France (FEIST & FEIST, 1997), which has the same basic structure but with antheridia, is the oldest representative of *Pinnoputamen. Costacidium* LANGER was referred by LANGER (1991) to the Pinnoputamenaceae; however, the differences from *Pinnoputamen* remain unclear.] *Lower Devonian (Lochkovian)–Middle Devonian (Givetian):* Europe, China.——FIG. 48*a–c.* **P. yunnanensis* Z. WANG & LU, Middle Devonian, southern China; *a,* lectotype, lateral view; *b,* apical view, ×60 (new, courtesy of Z. Wang & H. Lu); *c,* lateral view, schematic interpretation with bifurcated branch, ×70 (adapted from Feist & Grambast-Fessard, 1991, fig. 2-1).——FIG. 48*d–f. P.* sp., Lower Devonian, southern France; *d,* apical view; *e,* lateral view with a branch bearing antheridia, ×48 (Feist & Feist, 1997, fig. 1a, 1c); *f,* internal mold of a gyrogonite surrounded by its utricle, ×48 (new).

FIG. 47. Chovanellaceae (p. 97).

Order CHARALES
Lindley, 1836

[Charales LINDLEY, 1836, p. 414]

Gyrogonites composed of sinistrally spiralled cells. Apical structure variable. *Middle Devonian*[1]*–Holocene.*

Suborder PALAEOCHARINEAE
Feist & Grambast-Fessard, 1991

[Palaeocharineae FEIST & GRAMBAST-FESSARD, 1991, p. 201]

Gyrogonites with more than 5 sinistrally spiralled cells. *Middle Devonian*[1]*–Middle Triassic.*

---

[1]The assignment of *Palaeonitella cranii* (KIDSTON & LANG) PIA to the Eocharaceae extends the range of the Charales down to the Lower Devonian (Pragian; Kelman & others, 2004; see p. 120 herein for reference listing).

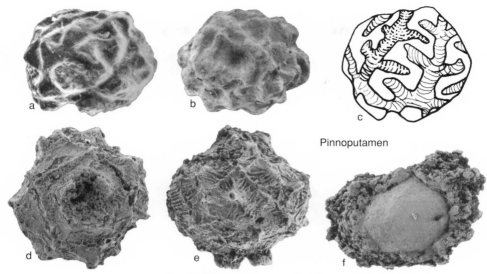

FIG. 48. Pinnoputamenaceae (p. 97).

Family EOCHARACEAE
Grambast, 1959

[Eocharaceae GRAMBAST, 1959a, p. 559]

Gyrogonites with sinistrally spiralled cells variable in number from 8 to 13. Apical pore present. Apex flat. [The attribution of *Octochara* GESS & HILLER, 1995, p. 420, and *Hexachara* GESS & HILLER, 1995, p. 422, to the Eocharaceae, as suggested by GESS and HILLER (1995), is hypothetical due to the lack of data on the cell number and apical structure of gyrogonites. These genera have been reported from the Upper Devonian of South Africa. The presence of the family in the Triassic is attested by KISIELEVSKY (1996) based on the presence of an undescribed taxon.] *Middle Devonian[1]–Middle Triassic.*

Eochara CHOQUETTE, 1956, p. 1,373 [*E. wickendenii* CHOQUETTE, 1956, p. 1,373, fig. 1–7; OD]. 8 to 13 spiral cells in type species, and basal plate visible from exterior. *Middle Devonian:* Canada, USA, China.——FIG. 49,*1a–c.* *E. wickendenii* CHOQUETTE, Cooper Quarry, Missouri, USA; *a,* apical view, C.1238-2, ×75; *b,* lateral view, C.1238-3, ×70; *c,* basal view, C.1238-4, ×75 (new).

Family PALAEOCHARACEAE Pia, 1927

[Palaeocharaceae PIA, 1927, p. 90]

Gyrogonite with 6 to 7 sinistrally spiralled cells. Apical pore present. Apex protruding.

Carboniferous (Pennsylvanian)–lower Permian.

Palaeochara BELL, 1922, p. 160 [*P. acadica* BELL, 1922, p. 160, pl. I,*3–9;* OD; holotype, GSC 988, designated PECK & EYER, 1963b, p. 843, pl. 101,*10–12*]. Apical part of gyrogonite protrudes into beak, conical to very elongated. *Carboniferous (Pennsylvanian)–lower Permian:* Canada, Germany, China.——FIG. 49,*2a–c.* *P. acadica* BELL, Pennsylvanian, Canada, holotype; *a,* apical view; *b,* lateral view; *c,* basal view, ×125 (Peck & Eyer, 1963b, pl. 101,*12,11,10*).

Suborder CHARINEAE
Feist & Grambast-Fessard 1991

[Charineae FEIST & GRAMBAST-FESSARD, 1991, p. 201]

Gyrogonite with 5 sinistrally spiralled cells. *Carboniferous (Pennsylvanian)–Holocene.*

Family POROCHARACEAE
Grambast, 1962

[Porocharaceae GRAMBAST, 1962b, p. 65]

Gyrogonites with 5 sinistrally spiralled cells, not enclosed in utricle; spiral cell endings delimit an apical pore generally open, although pore tends to be closed in some stellatocharoid genera. Basal plate undivided or with 2 to 3 pieces. [All the described species are without any ornamentation.]

1a

1b

1c

Eochara

2b

Palaeochara

2a

2c

FIG. 49. Eocharaceae and Palaeocharaceae (p. 99).

Carboniferous (Pennsylvanian)–Paleogene (Paleocene, ?Eocene).

The Porocharaceae are mostly Mesozoic. GRAMBAST (1962b) has divided the Porocharaceae into two subfamilies on the basis of the apex morphology: presence of an apical neck (Stellatocharoideae) or of a truncated or pointed apex (Porocharoideae). KOZUR (1973) erected a third subfamily division, Clavatoritinae (later correctly named Clavatoritoideae by BILAN, 1988), grouping gyrogonites with a pointed apex not elongated into a neck; Cuneatocharoideae Z. WANG and HUANG in Z. WANG (1978a), based on the same characters, is a junior synonym of the Clavatoritoideae.

Although Porocharaceae are characterized mainly by an open apical pore, some Permian Stellatocharoideae have a very small or even closed apex at the end of the apical neck. In such instances, the apical ends of the spiral cells join themselves at a point rather than along a broken line, as they do in the Characeae. On the other hand, the Permian representatives having a closed apex do not represent a distinct group, as specimens with open and closed apical pores may coexist in a given population (Z. WANG, 1984).

Subfamily POROCHAROIDEAE
Grambast, 1961

[Porocharoideae GRAMBAST, 1961, p. 200; *emend.*, Z. WANG & HUANG in Z. WANG, 1978a, p. 66]

Gyrogonite of Porocharaceae with a truncate summit. Apical pore sunken. *Carboniferous (Pennsylvanian)–Paleogene (Paleocene, ?Eocene).*

The Porocharoideae are a homogeneous group, including approximately fifty species for only four genera. The inclination of the endings of the spiral cells into the center of the apex, which is the chief character of both *Euaclistochara* WANG, HUANG, & WANG and *Jarzevaella* SHAIKIN, may occur in other genera, especially in *Porochara s.s.* These genera have been abandoned (FEIST & GRAMBAST-FESSARD, 1982; SCHUDACK, TURNER, & PETERSON, 1998).

Porochara MÄDLER, 1955, p. 271; *emend.*, SCHUDACK, 1986, p. 23 [*Aclistochara kimmeridgensis* MÄDLER, 1952, p. 26, pl. B,*13–19;* OD] [=*Euaclistochara* Z. WANG, HUANG, & S. WANG, 1976, p. 71 (type, *E. lufengensis* Z. WANG, HUANG, & S. WANG, 1976, p. 72, pl. 3,*14–19,* OD), *partim; Jarzevaella* SHAIKIN, 1977, p. 107 (type, *J. boltiskaensis* SHAIKIN, p. 107,fig. 1–2, OD), *partim; Musacchiella* FEIST & GRAMBAST-FESSARD, 1984, p. 301 (type, *M. douzensis* FEIST & GRAMBAST-FESSARD, 1984, p. 302, fig. 4a–c, OD)]. Apical opening small to medium; spiral ends sometimes bending toward center of apical pore; basal plate multipartite; general shape varying from ellipsoidal to subglobular. Size variable. [SCHUDACK (1986) described multipartite basal plates in type specimens of *P. kimmeridgensis*, and thus *Musacchiella* became superfluous as a junior synonym. Species whose basal plates have been recognized as multipartite extend from the Bathonian to the Berriasian. In addition, species attributed to *Porochara* but without indications on basal plate morphology are provisionally maintained in this genus.] *?upper Permian, Middle Jurassic–Lower Cretaceous, Paleogene (?Eocene):* worldwide.——FIG. 50,*3a–b.* *P. kimmeridgensis* (MÄDLER) MÄDLER, Kimmeridgian, Germany; *a,* topotype, lateral view, C.1234-1, ×60 (new); *b,* paratype, multipartite basal plate from inside gyrogonite, ×225 (Schudack, 1986, pl. 1,*12*).——FIG. 50,*3c–e. P. (Musacchiella) douzensis* (FEIST & GRAMBAST-FESSARD) SCHUDACK, Bathonian, France; *c,* apical view, ×50; *d,* basal view, ×50; *e,* longitudinal section, ×54 (Feist & Grambast-Fessard, 1984, fig. 3B, 4C, 2A).

Feistiella SCHUDACK, 1986, p. 23 [*F. bijuescensis* SCHUDACK, 1986, p. 23, pl. 1,*1–11;* OD] [=*Euaclistochara* Z. WANG, HUANG, & S. WANG, 1976, p. 71, *partim* (type, *E. lufengensis* Z. WANG, HUANG, & S. WANG, 1976, p. 72, pl. 3,*14–19,* OD); *Jarzevaella* SHAIKIN, 1977, p. 107 (type, *J. boltiskaensis* SHAIKIN, 1977, p. 107, fig. 1–2, OD), *partim; Porochara* MÄDLER, 1955, p. 271 (type, *Aclistochara kimmeridgensis* MÄDLER, 1952, p. 26), *partim*]. Apical opening small or medium; basal plate undivided; general shape varying from ellipsoidal to subglobular. Size variable. [This genus is most similar to *Porochara* in its general shape and in the morphology of the somewhat sunken apical opening. It differs in the particular character of an undivided basal plate and by the larger size of the Upper Cretaceous and Paleocene species.] *?upper Permian, Middle Jurassic–Paleogene (Paleocene, ?Eocene):* worldwide.——FIG. 50,*2a–d.* *F. bijuescensis* SCHUDACK, Berriasian, Spain; *a,* holotype, lateral view, ×57; *b–c,* holotype, apical, basal views, ×60; *d,* basal plate, ×250 (Schudack, 1986, pl. 1,*1,4,5,6*).

Stomochara L. GRAMBAST, 1961, p. 201[*Gyrogonites moreyi* PECK, 1934b, p. 54, pl. *1,1–3,5,6;* OD; =*Gyrogonites robertsi* PECK, 1934b, p. 54] [=*Catillochara* PECK & EYER, 1963b, p. 838, obj.; *Horniella* SHAIKIN, 1966, p. 158 (type, *Gyrogonites robertsi* R. PECK, 1934b, p. 54, fig. 10–12, OD), *non* A. TRAVERSE, 1955, p. 55 (type, *H. clavaticostata* A. TRAVERSE, 1955, p. 55, pl. 48,*65,* OD); *Altochara* SAIDAKOVSKY, 1968, p. 103 (type, *A. continua* SAIDAKOVSKY, 1968, p. 104, pl. 15,*22–23,* OD)]. Apical opening fairly large and ranging from strongly stellate to almost round; gyrogonites taper and may possess beak with small, truncate, apical area; basal plate undivided (PECK & EYER, 1963b, pl. 101,*6*). [PECK & EYER (1963b) restudied the types of *Gyrogonites moreyi* PECK and *G. robertsi* PECK with approximately 600 gyrogonites from the Pennsylvanian and Permian of the central United States. They concluded that all the Pennsylvanian and Permian gyrogonites studied should be placed in a single species, *G. moreyi,* thus placing *G. robertsi* into synonymy.] *Carboniferous (Pennsylvanian)–Triassic:* Bulgaria, Germany, Poland, Ukraine, USA, China.——FIG. 50,*1a–e.* *S. moreyi* (PECK) GRAMBAST, Pennsylvanian, USA; *a–b,* holotype, lateral and apical view, ×54 (Peck, 1934b, fig. 1–2); *c,* lateral view, C.1235-1; *d,* apical view, C.1235-2, ×105; *e,* basal plate in situ, C.1235-3, ×325 (new).

Vladimiriella SAIDAKOVSKY, 1971, p. 122 [*Tolypella globosa* SAIDAKOVSKY, 1960, p. 56, pl. I,*4a;* OD] [=*Porosphaera* Z. WANG & HUANG, 1978, p. 273, obj., *non* DUMORTIER, 1822, p. 91]. Apical opening small; general shape spherical, with rounded apex and base; size medium. [SAIDAKOVSKY (1971) erected a new Porocharaceae genus for species previously assigned to *Tolypella* or *Sphaerochara* (Characeae), as they possess an apical pore. The genus *Porosphaera,* based on the same type, is a junior objective synonym of *Vladimiriella.*] *Triassic:* Bulgaria, Germany, Poland, Sweden, Ukraine, China.——FIG. 50,*4a–b.* *V. globosa* (SAIDAKOVSKY) SAIDAKOVSKY, Dnieper-Donets, Ukraine; *a,* lateral view, ×120 (Saidakovsky, 1960, fig. 4a); *b,* lateral view, ×108 (Bilan, 1988, pl. VIII,*1*).

Subfamily CLAVATORITOIDEAE
Kozur, 1973

[*nom. correct.* KOZUR in BILAN, 1988, p. 107, *pro* Clavatoritinae KOZUR, 1973, p. 26] [=Cuneatocharoideae Z. WANG & HUANG in Z. WANG, 1978a, p. 66]

Gyrogonite of Porocharaceae with pointed summit that is not, however, drawn into a

1e
1c
1d
Stomochara

2a
Feistiella
2b
2c
2d
3c
Porochara
3e

1a
1b

3a
3d

4a
Vladimiriella
4b
3b

Fig. 50. Porocharaceae (p. 101).

Clavatorites

1a
1b
1c
1d
1e
1f

2a   Stenochara   2b   2c   2d

FIG. 51. Porocharaceae (p. 103–104).

neck. Apical opening small. *Triassic–Lower Cretaceous.*

Clavatorites HORN AF RANTZIEN, 1954, p. 47 [*Cl. hoellvicensis* HORN AF RANTZIEN, 1954, p. 48, pl. IV,4; OD] [=*Cuneatochara* SAIDAKOVSKY, 1962, p. 1,144 (type, *C. acuminata* SAIDAKOVSKY, 1962, p. 1,144, pl. 1,1,7,8, OD)]. Apical part of gyrogonite forming cuneiform apical projection with small, circular aperture at its top; basal plate not described; general shape ovoid; size small to medium. [GRAM-BAST (1962b, p. 83) stated that the genus *Clavatorites* should be rejected because the type, based on a single badly preserved specimen, was not clearly established. KOZUR (1974) recognized the genus and considered *Cuneatochara* SAIDAKOVSKY as a junior synonym.] *Triassic:* Sweden, Bulgaria, Germany, Poland, Ukraine, China, Kazakhstan.——FIG. 51,1a. * *C. hollvicensis* HORN AF RANTZIEN, Sweden; holotype, lateral view, SGS 1952-9-1762-2, ×70 (Horn af Rantzien, 1954, pl. IV,4).——FIG.

51,1b–c. *C. (Cuneatochara) acuminatus* SAIDA-KOVSKY, Lower Triassic, Ukraine; *b,* holotype, lateral view, PMUK 570; *c,* apical view, ×110 (Saidakovsky, 1962, pl. I,7–8).——FIG. 51,1d–f. *C. (Cuneatochara) wuerttembergensis* BREUER, Triassic, Germany; *d,* holotype, lateral view, MNS P1456, ×80; *e,* apical view, ×100; *f,* basal view of oospore, ×100 (Breuer, 1988, fig. 2a–2c).

Stenochara GRAMBAST, 1962b, p. 66, *nom. nov. pro Praechara* HORN AF RANTZIEN, 1954, p. 57, *non* BIRINA, 1948 (type, *Praechara chovanensis* BIRINA, 1948, p. 154, pl. 1,1–2) [*Praechara mädleri* HORN AF RANTZIEN, 1954, p. 62, pl. 5,6–8; OD]. Apical part of gyrogonite forming low projection, with small, star-shaped or rounded aperture at its top. General shape ovoid, with apex slightly conical and base rounded. Basal plate unknown. Size small to medium. [Differs from *Cuneatochara* in its apical part, which is less protruding and does not form an acute angle.] *Triassic–Lower Cretaceous:* Bulgaria, Germany, Poland, Portugal, Sweden, Ukraine,

China, Kazakhstan.——Fig. 51,*2a*. *S. maedleri* (Horn af Rantzien) Grambast, Triassic, Sweden; holotype, lateral view, ×70 (Horn af Rantzien, 1954, pl. V,*6*).——Fig. 51,*2b–d*. *S. zavialensis* Grambast-Fessard, Lower Cretaceous, Portugal; *b*, holotype, lateral view, ×70; *c*, paratype, apical view; *d*, basal view, ×80 (Grambast-Fessard, 1980, pl. 3,*10,12,11*).

Subfamily STELLATOCHAROIDEAE Grambast, 1962

[Stellatocharoideae Grambast, 1962b, p. 68] [=Maslovicharoideae Saidakovsky, 1966, p. 114; Stellatocharaceae Conkin & Conkin, 1977, p. 181]

Gyrogonite of Porocharaceae with apical part drawn into neck that is conical or truncated at distal end; apical pore variable in diameter; in some genera very small or even closed. Apical pore rounded, pentagonal, or stellatiform. Basal plate multipartite or unknown. *Carboniferous (Pennsylvanian)– Paleogene (Paleocene).*

Stellatochara Horn af Rantzien, 1954, p. 26 [**S. sellingii* Horn af Rantzien, 1954, p. 33, pl. 1,*1–3*; OD] [=*Maslovichara* Saidakovsky, 1962, p. 1,143 (type, *M. gracilis* Saidakovsky, 1962, p. 1,143, pl. 1,*1–2*, OD)]. Spiral cells progressively bent at rim of apex, forming wide apical neck, less than one-third of gyrogonite length. Apical neck truncated at extremity; apical pore rounded, pentagonal, or star shaped, generally small; basal plate multipartite. General shape frequently ovoid, occasionally ellipsoid or subglobular. Size small to medium. [The genus is well characterized by its apical elongated neck; however the trait is not well marked in the type species *S. sellingii.* The Jurassic and Cretaceous species, which present a truncated apex and were assigned to *Stellatochara* by Peck (1957) and Bhatia and Mannikeri (1977), belong to *Porochara.* Horn af Rantzien (1954) noted the similarities in the gyrogonites of *Stellatochara* and Clavatoraceae genera; in both instances, the gyrogonite is bottle shaped with a cylindrical apical neck. Grambast (1962b) agreed with Horn af Rantzien (1964) and expressed the opinion that the ancestors of the Clavatoraceae are to be sought among the Stellatocharoideae. Transitional forms between the Triassic Stellatocharoideae and the Upper Jurassic Clavatoraceae, however, are presently unknown. The Upper Jurassic *S. rostrata* (Mädler) Schudack, 1993b, as well as the Lower Cretaceous *S. reyi* Grambast-Fessard, 1980, and *S. nehdensis* Schudack, 1987, have an apex with apical projection abruptly turning upward, which is typical of *Stellatochara.* These taxa most likely represent clavatoracean gyrogonites, exceptionally calcified when the utricle was, for some reason, uncalcified, and they therefore should not be referred to *Stellatochara.*] *Triassic:* Germany, Poland, Sweden, Ukraine, China, Kazakhstan.——Fig. 52,*4a–d*. **S.*

sellingii Horn af Rantzien, Triassic, Sweden; *a*, holotype, lateral view RMS-1952-9-1805-44, ×70 (new); *b–c*, paratype, apical, basal views, RMS-1952-9-1805-48, ×120 (new); *d*, longitudinal section, ×90 (Horn af Rantzien, 1954, pl. II,*4*).——Fig. 52,*4e*. *S. germanica* Kozur, Triassic, Germany; lateral view, ×110 (Breuer, 1988, fig. 2d).

Auerbachichara Kisielevsky, 1967, p. 37; *emend.,* Saidakovsky, 1968, p. 102 [**A. saidakovskyi* Kisielevsky, 1967, p. 38, pl. 1,*1–2*; OD] [=*Shaikinella* Kisielevsky, 1993b, p. 87 (type, *S. consummata* Kisielevsky, 1993b, p. 89, pl. VIII,*1–2*, OD)]. Spiral cells progressively bent at summit, forming short and broad apical neck; apical ends of spiral cells forming more or less developed denticles around apical aperture; apical aperture large, pentagonal or star shaped. Basal plate unknown. General shape ovoid. Size small. [Differs from *Stellatochara* in its less protruding neck and in its larger apical pore.] *Permian–Triassic:* Germany, Poland, Ukraine, Russia, China, Kazakhstan.——Fig. 52,*1a*. **A. saidakovskyi* Kisielevsky, Lower Triassic, Russia; lateral view, ×105 (adapted from Saidakovsky, 1968, pl. XV,*18*).——Fig. 52,*1b–c*. *A. starozhilovae* Kisielevsky, Triassic, Poland; lateral, apical views, ×108 (Bilan, 1988, pl. X,*1a–1b*).

Latochara Mädler, 1955, p. 271; *emend.,* Feist in Feist & Cubaynes, 1984, p. 595 [**Aclistochara latitruncata* Peck, 1937, p. 89, pl. 14,*1–4;* OD] [=*Minhechara* Wei in Hao & others, 1983, p. 173 (type, *M. columelaria* Wei in Hao & others, 1983, p. 174, pl. 43,*11–17,* OD)]. At rim of summit, spiral cells level off, turn inward, then turn abruptly upward into almost vertical position to form small pyramidal projection in center of summit (Peck, 1957); apical pore very small. Basal plate multipartite. General shape varying from subglobular to ovoid. Size small to medium. [*Minhechara,* based only on the wider apical pyramidal projection, is not distinguishable from *Latochara* (Feist & Grambast-Fessard, 1991).] *Triassic–Paleogene (Paleocene):* France, Ukraine, USA, China.——Fig. 52,*2a–c*. **L. latitruncata* (Peck) Mädler, Upper Jurassic, USA; *a,* lateral view, C.1236-1; *b,* multipartite basal plate from inside gyrogonite, C.1236-3, ×145; *c,* apical view, C.1236-2, ×80 (new).

Leonardosia Sommer, 1954, p. 186; *emend.,* Saidakovsky, 1989, p. 91 [**L. langei* Sommer, 1954, p. 187, pl. 16,*12;* OD] [=*Paracuneatochara* Z. Wang, 1984, p. 55 (type, *P. jinxiensis* Z. Wang, 1984, p. 56, pl. I,*1–15,* OD); *Acutochara* Saidakovsky, 1993, p. 78 (type, *A. chinensis* Saidakovsky, 1993, p. 79, fig. 4, OD; holotype, NIGP PB 11298, Wang, 1984, pl. II,*8*); *Leonidiella* Kisielevsky, 1993c, p. 98 (type, *L. embensis* Kisielevsky, 1993c, p. 98, pl. XII,*1–2,* OD); *Luichara* Kisielevsky, 1993c, p. 100 (type, *L. molostovskae* Kisielevsky, 1993c, p. 100, pl. XII,*5–6,* OD)]. Apical neck very long, more than one-third of gyrogonite length; Apical neck broad at base, then decreasing in width toward top. Apical pore small or closed. Basal plate unknown. General shape subglobular. Size large. [In the apical neck,

1a

1c

2a

1b
Auerbachichara

2b

3a

3c
Leonardosia

2c
Latochara

3b

4e

4c

4b

Stellatochara

4a

4d

Fig. 52. Porocharaceae (p. 104–106).

cells are so tightly conjoined that the small pore at their apical ends tends to disappear. This condition differs from the closure of the apex in the Characeae. Original description by SOMMER (1954), based on impressions, shows a reverse course of the spiral cells. *Acutochara* SAIDAKOVSKY, 1993, which is defined only by the wavy outline of the apical neck that may be due to the preservation as a cast, is not distinct from *Leonardosia*.] *Carboniferous (Pennsylvanian)–upper Permian:* Russia, Brazil, Paraguay, China, Kazakhstan.——FIG. 52,*3a. *L. langei* SOMMER, Permian, Brazil; holotype, lateral view of dextrally spiralled impression of enveloping cells, ×45 (Sommer, 1954, pl. 16,*12*).——FIG. 52,*3b–c*. *L. (Paracuneatochara) jinxiensis* (Z. WANG) FEIST & GRAMBAST-FESSARD, upper Permian, China; *b*, lateral view; *c*, basal view, ×60 (Z. Wang, 1984, pl. II,*5–6*).

Family CLAVATORACEAE Pia, 1927

[Clavatoraceae PIA, 1927, p. 91]

Gyrogonites with 5 sinistrally spiralled cells, enclosed in utricle, made of generally calcified cells of vegetative origin. Gyrogonites with apical pore at end of neck or collar. [Gyrogonites resembling those of the Porocharaceae Stellatocharoideae, from which the Clavatoraceae probably evolved. Characters of particular importance are the symmetry and the number of layers in the utricle. Reported only from the Mesozoic.] *Upper Jurassic–Upper Cretaceous (Maastrichtian).*

The family Clavatoraceae was established by PIA (1927) after the genus *Clavator* REID & GROVES, 1916. PECK (1938), who described the genus *Atopochara,* placed it in a new family, the Atopocharaceae, which has since been abandoned. GRAMBAST (1969) created three subfamilies within the Clavatoraceae, based upon utricle symmetry and number of layers of the utricle wall: Echinocharoideae, Clavatoroideae, and Atopocharoideae. Z. WANG and LU (1982) subdivided the Atopocharoideae into two tribes, the Atopocharae and Globatorae, and the Clavatoroideae into Clavatorae and Clypeatorae; the latter was divided into two subtribes, the Clypeatorinae and Septorellinae. These subdivisions, however, do not appear needed; and they have not generally been followed. SCHUDACK (1993b) has shown that the structure of the utricle in the

Echinocharoideae was of the same type as that in the Atopocharoideae; the former subfamily has thus been abandoned.

In the classification of the Clavatoraceae proposed by MARTIN-CLOSAS and SERRA-KIEL (1991), the evolutionary lineages are interpreted as evolutionary species, in the sense of WILEY (1978). Although attractive in correctly reflecting progressive evolution within the phylum, this interpretation would however entail a total turnover of the taxonomy not completely in agreement with the rules of nomenclature (FEIST & Z. WANG, 1995).

Subfamily CLAVATOROIDEAE Pia, 1927

[*nom. transl.* GRAMBAST, 1969, p. 880, *ex* Clavatoraceae PIA, 1927, p. 91; *emend.,* GRAMBAST, 1969, p. 880]

Gyrogonite enclosed in utricle typically bilaterally symmetrical and composed of inner nodular layer and external structural layer formed of elongated units. External layer not developed in some genera. Some specialized genera develop secondary triradiate or four-rayed symmetry. *Upper Jurassic–Upper Cretaceous.*

Clavator REID & GROVES, 1916, p. 253, pl. 8; *emend.,* HARRIS, 1939, p. 14 [*C. reidii* GROVES, 1924, p. 116; SD GROVES, 1924, p. 116]. Utricle bilaterally symmetrical with 2 calcified layers, inner smooth or nodular, outer made of 12 or fewer elongated vertical or spiralled units. Vegetative apparatus strongly calcified, with central tube surrounded by 12 dextrally coiled cortical tubes composed of alternate long and short units, latter giving rise to clusters of spines that more or less completely cover cortex. *Upper Jurassic (Tithonian)–Lower Cretaceous (Aptian):* USA, Germany, United Kingdom, Switzerland.——FIG. 53,*2a–b.* *C. reidii* GROVES, Berriasian, United Kingdom; utricles, lateral views, MPK 8892 and 8895, ×45 (Feist, Lake, & Wood, 1995, pl. I,*11–12*).

Ascidiella GRAMBAST, 1966b, p. 2,210 [*A. iberica* GRAMBAST, 1966b, p. 2,210, pl. I,*1–3*; OD]. Utricle with strong bilateral symmetry and lateral expansion resembling a horn on shoulder near apex. A pore opening at end of horn. Numerous accessory pores present, with units of outer layer of utricle radiating from them. Pores are outlets for internal canals. Internal nodular layer of utricle well developed. [GRAMBAST (1966b) indicated that *Dictyoclavator* may have been ancestral type of *Ascidiella.*] *Lower Cretaceous (Barremian–Aptian):* United Kingdom, Portugal, Spain, Lebanon.—— FIG. 54,*1a–b.* *A. iberica* GRAMBAST, Barremian,

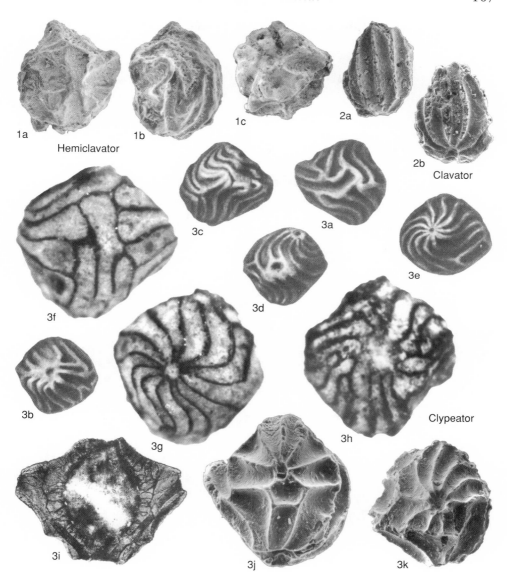

FIG. 53. Clavatoraceae (p. 106–110).

Spain; *a,* holotype, lateral view, C.6333-6, ×38 (new); *b,* longitudinal section, ×35 (Grambast, 1966b, pl. I,*4*).——FIG. 54,*1c. A. irregularis* GRAMBAST-FESSARD, Aptian, Portugal; paratype, lateral view, ×28 (Grambast-Fessard, 1986, pl. I,*5*).——FIG. 54,*1d. A. inflata* GRAMBAST-FESSARD, Barremian, Spain; paratype, apical view, ×25 (Grambast-Fessard, 1986, pl. I,*3*).

Clypeator GRAMBAST, 1962b, p. 69; *emend.,* L. GRAMBAST, 1970, p. 1,967 [**Perimneste corrugata* PECK, 1941, p. 295, pl. 42,*15–24;* OD]. Utricle bilaterally symmetrical, with 2 opposite shields, each composed of 9 to 13 superficial units radiating from 2 lateral pores. Pores at end of internal canals, generally opening at tip of lateral projections. On 1 or 2 sides, 2 or 3 cells are intercalated between basal cell and lateral pore. *Upper Jurassic–Lower Cretaceous (Albian):* North America, Bulgaria, Germany, United Kingdom, Portugal, Romania, Russia, Spain, China, South Korea.——FIG. 53,*3a–i. *C. corrugatus* (PECK) GRAMBAST, Aptian, North America; *a–e,* different views of one specimen, ×40

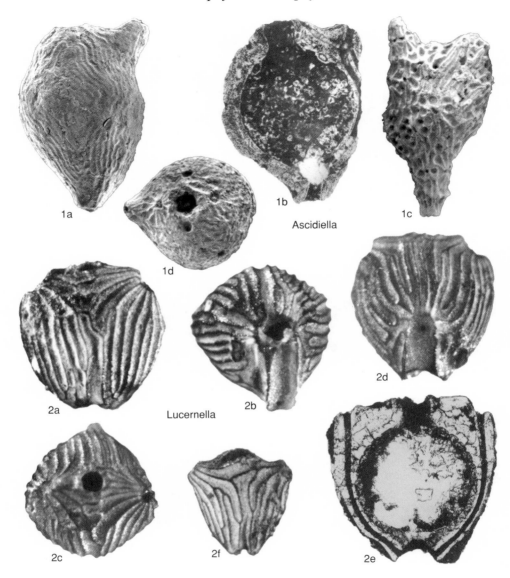

FIG. 54. Clavatoraceae (p. 106–110).

(Peck, 1957, pl. 3,*1–5*); *f–g*, topotype, ventral, lateral views of same specimen; *h–i*, basal view, longitudinal section, ×70 (Grambast, 1970, pl. IV,*3a–3b,2d,4*).——FIG. 53,*3j*. *C. discordis* SHAIKIN, Berriasian, Germany; lateral view, CF.2003c-1, ×75 (new).——FIG. 53,*3k*. *C. combei* GRAMBAST, Hauterivian, United Kingdom; lateral view, MPK 8906, ×50 (new).

Dictyoclavator GRAMBAST, 1966b, p. 2,210 [**Clavator fieri* DONZE, 1955, p. 288, pl. XIII,*4–5;* OD]. Utricle globular, with a well-marked adaxial furrow underlining bilateral symmetry. Outer layer not developed. Inner layer composed of irregularly disposed short units. *Upper Jurassic (Kimmeridgian)–Lower Cretaceous (Valanginian):* France, Portugal, Spain, Switzerland.——FIG. 55,*1a–b*. **D. fieri* (DONZE) GRAMBAST, Berriasian, France, topotypes; *a*, lateral view, C.1218-1; *b*, apical view, C.1218-2, ×30 (new).——FIG. 55,*1c*. *D. ramalhoi* GRAMBAST-FESSARD, Kimmeridgian, Portugal; adaxial view with median furrow, ×40 (Grambast-Fessard & Ramalho, 1985, pl. I,*4*).

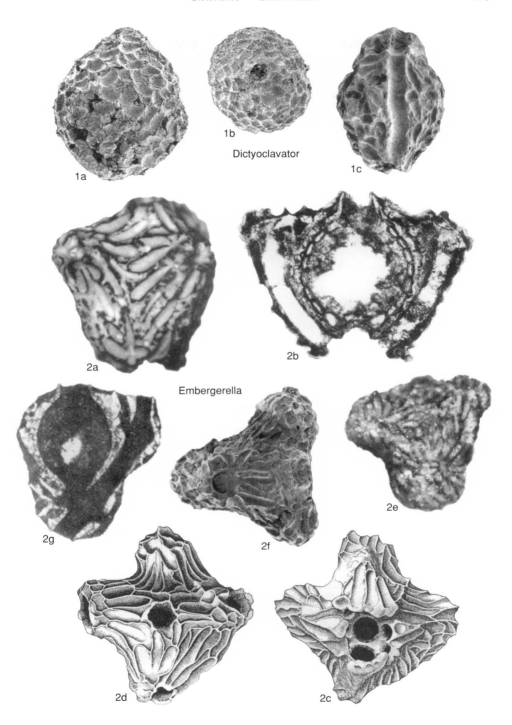

Dictyoclavator

Embergerella

Fig. 55. Clavatoraceae (p. 108–110).

Embergerella GRAMBAST, 1969, p. 881 [**E. cruciata* GRAMBAST, 1969, p. 881, pl. II,*8–14;* OD]. Utricle quadrangular to triangular from apex to base, composed in upper part of 3 or 4 strongly developed projections. At ends of projections are openings of canal system, canals originating near base. Surface units short and consisting of asymmetrical rosettes radiating from openings. [*Embergerella* differs from *Triclypella* in shape, development of surface units, and development of canal system.] *Upper Jurassic–Upper Cretaceous (Cenomanian):* France, Spain, Russia.——FIG. 55,*2a–d.* **E. cruciata* GRAMBAST, Barremian, Spain; *a,* holotype, lateral view; *b,* longitudinal section, ×55 (Grambast, 1969, pl. II,*8a,13*); *c,* basal view; *d,* apical view, C.747-7, ×55 (new).——FIG. 55,*2e–g. E. triquetra* GRAMBAST, Barremian; *e,* holotype, lateral view; *f,* apical view; *g,* longitudinal section with main canal and gyrogonite, ×60 (Grambast, 1969, pl. III, *18a,15b,20*).

Flabellochara GRAMBAST, 1959a, p. 559 [**Clavator harrisi* PECK, 1941, p. 292, pl. 42,*28–34;* OD]. Utricle bilaterally symmetrical with 2 opposite fans originating from a basal vertical unit. Fans each composed of 7 to 11 radiating cells. On adaxial side, single elongated cell intercalated between 2 fans. *Lower Cretaceous:* USA, Argentina, Bulgaria, France, Germany, United Kingdom, Italy, Spain, Switzerland, Ukraine, China, Uzbekistan.——FIG. 56,*3a–b.* **F. harrisi* (PECK) GRAMBAST, Aptian, North America; *a,* topotype, lateral view, ×40 (Peck, 1957, pl. 2,*9*); *b,* topotype, lateral view, C.1240-1, ×45 (new).——FIG. 56,*3c. F. grovesi* (HARRIS) GRAMBAST, Berriasian, United Kingdom; lateral view, C.1219-1, ×45 (new).

Hemiclavator Z. WANG & LU, 1982, p. 98 [**H. neimongolensis* Z. WANG & LU, 1982, p. 98, pl. IV,*1–5;* OD; lectotype, PB8738OD, pl. IV, *1b,1c,1d,* designated FEIST & GRAMBAST-FESSARD herein]. Utricle with 2 different sides: 1 with vertical cells as in *Clavator* species, the other with long units radiating from central pore. Nodular layer generally visible laterally as well as in apical part of utricle. *Lower Cretaceous (Barremian):* Spain, China.——FIG. 53,*1a–c.* **H. neimongolensis* Z. WANG & LU, China; lectotype; *a,* lateral side with radiating units; *b,* lateral side with vertical units; *c,* basal view, ×50 (Z. Wang & Lu, 1982, pl. IV,*1b–1d*).

Heptorella FEIST & GRAMBAST-FESSARD, *nom. nov.* herein, *nom. nov.* pro *Septorella* GRAMBAST, 1962b, p. 69, *non* ALLESCHER in HENNINGS, 1897, p. 242, Fungi (type, *S. salacia,* OD) [**Septorella brachycera* GRAMBAST, 1962b, p. 69, pl. I,*a–d;* OD]. Utricle with 6 to 9 lateral pores, superficial or at ends of projections. Lateral pores are outlets for internal canals originating from basal chamber. Outer layer with numerous vertical, long units in basal part of utricle. Apical part composed of shorter units converging to apical pore. A horizontal corticated tube, weakly developed in *H. campylopoda,* joined to basal part of utricle. [*Septorella* GRAMBAST, 1962b, is a junior homonym of *Septorella* ALLESCHER, 1897.]

Derivatio nominis: Heptorella, from the Greek *hepta* (seven), referring to the frequent number of lateral horns of utricles in the type species.] *Upper Cretaceous (Campanian–Maastrichtian):* France, Spain. ——FIG. 56,*1a–c.* **H. brachycera* GRAMBAST, Maastrichtian, southern France; *a,* holotype, lateral view, ×50 (Grambast, 1962b, fig. 1b); *b,* paratype, apical view, ×40; *c,* longitudinal section, ×45 (Grambast, 1971, pl. III,*3b,* pl. II,*4*).——FIG. 56,*1d–f. H. ultima* GRAMBAST, southern France; *d,* holotype, lateral view; *e,* paratype, basal view, ×30 (Grambast, 1971, pl. VI,*1a,* pl. VII,*1c*); *f,* dwarf form, ×30 (Grambast, 1977b, fig. 4b).

Lucernella GRAMBAST & LORCH, 1968, p. 48 [**L. ampullacea* GRAMBAST & LORCH, 1968, p. 48, pl. I,*1–3,* pl. II,*1–9;* OD]. Utricle bilaterally symmetrical, with 2 accessory pores located at top of shoulders of apex. Accessory pores are outlets for 2 internal canals originating at basal chamber. Adaxial face of utricle joined to fragment of branch or with prominent furrow marking its place. Internal nodular layer of utricle well developed. External layer made of vertical units except in apical zone where furrows radiate from accessory pores. *Lower Cretaceous (Aptian):* Lebanon.——FIG. 54,*2a–e.* **L. ampullacea* GRAMBAST & LORCH, holotype; *a,* dorsal (abaxial) view, ×49; *b,* basal view, ×47; *c,* apical view, ×44; *d,* ventral view, ×49; *e,* longitudinal section, ×50 (GRAMBAST & LORCH, 1968, pl. I,*1a,1d,1c,1b,* pl. II,*8*).——FIG. 54,*2f. L. deltea* GRAMBAST & LORCH; paratype, dorsal view, ×60 (Grambast & Lorch, 1968, pl. III,*1a*).

Nodosoclavator MASLOV, 1961, p. 679; *emend.,* GRAMBAST, 1966c, p. 269 [**Clavator nodosus* PECK, 1957, p. 15, pl. 8,*3–18;* OD]. Utricle with external layer restricted to basal portion of gyrogonite, nodular layer with tubercles well developed and irregularly disposed or more or less aligned with spirals and covering gyrogonite. Gyrogonites strongly beaked by abrupt upturn of spiral units at distal ends. Vegetative parts commonly preserved at base of utricle. [*Nodosoclavator* differs from *Clavator* in that outer structural layer is restricted to the basal part of the utricle or even missing. *Nodosoclavator* is one of the oldest representatives of the Clavataraceae family. The nodosoclavatoroid utricles (SCHUDACK, 1989) are incompletely developed utricles of other Clavatoroideae, which may represent the *Nodosoclavator* stage and do not put the validity of the genus in question.] *Upper Jurassic (Oxfordian)–Lower Cretaceous (Aptian):* USA, France, Germany, United Kingdom, Portugal, Spain, Switzerland, Ukraine, China, Algeria.——FIG. 57,*1a–b.* **N. nodosus* (PECK) MASLOV, Aptian, North America; *a,* holotype, lateral view; *b,* paratype, lateral view, ×60 (Peck, 1957, pl. 8,*5–6*).——FIG. 57,*1c–d. N. adnatus* MARTIN-CLOSAS & GRAMBAST-FESSARD, Barremian, Spain; *c,* lateral view with part of branchlet, ×50; *d,* interpretation of external utricle structure in connection with branchlet, ×50 (Martin-Closas & Grambast-Fessard, 1986, pl. II,*10,* text-fig. 4).

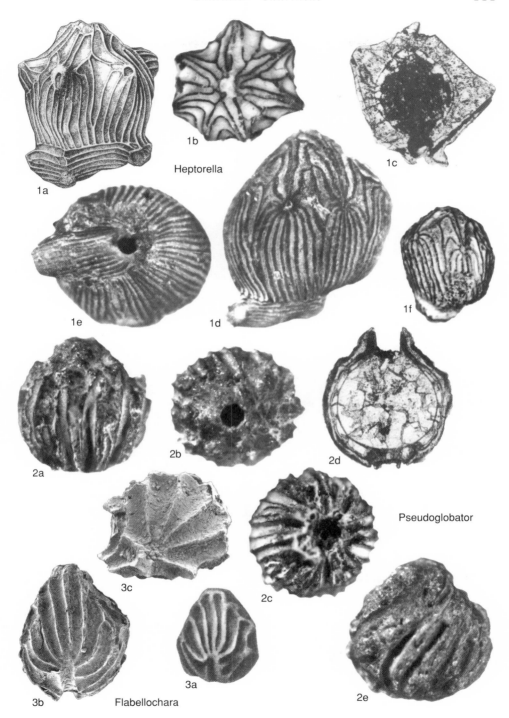

1a

1b

Heptorella

1c

1e

1d

1f

2a

2b

2d

Pseudoglobator

3c

2c

3b   Flabellochara

3a

2e

FIG. 56. Clavatoraceae (p. 110–112).

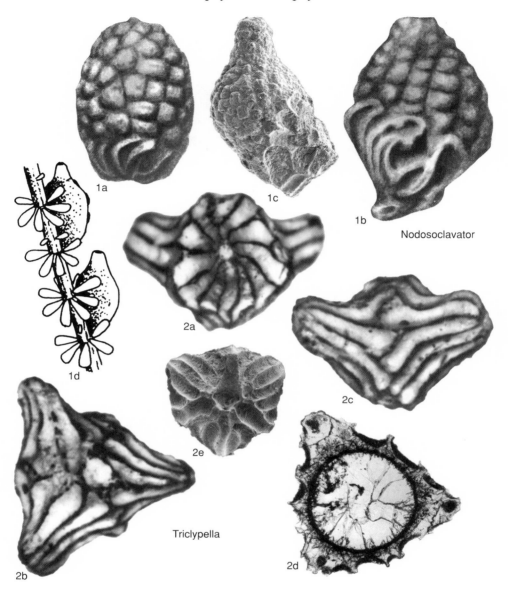

FIG. 57. Clavatoraceae (p. 110–113).

Pseudoglobator GRAMBAST, 1969, p. 881 [**P. fourcadei* GRAMBAST, 1969, p. 881, pl. IV,*22–28;* OD]. Utricle globular, not bilaterally symmetrical, without lateral expansions or canals. Internal layer formed of large nodules, external layer of numerous units, not articulated, long, vertical, or slightly spiralled. *Lower Cretaceous (Barremian):* Spain.——FIG. 56,*2a–e.* **P. fourcadei* GRAMBAST; *a–c,* holotype, lateral, apical, basal views; *d,* longitudinal section; *e,*

paratype, lateral view, ×40 (Grambast, 1969, pl. IV,*22a–c,27,23a*).

Triclypella GRAMBAST, 1969, p. 881 [**T. calcitrapa* GRAMBAST, 1969, p. 881, pl. I,*1–7;* OD]. Utricle with 3 laterally directed projections developed in upper half. At ends of projections are openings of internal canals that originate near base. Surface units forming shields radiate from ends of projections. [Differs from *Clypeator* by presence of a third projection developed in the symmetry plane.] *Lower Cretaceous (?Hauterivian, Barremian):* Argentina, United Kingdom, Spain, China.——FIG. 57,*2a–e.* *T. calcitrapa* GRAMBAST; *a,* holotype, lateral view with 1 shield, Barremian, Spain; *b–c,* holotype, apical, lateral views, Barremian, Spain; *d,* transverse section, Barremian, Spain, ×70 (Grambast, 1969, pl. I,*1c,1a–1b,7*); *e,* basal view, ?Hauterivian, United Kingdom, ×45 (Feist, Lake, & Wood, 1995, pl. II,*2*).

Subfamily ATOPOCHAROIDEAE
Peck, 1938

[*nom. transl.* GRAMBAST, 1969, p. 880, *pro* Atopocharaceae PECK, 1938, p. 173; *emend.,* SCHUDACK, 1993b, p. 93]

Utricle with a well-developed, 3-rayed symmetry. Utricle composed of 2 superposed groups of branched units. 3 or 6 similarly branched units of internal group trifurcately ramified, whereas external group more variable or even completely reduced. *Upper Jurassic–Upper Cretaceous.*

Atopochara PECK, 1938, p. 173; *emend.,* PECK, 1941, p. 289 [**A. trivolvis* PECK, 1938, p. 174, pl. 28,*8–12,* text-fig. 1; OD]. Utricle composed of 3 equivalent groups of units. Each group composed of 3 short vertical units originating near basal opening and ending near equator; 2 to 5 small units grouped on or near equator and several sinistrally spiralled units extending distally from equator to apex. Gyrogonite thin walled, fragile. [GRAMBAST (1967) stated that *Atopochara* developed directly from *Perimneste* by suppression of primordial basal cells of each ramulus and of all vestigial antheridia except that in right-hand fork.] *Cretaceous:* worldwide.——FIG. 58,*1a–c.* *A. trivolvis* PECK, Aptian, North America; *a,* holotype, lateral view, ×33 (Peck, 1938, pl. 28,*12*); *b–c,* topotype, basal view, apical view, ×40 (Grambast, 1968, pl. III,*16b,1c*).——FIG. 58,*1d–e. A. triquetra* (GRAMBAST) FEIST, Lower Cretaceous, Spain; *d,* paratype, lateral view; *e,* paratype, basal view, ×50 (Grambast, 1968, pl. II,*13a,12b*).——FIG. 58,*1f. A. multivolvis* PECK, Cenomanian, southern France; lateral view, ×35 (Feist, 1981, fig. 1f).——FIG. 58,*1g–h. A. trivolvis* PECK; interpretations of cellular structure of utricle (*white,* antheridia) (Grambast, 1967, fig. d,f).

Diectochara MUSACCHIO, 1971, p. 29 [**D. andica* MUSACCHIO, 1971, p. 31, text-fig. 4, pl. I,*8–10,* pl. II,*24–29,* pl. III,*30–38*; OD]. Utricle made of long, noncontiguous, unbranched tubes forming 2 superposed series of 6 cells each, outer being more elongated. Vegetative apparatus preserved, composed of vertical, long units. [The utricle structure in this genus is even less distinctive than in *Echinochara.*] *Lower Cretaceous (Barremian):* Argentina.——FIG. 59,*2a–c.* *D. andica* MUSACCHIO; *a,* topotype, acidized specimen, C.1217-1, ×25 (new); *b,* paratype, gyrogonite and antheridia, ×54

(Musacchio, 1971, pl. I,*9*); *c,* topotype, internal view of half of whorl of utricles with 3 gyrogonites and 1 antheridium, C.1217-2, ×23 (new).

Echinochara PECK, 1957, p. 21; *emend.,* SCHUDACK, 1993b, p. 94 [**E. spinosa* PECK, 1957, p. 22, pl. I,*1–22,* pl. 2,*21–25;* OD]. Utricle made of short, contiguous, branched or not branched cortical tubes, more or less fused to gyrogonite; these tubes form 2 groups of units: internal ones, 3 or 6 in number, trifurcately ramified; external units (also 3 or 6) more variable. Vegetative apparatus preserved, with external filaments more or less dextrally coiled. [In *E. pecki* (MÄDLER) GRAMBAST, the tubes are contiguous and joined to the gyrogonite and constitute a true utricle completely enclosing the gyrogonite.] *Upper Jurassic–Lower Cretaceous:* North America, Germany, Switzerland, Spain.——FIG. 58,*2a–c.* *E. spinosa* PECK, Kimmeridgian, North America; *a,* paratype, 3 fertile nodes with spiral internal fillings of gyrogonites (etched specimen), ×16; *b,* section through 2 fertile nodes of branchlet, ×18 (Peck, 1957, pl. 1,*2, 6*); *c,* holotype, lateral, view of gyrogonite filling and utricle cells (etched specimen), ×40 (Peck, 1957, pl. 1,*2,6,* pl. 2,*23*).——FIG. 58,*2d–e. E. pecki* (MÄDLER) GRAMBAST, upper Kimmeridgian, Germany, topotypes; *d,* apical view of utricle whorl around central axis, CF.2950-1, ×40; *e,* internal view of utricle with casts of spiral cells, CF.2950-2, ×60 (new).

Globator L. GRAMBAST, 1966a, p. 1,932 [**G. trochiliscoides* L. GRAMBAST, 1966a, p. 1,932, fig. 1–3; OD]. Utricle composed of 3 equivalent groups of units. Each group composed of 3 units at base, with 5 units resting on them. Type species unique in having only 15 units, 3 basal units not represented. *Upper Jurassic (Tithonian)–Lower Cretaceous (Barremian):* France, Germany, United Kingdom, Italy, Spain, Switzerland, Algeria.——FIG. 59,*1a–d.* *G. trochiliscoides* GRAMBAST, Barremian, Spain, topotype; *a,* lateral view; *b,* basal view; *c,* apical view, ×35 (L. GRAMBAST, 1966a, fig. 1–3); *d,* longitudinal section, ×45 (GRAMBAST, 1966b, pl. III,*6*).——FIG. 59,*1e. G. rectispirale* FEIST, Tithonian, United Kingdom; holotype, lateral view, MPK 8919, ×45 (Feist, Lake, & Wood, 1995, pl. I,*5*).——FIG. 59,*1f–g. G. protoincrassatus* MOJON, Berriasian, United Kingdom; *f,* lateral view, MPK 8921; *g,* apical view, MPK 8890, ×45 (Feist, Lake, & Wood, 1995, pl. I,*8,4*).

Perimneste HARRIS, 1939, p. 54 [**P. horrida* HARRIS, 1939, p. 54, text-fig. 8o–q, 9–13, pl. 13–15, pl. 16,*6,8,9;* OD]. Utricle consisting of 3 similar groups of branching ramuli bearing antheridia. Each right-hand side branch of ramulus bearing fork of 2 long units with antheridium in angle. Supplementary antheridia may occur at any point where 2 cells form sufficiently open angle. Utricle units not contiguous. *Lower Cretaceous (Berriasian–Barremian):* Germany, United Kingdom, Spain, Switzerland, China.——FIG. 60a–e. *P. horrida* HARRIS, Berriasian, Germany; *a,* lateral view, CF.2003, ×45 (new); *b,* specimen with outer wall dissolved by acid to show utricular ramulus, ×40;

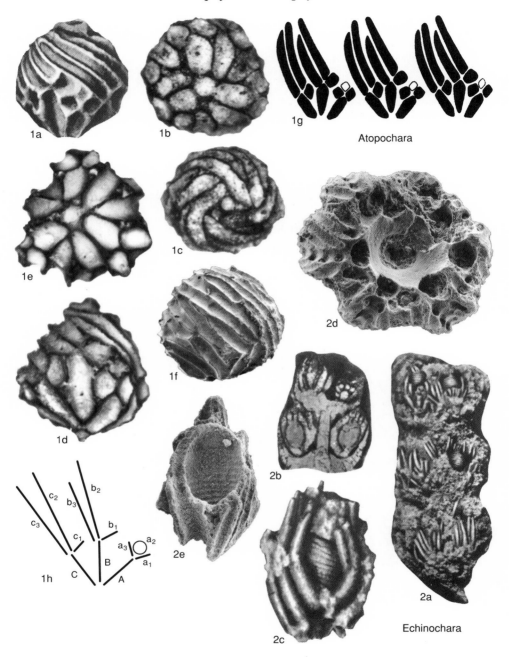

1a

1b

1g

Atopochara

1c

1e

2d

1f

1d

2b

2e

2a

1h   c₂   b₂   b₃   c₃   c₁   b₁   a₃   a₂   a₁   B   C   A

2c

Echinochara

F𝐈𝐆. 58. Clavatoraceae (p. 113).

c–d, analysis of cellular structure of utricle (antheridia: *white*) (Grambast, 1967, pl. I,*2;* text-fig. a,e); *e,* detail of antheridial cast, CF.2003, ×90 (new). ——F𝐈𝐆. 60*f. P. vidua* G𝐑𝐀𝐌𝐁𝐀𝐒𝐓, Barremian, Spain; transverse section of utricle, ×35 (Grambast, 1967, pl. IV,*20*).——F𝐈𝐆. 60*g. P. ancora* G𝐑𝐀𝐌𝐁𝐀𝐒𝐓, lower Barremian, Spain, holotype; lateral view, ×50 (Grambast, 1967, pl. III,*13a*).

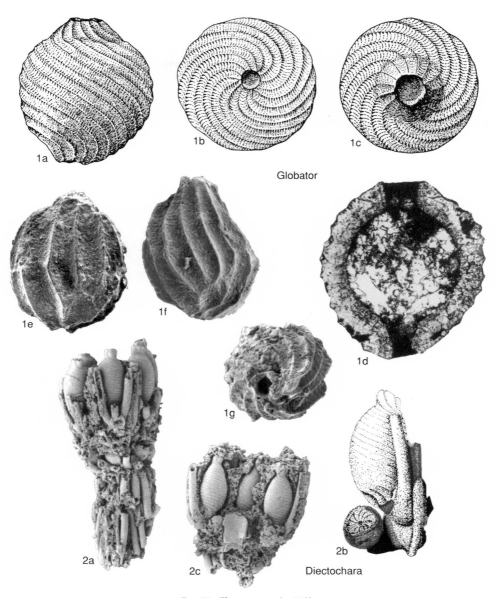

Globator

Diectochara

FIG. 59. Clavatoraceae (p. 113).

Family RASKYELLACEAE
L. Grambast & N. Grambast, 1955

[*nom. transl.* GRAMBAST, 1957, p. 357, *ex* Raskyelloideae L. GRAMBAST & N. GRAMBAST, 1955, p. 1,001] [=Raskyellae Z. WANG, 1978a, p. 67]

Gyrogonite with 5 sinistrally spiralled cells, not enclosed in utricle; spiral endings bearing 5 apical cells, joined in apex center and constituting deciduous operculum. Loss of operculum creates rose-shaped apex opening. Spirals smooth or with tubercles. *Upper Cretaceous–Neogene (lower Miocene).*

MÄDLER (in MÄDLER & STAESCHE, 1979) and Z. WANG (1978b) compared the 5-celled operculum of the Raskyellaceae with nodules present at apical ends of spirals in some genera, such as *Nitellopsis* and

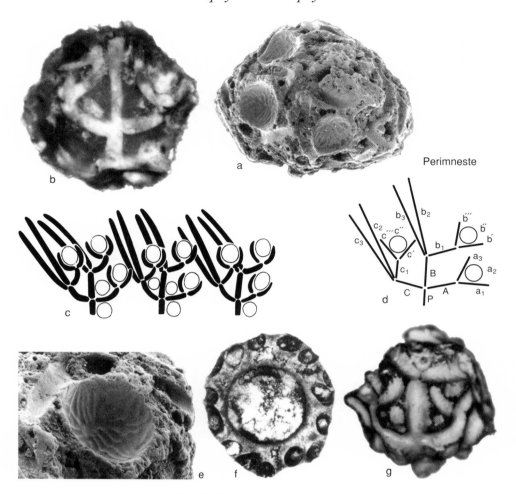

FIG. 60. Clavatoraceae (p. 113–114).

Gyrogona, in the family Characeae; however, actual apical nodules have never been reported in the Raskyellaceae. The opercular units are separated from the spirals by true walls, as visible on the inside of the apex of a gyrogonite of *Raskyella*. The 5 apical cells are separated from the spirals and from one another by undulating walls similar to those separating the spirals.

Raskyella L. GRAMBAST & N. GRAMBAST, 1954, p. 669 [*R. peckii* L. GRAMBAST & N. GRAMBAST, 1954, p. 670, fig. 1; OD]. Gyrogonites with opercular apical cells in most instances superficial and alternating with spirals in position. General shape spheroidal to prolate, with apex truncated and base rounded or tapered. Spirals smooth or with nodules. Internal cellular folds present. Basal plate not well calcified and not visible from exterior. Size medium to large. *Paleogene (Eocene):* France, Hungary, Spain, Algeria, China.——FIG. 61*a–d.* *R. peckii* L. & N. GRAMBAST, France, topotypes; *a,* apical view with opercular cells, C.33-18; *b,* lateral view, C. 33-19; *c,* base, C.33-20, ×35 (new); *d,* apical view without opercular cells, ×40 (GRAMBAST, 1957, pl. V,*9*).——FIG. 61*e–g. R. vadaszi* (RASKY) GRAMBAST, France; *e,* ×40, lateral view (Grambast, 1957, pl. V,*3*); *f,* exterior apical view, ×90; *g,* interior apical view showing folded sutures between apical and spiral cells, ×110 (Anadón & Feist, 1981, pl. 2,*1–2*).

FIG. 61. Raskyellaceae (p. 116).

Rantzieniella GRAMBAST, 1962b, p. 72 [**R. nitida* GRAMBAST, 1962b, p. 74, fig. 3a–c; OD]. Gyrogonites with superficial or slightly inserted opercular apical cells positioned in alignment with spiral ends. General shape perprolate, with apex and base truncated. Spirals smooth. Internal cellular folds present. Basal plate weakly calcified, wider than high, and not visible from exterior. Size medium to large. [Differs from *Raskyella* chiefly in cylindrical shape of gyrogonite and position of opercular units.] *Neogene (lower Miocene):* France, Switzerland, China.——FIG. 62,*2a–d. *R. nitida* GRAMBAST, France; *a,* holotype, lateral view, C.536-1; *b,* apical view, C.536-8; *c,* basal view, C.536-9, ×50 (new); *d,* internal view of gyrogonite showing folded sutures between spiral cells, ×250 (Feist-Castel, 1973, pl. 15,5).

Saportanella GRAMBAST, 1962b, p. 72 [**S. maslovi* GRAMBAST, 1962b, p. 72, fig. 2a–f; OD]. Gyrogonites with superficial or slightly inserted opercular apical cells positioned in alignment with spiral ends. General shape prolate-spheroidal to prolate, with apex truncated and base truncated or tapered. Spirals smooth. Internal cellular folds absent. Basal plate generally thick, higher than wide, visible from the exterior. Size small to large. *Upper Cretaceous:* France, Spain, Peru, Mongolia.——FIG. 62,*1a–f. *S. maslovi* GRAMBAST, France, topotypes; *a,* lateral view, C.450-49; *b,* apical view, C.450-450; *c,* base, C.450-51, ×35; *d,* basal plate, C.754-1, ×155 (new); *e,* longitudinal section, ×50; *f,* longitudinal section of basal part, with basal plate in situ and lamellar structure of calcified wall, ×90 (Grambast, 1971, pl. XIII,*2,10*).

1d

1f

1e

1b

1a

Saportanella

1c

2a

2b

2d

2c

Rantzieniella

Fig. 62. Raskyellaceae (p. 117).

Family CHARACEAE Agardh, 1824

[Characeae AGARDH, 1824, p. XXVII]

Gyrogonite with 5 sinistrally spiralled cells, not enclosed in utricle; spiral cells joined at apex along a broken line. Pore of dehiscence wide, in form of a cog wheel. Spiral cells smooth or variously ornamented. *Upper Triassic–Holocene.*

Range

The *Aclistochara* species reported by LIU and CHEN (1992) from the Upper Triassic of Western China are the oldest known Characeae. Previously, all the Triassic species placed in the Characeae had been attributed to the family Porocharaceae (GRAMBAST, 1963; SAIDAKOVSKY, 1971).

The Characeae were rare until the Late Cretaceous, the time of their first great diversification. After the end of the Cretaceous extinctions, a new stage of diversification occurred in the Paleocene, and their development continued through the Tertiary. From the late Miocene onward the Characeae is the only remaining family; this includes 7 extant genera represented by 77 species (WOOD & IMAHORI, 1965 in 1964–1965).

Classification

The Characeae presently include 43 genera, more than all the other charophyte families. All the extant genera have been recorded as fossils with certainty. Even the noncalcified *Nitella* seems to have been in existence since the Jurassic, as suggested by the characters of the oospore membrane of *N. sahnii* HORN AF RANTZIEN, 1957. The Characeae are divided into two subfamilies, Charoideae and Nitelloideae, sometimes considered at the family or tribe level. This subdivision, first established in living species, is based on characters that are not always preserved in the fossils. The uncalcified coronula cells, whose number is invariably 10 in the Nitelloideae and 5 in the

Charoideae, have been recorded only by casts in early Tertiary species of *Microchara* and *Peckichara*. The vegetative parts, which also characterize well the two subdivisions in the living forms, are not of great utility since fossil gyrogonites are rarely connected to the fragments of thallus that are found with them in the sediments. The basal plate, corresponding to the calcified sister cells of the oosphere (GRAMBAST, 1956a), is the only relatively significant character that is represented in extant as well as frequently in fossil members; in the Nitelloideae, the basal plate is multipartite in both *Nitella* and *Tolypella* (section *Tolypella*) but simple in *Sphaerochara* (synonym of *Tolypella* section *Rothia* in the classification of extant forms). The inclusion of *Sphaerochara* in the Nitelloideae is based on morphological characters of the subfamily and on molecular data that place the two *Tolypella* sections in the same clade (MCCOURT, KAROL, & others, 1996). In the Charoideae, the basal plate is simple, but it is multipartite in *Aclistochara* and related genus *Songliaochara* (LU & LUO, 1990). The inclusion of both genera in the Charoideae is based on the apical structure and postulated relationships of *Aclistochara* with *Lamprothamnium* (SOULIÉ-MÄRSCHE, 1989; FEIST & GRAMBAST-FESSARD, 1991). That the two types of basal plates are represented in both subfamilies suggests that Charoideae and Nitelloideae are less distinct than suggested by the morphological cladistic analysis that was based mainly on the basal plate morphology (MARTÍN-CLOSAS & SCHUDACK, 1991). The attribution to one of these subfamilies is possible only in two instances: when fossil species may be attributed with certainty to an extant genus and when the fossils have significant characters of a particular subfamily. Such are the corticated fragments of thallus-bearing oogonia of the Oligocene *Gyrogona,* allowing their inclusion among the Charoideae. Similarly, the uncalcified, uncorticated, and bifurcated

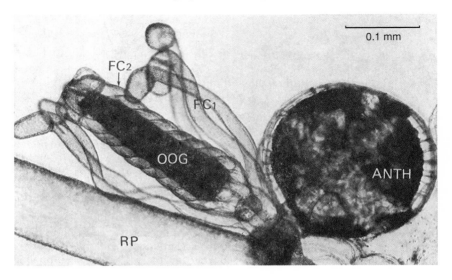

Fig. 63. Modifications of oogonial bud of *Chara vulgaris* L. after isolation of young plagiotropic branchlet, setting up two successive stages of spiral cells of oogonium; *ANTH,* antheridia; *FC,* spiral cells of oogonium; *FC1, FC2,* spiral cells belonging to successive whorls; *OOG,* oogonium; *RP,* plagiotropic branchlet (Ducreux, 1975, pl. VIII,3).

branchlets of the Devonian *Palaeonitella* (Kidston & Lang, 1921; Kelman & others, 2004[1]) suggest affinities with the Nitelloideae. Among the fossil Characeae, all species with a simple basal plate (except *Sphaerochara*) are assigned to the Charoideae; those with a multipartite basal plate are included in the Nitelloideae (except *Aclistochara*). The Characeae do not have utricles, but under experimental conditions involving extant species they produce supernumerary vegetative whorls that evoke this organ (Fig. 63; see also discussion on p. 23 herein).

With three extant genera, the Nitelloideae represent a small, well-characterized group. On the other hand, the Charoideae contain 40 genera, 4 of which are still living, and they have a great diversity.

Subfamily CHAROIDEAE Braun, 1897

[*nom. correct.* Feist & Grambast-Fessard, herein, *pro* subfamily Chareae Braun in Migula, 1897, p. 94]

Gyrogonite of Characeae with undivided basal plate, except *Aclistochara*. In extant species, 5 large noncalcified coronula cells in 1 tier; thallus corticated or not corticated. *Upper Triassic–Holocene.*

The subdivision of the Charoideae into 3 morphological types (Feist & Grambast-Fessard, 1982), adopted herein, is based mainly on the detailed structure of the apex of the gyrogonites. It is worth noting that specimens may contain characters dissimilar to the generic criteria, due to variable degrees of calcification in the gyrogonites. At the present time, the groupings listed below (Table 8), although useful in practice for identifying the genera, do not seem to be based on phylogenetic relationships.

Chara Linnaeus, 1753, p. 1,156; *emend.,* Agardh, 1824, p. 27; *emend.,* A. Braun, 1849, p. 292 [**C. tomentosa;* OD; see also Horn af Rantzien & Olsen, 1949, p. 99] [=*Chara* Vaillant, 1719, *partim* (type, *Chara vulgaris foetida,* OD); *Chara* Linnaeus, 1753, p. 1,156, obj. (includes the family Characeae); *Characias* Rafinesque, 1815, p. 209, *nom. nud., non* Gray, 1821, p. 259 (type, *C. purpurea,* OD); *Characella* Gaillon, 1833, p. 33 (type, *C. vulgaris,* OD); *Charopsis* Kützing, 1843, p. 319 (type, *Chara braunii* Gmelin, 1826, p. 646, OD); *Characeites* Tuzson, 1913, p. 209 (type, *C. verrucosa* Tuzson, 1913, p. 210, OD); *Protochara* Womersley & Ophel, 1947, p. 311 (type, *P. australis,* OD); *Grambastichara* Horn af Rantzien,

[1]Kelman, Ruth, Monique Feist, Nigel H. Trewin, & Hagen Hass. 2004. Charophyte algae from the Rhynie Chert. Transactions of the Royal Society of Edinburgh (series IV) 4:445–455.

TABLE 8. Apical features in the genera of the Characeae (new).

Types of apex	Lamprothamnoid	Psilocharoid	Nitellopsidoid
apex outline	prominent in center	flat or convex	convex, rounded
periapical depression	well marked	absent, except in Lychnothamnus and Pseudoharrisichara	generally present
periapical narrowing	absent	absent	generally present
apical nodules	absent	absent or weak	present
genera	Aclistochara, Grovesichara, Hetaochara, Lamprothamnium, Mongolichara, Nemegtichara, Pseudolatochara, Stylochara, Wangichara	Amblyochara, Chara Collichara, Dughiella Harrisichara, Henanochara, Hornichara, Linyiechara, Lychnothamnus, Maedleriella, Mesochara, Microchara, Multispirochara, Nothochara, Peckisphaera, Pseudoharrisichara, Psilochara, Rhabdochara, Saidakovskyella, Shandongochara, Strobilochara	Bysmochara, Gyrogona, Neochara, Nitellopsis, Nodosochara, Peckichara, Platychara, Songliaochara, Stephanochara, Zhejiangella

1959b, p. 68 (type, *Chara tornata* REID & GROVES, 1921, p. 187, pl. V,*1–3*, OD); *Charites* HORN AF RANTZIEN, 1959b, p. 57 (type, *Chara molassica* STRAUB, 1952, p. 466, pl. A,*1–3*, OD); *Amphorochara* KRASSAVINA, 1978, p. 227 (type, *A. grambasti* KRASSAVINA, 1978, p. 227, pl. 1, OD); *Granulachara* LU & LUO, 1990, p. 142 (type, *Kosmogyra ovalis* MÄDLER, 1955, p. 302, pl. 26,*28–30,* OD)]. Apex psilocharoid, convex, with cellular apical ends enlarged, generally shaped into a cap without apical nodules; in ornamented species (occurring as fossils) apical tubercles present, similar to those of lateral parts of gyrogonite. General shape of gyrogonite ellipsoid to cylindroid, sometimes very elongated. Basal plate pyramidal, its thickness being more than half of width. Size small to medium. [A great number of species were designated formerly under the name *Chara* without any real taxonomic significance, meaning roughly Characeae or charophytes. VAILLANT (1719) published the name *Chara* and gave a type and an illustration, but the genus was officially and validly published by LINNAEUS in 1753.] *Upper Cretaceous–Holocene:* worldwide.——FIG. 64,*1a–d*. **C. tomentosa* L., Holocene, Sweden; *a,* lateral view; *b,* apical view; *c,* basal view, ×44; *d,* basal plate, ×350 (Soulié-Märsche, 1989, pl. XXI,*2,4,5,* pl. XV,*1*).——FIG. 64,*1e. C. notata* GRAMBAST & PAUL, lower Miocene, France; lateral view, ×80 (Feist & Ringeade, 1977, pl. XII,*7*).——FIG. 64,*1f. C. antennata* GRAMBAST, upper Eocene, United Kingdom; lateral view, ×80 (Feist-Castel, 1977a, pl. 22,*1*).——FIG. 64,*1g. C. microcera* GRAMBAST & PAUL, upper Oligocene, France; longitudinal section, basal plate upside down, ×70 (Castel, 1967, pl. XXI,*13*).

Aclistochara PECK, 1937, p. 86; *emend.,* PECK, 1957, p. 24 [**A. bransoni* PECK, 1937, p. 87, pl. 14,*8–11;* OD] [=*Obtusochara* MÄDLER, 1952, p. 36, *partim* (type, *O. prima* MÄDLER, 1952, p. 36, pl. B,*53–55*); *Jurella* KYANSEP-ROMASCHKINA, 1974, p. 28 (type, *J. abshirica* KYANSEP-ROMASCHKINA, 1974, p. 28, pl. 2,*2,6,* OD); *Caucasuella* KYANSEP-ROMASCHKINA, 1980, p. 81 (type, *C. gulistanica* KYANSEP-ROMASCHKINA, 1980, p. 82, pl. I,*4–7,* pl. II,*1–3,* OD); *Xinjiangichara* LU & LUO, 1990, p. 80 (type, *X. wuqiaensis* LU & LUO, 1990, p. 81, pl. 10,*10–16,* OD)]. Apex lamprothamnoid with deep periapical furrow. Diameter of apical zone varying from 100 to 160 μm. Spirals turn onto truncate apex to form its outer rim, then bend down into central depression, finally turning sharply into center of summit depression and expanding to fill space; horizontal part of apex thin and transparent to swollen and bulbous. Abrupt downward turning and thinning producing circular furrow around expanded ends of spirals (PECK, 1957). General shape of gyrogonite ovoid to ellipsoid, with truncate apex. Spirals smooth, concave to gently convex. Basal plate generally not described; in some species, basal plate multipartite (LU & LUO, 1990). [*Aclistochara* resembles Porocharaceae and Raskyellaceae in some respects, the periapical zone with a small diameter and being located within a depression; *Aclistochara* has an apical opening closed by the calcified tips of the spiral cells, which differs from the Porocharaceae (where this zone is open) and from the Raskyellaceae (where it is closed by an operculum composed of five supplementary cells). Because of similarities in periapical morphology some *Aclistochara* were referred to Raskyellaceae (*Jurella*

1d   Chara   1a   1b   1g   1e   1f   1c   2a   2c   2d   2b   Amblyochara   3a   3d   3c   Aclistochara   3b

FIG. 64. Characeae (p. 120–123).

and *Caucasuella* KYANSEP-ROMASCHKINA; KYANSEP-ROMASCHKINA, 1974); or, on the contrary, some Porocharaceae were ascribed to the genus *Aclistochara* (BHATIA & MANNIKERI, 1977). SCHUDACK (1990) put *Obtusochara* into synonymy with *Aclistochara;* however, several species are referable to different genera (*Lamprothamnium, Mesochara, Mongolichara*), and thus they have not been considered here for the range of *Aclistochara.*] *Upper Triassic–Upper Cretaceous:* USA, Armenia, Germany, United Kingdom, China, Kazakhstan, Mongolia, Tanzania.——FIG. 64,*3a–d.* **A. bransoni* PECK, Middle Jurassic, USA, topotypes; *a,* lateral view, C.1212-1; *b,* lateral view, C.1221-1; *c,* basal view, C.1221-2, ×72; *d,* apical view, detail, C.1222-1, ×130 (new).

Amblyochara GRAMBAST, 1962b, p. 79 [**A. begudiana* GRAMBAST, 1962b, p. 79, fig. 4; OD]. Apex psilocharoid, with spirals retaining their width but tending to flatten as they turn onto summit. General shape subovoid with apical part gently rounded or slightly projecting; base tapered, basal pore at end of funnel-shaped depression; basal plate parallelepidal shaped, being generally less high than one-quarter of width. Size medium to large. [Genus differs from *Rhabdochara,* which has a more flattened apex and a conical and hollow basal plate, and from *Lychnothamnus,* whose gyrogonites present a periapical groove and a thicker basal plate.] *Cretaceous–Neogene (Pliocene):* Europe, USA, South America (widespread), South Korea, Mongolia, China.——FIG. 64,*2a–c.* **A. begudiana* GRAMBAST, Upper Cretaceous, France, topotypes; *a,* lateral view, C.450-46; *b,* apical view, C.450-47; *c,* basal view, C.450-48, ×40 (new).——FIG. 64,*2d.* *A. rolli* (KOCH & BLISSENBACH) GRAMBAST, Upper Cretaceous, Chile; lateral view, C.1223-1, ×40 (new).

Bysmochara GRAMBAST & GUTIÉRREZ, 1977, p. 10 [**B. conquensis* GRAMBAST & GUTIÉRREZ, 1977, p. 11, pl. II,*10–14,* pl. III,*1–4,* pl. XIV,*4;* OD]. Apex nitellopsidoid; at periphery of apex, spiral cells becoming markedly thinner and narrower, producing distinct furrow that surrounds prominent rosette made of swollen endings. General shape ovoid or ellipsoid; spirals smooth. Basal plate as thick as wide, lower face visible from exterior. Size medium to large. [Genus differs from *Nitellopsis* in having a thicker basal plate and no basal funnel.] *Upper Cretaceous:* Spain.——FIG. 65,*3a–e.* **B. conquensis* GRAMBAST & GUTIÉRREZ; *a,* lateral view, holotype; *b,* apical view; *c,* basal view, ×30; *d,* basal plate, lateral view; *e,* basal plate, basal view, ×170 (Grambast & Gutiérrez, 1977, pl. II,*11,* pl. III,*2,4,* pl. II,*13,14*).

Coenoclavator Z. WANG & LU, 1982, p. 99 [**C. hubeiensis* WANG & LU, 1982, p. 99, pl. IV,*13–15;* OD]. Rejected genus. [Gyrogonites found in the Eocene, covered with calcified incrustation and bearing thallus fragments at their base, were designated under this name and attributed to the Clavatoraceae. The structureless covering and the absence of an apical pore (Z. WANG & LU, 1982, pl. 4,*13*) do not correspond to a true utricle and are

referable to the Characeae (FEIST & COLOMBO, 1983). In the earlier classifications, taxa with similar structures were regarded as *Lagynophora.*]

Collichara S. WANG & ZHANG in S. WANG & others, 1982, p. 49 [**C. taizhouensis* S. WANG & ZHANG in S. WANG & others, 1982, p. 49, pl. 26,*9–15;* OD; lectotype, NIGP PB5827, S. WANG & ZHANG in S. WANG & others, 1982, pl. 26,*1a–c,* designated FEIST & GRAMBAST-FESSARD herein]. Apex psilocharoid; apical endings slightly thickened, without appreciable peripheral thinning and narrowing. Gyrogonite spheroidal to subprolate, with short, broad apical neck; number of convolutions high (more than 10); spirals smooth, concave to flat. Base rounded or slightly pointed. Basal plate conical, thickness being about half width. Size small to medium. *Upper Cretaceous–Paleogene (Paleocene):* Asia, China.——FIG. 65,*2a–c.* **C. taizhouensis* S. WANG & ZHANG, Upper Cretaceous, China, lectotype; *a,* lateral view; *b,* apical view; *c,* basal view, ×40 (new, courtesy of Z. Wang).

Dughiella FEIST-CASTEL, 1975, p. 89 [**D. bacillaris* FEIST-CASTEL, 1975, p. 90, text-fig. 1–3; pl. I,*1–9;* OD]. Apex psilocharoid; spirals barely thinner as they pass onto summit then slightly thickened at center. Gyrogonite spheroidal; spirals smooth or in some species bearing well-calcified rods even in apical part. Basal plate prismatic, visible from exterior, thickness being more than half width. Size medium to large. [Genus differs from *Gyrogona* in lack of apical modification and having the basal plate visible from the exterior.] *Upper Cretaceous–Paleogene (Paleocene):* Belgium, France, Spain, Morocco, ?India.——FIG. 65,*1a–f.* **D. bacillaris* FEIST-CASTEL, Paleocene; *a–b,* holotype, paratype, lateral views, France, ×30; *c,* longitudinal section, France, ×45; *d–e,* apical, basal view, France, ×30 (Feist-Castel, 1975, fig. 1–3, pl. I, *5, 8*); *f,* apical view, Belgium, ×30 (Grambast-Fessard, 1980, pl. I,*4*).——FIG. 65,*1g–i. D. obtusa* GRAMBAST & GUTIÉRREZ, Upper Cretaceous, Spain; *g,* holotype, lateral view; *h,* apical view, *i,* basal view, ×40 (Grambast & Gutiérrez, 1977, pl. XI,*9,12,14*).

Grovesichara HORN AF RANTZIEN, 1959b, p. 123 [**Chara distorta* REID & GROVES, 1921, p. 186, pl. V,*6;* OD]. Apex lamprothamnoid; spirals become thinner as they pass onto summit, then thicken again, ascending to center of apex. General shape irregular, oblate-spheroidal to subprolate; apex rounded, strongly prominent. Base rounded, in some species tapering. Basal plate strongly calcified, thickness being more than half of width; lower face of plate visible from exterior. Size medium to large. [Genus differs from *Gyrogona* in having less marked periapical modification as well as having the basal plate visible from the exterior and general shape more elongated.] *Upper Cretaceous–Neogene (Miocene):* Austria, France, United Kingdom, Spain, China, Mongolia.——FIG. 66,*1a–c.* **G. distorta* (REID & GROVES) HORN AF RANTZIEN, upper Eocene, United Kingdom; *a,* lateral view (Feist-Castel, 1977a, pl. 21,*7*); *b,* apical view, CF.1579-3; *c,* basal view, CF.1579-2, ×30 (new).

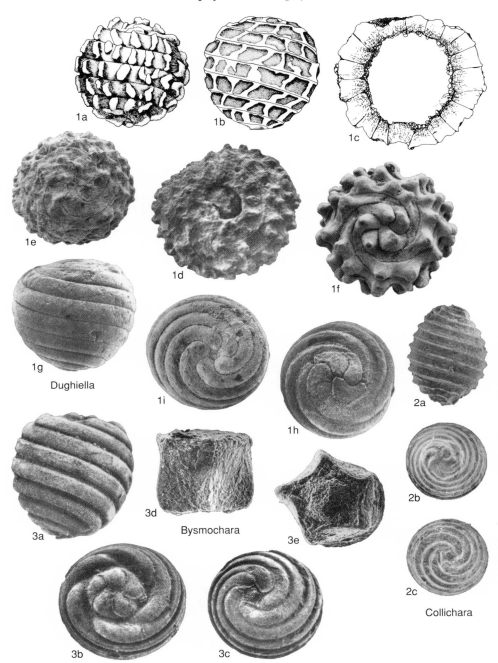

FIG. 65. Characeae (p. 123).

Gyrogona LAMARCK, 1822, p. 613 (LAMARCK, 1804, p. 355, *nom. nud.*); *emend.*, GRAMBAST, 1956b, p. 280 [*Gyrogonites medicaginula* LAMARCK, 1822, p. 614; OD; =*Gyrogonites medicaginula* LAMARCK, 1804, p. 356, *nom. nud.*] [=*Gyrogonites* LAMARCK, 1822, p. 613, obj. (LAMARCK, 1804, p. 355, *nom. nud.*), *non* PIA, 1927; *Brachychara* L. & N. GRAMBAST, 1954, p. 666 (type, *Gyrogonites medicaginula* LAMARCK, 1804, p. 356); *Brevichara* HORN AF RANTZIEN, 1956a, p. 245 (type, *B. hordlensis,* OD, *nom. null.; =Chara wrightii* REID & GROVES, 1921, p. 183, pl. IV,*1, non Chara wrightii* SALTER in FORBES, 1856, p. 160)]. Apex nitellopsidoid. Deep periapical furrow without notable narrowing of spirals, surrounding prominent rosette of well-marked nodules. Gyrogonite oblate to oblate-spheroidal; spirals smooth or variously ornamented. Base rounded; in some species, basal pore surrounded by widened funnel. Basal plate very thick, higher than wide, not visible from exterior. Size large. [Among the species reported by Z. WANG (1978a) from China, some, such as the Cretaceous *G. hubeiensis,* are more likely to be referable to *Platychara.*] *Paleogene (lower Eocene)–Neogene (upper Miocene):* Belgium, France, Germany, United Kingdom, Spain, China, India, ?USA; China (Xinxiang), *upper Miocene* (LU & LUO, 1990).——FIG. 66,*2a–c.* **G. medicaginula* LAMARCK, Stampian, France; *a,* neotype, designated herein, lateral view, C.146-1, ×25 (new); *b,* apical view, ×25 (Grambast & Grambast-Fessard, 1981, pl. IV,*12*); *c,* basal view, C.146-8, ×25 (new).—— FIG. 66,*2d–f. G. lamarcki* GRAMBAST, middle Eocene, France; *d,* basal plate, lateral view, ×100; *e,* basal plate, upper side, ×100; *f,* apical opening, ×20 (Grambast & Grambast-Fessard, 1981, pl. I,*11,10,7*).——FIG. 66,*2g. G. caelata* (REID & GROVES) GRAMBAST, middle Eocene, France; lateral view, ×30 (Grambast & Grambast-Fessard, 1981, pl. IV,*1*).——FIG. 66,*2h. G. lemani lemani* (BRONGNIART) PIA, middle Eocene, France; longitudinal section, ×40 (Grambast & Grambast-Fessard, 1981, pl. VI,*1*).

Harrisichara GRAMBAST, 1957, p. 347 [*Chara vasiformis* REID & GROVES, 1921, p. 185, pl. IV,*13;* OD]. Apex psilocharoid. Gyrogonite subovoidal, apex truncated or broadly rounded, base forming narrow, projecting cone or columnar shaped; spirals generally with tubercles or crests; ornamentation interrupted at periphery of apex. Basal plate very thin, about ten times as wide as high. Size small to large. [Occurrence of this genus in the Upper Cretaceous is questionable, as *H. cretacea* KARCZEWSKA & ZIEMBINSKA-TWORZYDLO, 1970, and *H. margaritata* Z. WANG, 1978b, do not have the basal projection characteristic of *Harrisichara.*] *?Upper Cretaceous, Paleogene (Paleocene–lower Oligocene):* Belgium, France, Germany, United Kingdom, Spain, China, India, Canada, USA, Peru.——FIG. 67,*1a.* **H. vasiformis* (REID & GROVES) GRAMBAST,

upper Eocene, United Kingdom; lateral view, ×50 (Feist-Castel, 1977a, pl. 21,*1*).——FIG. 67,*1b–f. H. tuberculata* (LYELL) GRAMBAST, lower Oligocene, United Kingdom; *b,* basal plate, ×300 (Grambast, 1957, text-fig. 2b); *c,* neotype, lateral view, spirals with nodules; *d,* lateral view, spirals with continuous crest, ×40 (Feist-Castel, 1977a, pl. 21,*5,4*); *e,* apical view, CF.1585-2; *f,* basal view, CF.1584-2, ×40 (new).

Hebeichara H. LIN, 1989, p. 76 [*H. sphaerides* H. LIN, 1989, p. 76, pl. 39,*1–7;* OD]. Incompletely known genus, referable either to *Sphaerochara* or *Tolypella,* according to the basal-plate morphology.

Henanochara ZHANG, JIANG, & MENG, in JIANG, ZHANG, & MENG, 1985, p. 164 [*H. squalida* JIANG, ZHANG & MENG, 1985, p. 164, pl. I,*7,11,12,* pl. II,*30;* OD]. Apex psilocharoid. Gyrogonite subprolate to prolate spheroidal with apex rounded or forming short neck; base rounded, truncated in center. Spirals numerous, unornamented, without modifications in apical part. Basal plug pentagonal, slightly wider than high, projecting out of basal pore. Size medium to large. [Whether this genus belongs to Characeae is questionable, and the described species might correspond to gyrogonites of Clavatoraceae without a developed utricle. *H. squalida* possesses an apical neck, a basal plate projecting out of the basal pore, and numerous convolutions of the spirals. Such features are present, for example, in *Atopochara trivolvis* gyrogonites (PECK, 1957, pl. 2,*5*).] *Lower Cretaceous:* China.——FIG. 66,*3a–c.* **H. squalida* ZHANG, JIANG, & MENG; *a,* holotype, lateral view; *b,* apical view; *c,* basal view, ×40 (Jiang, Zhang, & Meng, 1985, pl. 1,*7b,7a,7c*).——FIG. 66,*3d–e. H. nitida* ZHANG, JIANG, & MENG; *d,* lateral view; *e,* basal view, ×40 (Jiang, Zhang, & Meng, 1985, pl. 1,*9,8c*).

Hetaochara SHU & ZHANG, 1985, p. 68 [*H. cupula* SHU & ZHANG, 1985, p. 68, pl. 2,*6–10;* OD; lectotype, pl. 2,*9a–c,* designated FEIST & GRAMBAST-FESSARD herein]. Apex lamprothamnoid, with deep, periapical furrow and central part convex, not overtopping general surface. Gyrogonite stem shaped, lower part being abruptly narrowed and forming column with truncated ending. Summit truncated. Size small. Basal plate unknown. Differs from other genera by peculiar gyrogonite shape. [The validity of the genus is questionable as the atypical basal column, which comprises the entire lower half of the gyrogonite, could result from an abnormal calcification.] *Lower Cretaceous:* China.——FIG. 67,*2a–c.* **H. cupula* SHU & ZHANG, Mongolia, lectotype; *a,* lateral view; *b,* apical view; *c,* basal view, ×140 (Shu & Zhang, 1985, pl. 2,*9b,9a,9c*).

Hornichara MASLOV, 1963b, p. 444 [*H. kazakstanica* MASLOV, 1963b, p. 445, fig. 1; OD; lectotype, MASLOV, 1963b, fig. 1a–c, designated FEIST & GRAMBAST-FESSARD herein] [=*Krassavinella* FEIST in FEIST & RINGEADE, 1977, p. 346 (type, *K. blayaci*

1a

1b

1c

Grovesichara

2e

2a

2c

2b

2f

Gyrogona

2d

2g

2h

3a

Henanochara

3b

3c

3d

3e

Fig. 66. Characeae (p. 123–125).

FEIST in FEIST & RINGEADE, 1977, p. 346, pl. X,*1–5,* OD)]. Apex psilocharoid with thinning of entire apical zone. General shape ovoidal with apex prominent and base tapered with tendency to form a broad column. Spirals unornamented; basal pore in some species at end of funnel-shaped depression. Basal plate thin. Size small. [Genus differs from *Harrisichara* in having a more protruding apex and a wider basal column, from *Amblyochara* in its apical characters and smaller size, and from *Mesochara* in having a tapered base and basal plate morphology.] *Upper Cretaceous–Neogene (Pleistocene):* France, Georgia, Germany, Russia, Spain, Switzerland, China, India, Kazakhstan.——FIG. 67,*3a–c.* **H. kazakstanica* MASLOV, middle Oligocene, Kazakhstan; *a,* lectotype, lateral view; *b,* apical view; *c,* basal view, ×88 (adapted from Maslov, 1963b, fig. 1a–c).——FIG. 67,*3d–f. H. lagenalis* (STRAUB) FEIST, upper Oligocene, Switzerland; *d,* lateral view; *e,* apical view; *f,* basal view, ×80 (Feist-Castel, 1977b, pl. 1,*3,5,6*).

Kosmogyra STACHE, 1889, p. 134 [**K. superba* STACHE, 1889, p. 134, pl. IV,*2;* OD] Genus based essentially on gyrogonite ornamentation. The artificiality of this taxon has been discussed by L. GRAMBAST (1957), and it is no longer acknowledged. The original material has been lost.

Lagynophora STACHE, 1889, p. 132 [**L. liburnica* STACHE, 1889, p. 132, fig. 9, 14; OD]. Rejected genus. Gyrogonites described as bottle shaped and enclosed by vegetative parts. [Such enclosed gyrogonites belong in fact to the Characeae (BIGNOT & GRAMBAST, 1969) and may represent several genera: *Microchara* (CASTEL, 1969), *Peckichara* (RIVELINE & PERREAU, 1979), or *Harrisichara* (GRAMBAST-FESSARD, 1980). Because the type material is lost, *Lagynophora* cannot be assigned to one or another of these genera, so this taxon cannot be maintained.]

Lamprothamnium GROVES, 1916, p. 336 [*Chara papulosa WALLROTH, 1833, p. 107; OD] [=*Lamprothamnus* BRAUN in BRAUN & NORDSTEDT, 1882, p. 100 (type, *L. alopecuroides* BRAUN in BRAUN & NORDSTEDT, 1882, p. 100, fig. 185–188, OD), *non* HIERN in OLIVER, 1877, p. 130; *Yahuchara* TANG & DI, 1991, p. 98 (type, *Y. subcylindrica* TANG & DI, 1991, p. 98, pl. 1,*1–8,* OD)]. Apex lamprothamnoid, with deep periapical furrow. Diameter of apical zone varying from 160 to 280 μm. Spirals thin or absent at apical center. When preserved, apical parts of spirals concave, turning up sharply into apex center. General shape subprolate to perprolate, with apex truncated and base slightly narrowed. Spirals unornamented and with Y-calcification (see p. 10 herein). Basal plate variable in thickness. Size small to medium. [Genus differs from *Aclistochara* in having the diameter of the apical zone notably wider and an undivided basal plate, and from *Chara* in having a strongly depressed periapical zone. *Upper Cretaceous–Holocene:* worldwide.——FIG. 68,*1a–f.* **L. papulosum* (WALLROTH) GROVES, Holocene, France;

a, longitudinal section, ×50; *b,* lateral view, CF.2952-1, ×66 (new); *c,* apical view, ×150 (Feist & Grambast-Fessard, 1991, fig. 5b); *d,* basal view, CF.2952-2, ×66 (new); *e,* basal plate, lateral view, ×220 (Soulié-Märsche, 1989, pl. XXXII,*10*); *f,* detail of wall of spiral cells, CF.2952-2, ×260 (new).——FIG. 68,*1g–i. L. priscum* CASTEL & GRAMBAST, lower Eocene, France; *g,* lateral view, holotype; *h,* apical view, ×60 (Castel & Grambast, 1969, pl. XXXII,*4a,4c*); *i,* detail of the wall of spiral cells, ×300 (Feist & Grambast-Fessard, 1984, fig. 2G).

Linyiechara XINLUN in WANG Shui & others, 1978, p. 23 [**L. clara* XINLUN in WANG Shui & others, 1978, p. 24, pl. 4,*2–6;* OD; lectotype, NIGP 390037, pl. 4,*4a–c,* designated FEIST & GRAMBAST-FESSARD herein] [=*Guangraochara* YANG, 1987, p. 159 (type, *G. distincta* YANG, 1987, p. 159, pl. 1,*1–7,* OD)]. Apex psilocharoid. Spirals narrowing at periphery of apex, then widening again toward center without thickening. General shape subprolate, with apex rounded and base truncated. Spirals smooth or with irregular nodules. Basal plate slightly wider than thick, visible from exterior. Size medium. *Paleogene (Oligocene):* China.——FIG. 67,*4a–d.* **L. clara* XINLUN; *a,* longitudinal section, ×68; *b–d,* lectotype, lateral, apical, basal views, ×34 (Wang Shui & others, 1978, pl. 4,*6a,4b,4a,4c*).

Lychnothamnus (RUPRECHT, 1845) VON LEONHARDI, 1863, p. 57; *emend.,* A. BRAUN in BRAUN & NORDSTEDT, 1882, p. 100 [*Chara barbata MEYEN, 1827, p. 75; OD] [=*Lychnothamnites* MASLOV, 1966, p. 77 (type, *L. narynensis* MASLOV, 1966, p. 78, pl. IX,*9–11,* OD)]. Apex psilocharoid with periapical furrow. Apical ends of spirals concave, in some instances with poorly developed nodules. General shape subprolate to prolate with apex rounded and its central part slightly prominent; base rounded. Basal plate conical, its thickness being about half of width. Size medium to large. [Reminiscent of the genus *Stephanochara.*] *Paleogene (upper Eocene)–Holocene:* Europe, Mali, China, India, Australia.——FIG. 69,*3a–e.* **L. barbatus* (MEYEN) VON LEONHARDI, Holocene, Germany; *a,* lateral view, ×50; *b,* apical view, ×47; *c,* basal view, ×47; *d,* basal plate, lower side, ×250 (Soulié-Märsche, 1989, pl. XXXV, *2,5,8,10*); *e,* detail of the oospore membrane, CF.2953-5, ×580 (new).—— FIG. 69,*3f–g. L. longus* CHOI, upper Eocene, Spain; *f,* holotype, lateral view; *g,* paratype, apical view, CF.VF/8-6, ×60 (new).

Maedleriella GRAMBAST, 1957, p. 349 [*Chara monolifera PECK & REKER, 1947, p. 4, fig. 12–18; OD]. Apex psilocharoid, without distinct differentiation. General shape oblate to oblate-spheroidal; apex and base rounded or truncated; spirals with tubercles or crests, continuing up to apex with small break in periapical zone. Basal plate prismatic, height and width approximately equal, visible from exterior. Size small to medium. *Upper Cretaceous–Paleogene (upper Eocene):* USA, Peru, France, Germany, Spain, China, Mongolia, Algeria.——FIG.

1b

Harrisichara

1a

1d

1c

1e

1f

2a

2b

Hetaochara

2c

3b

3a

3d

3e

Hornichara

3c

4b

4a

4c

4d

Linyiechara

3f

FIG. 67. Characeae (p. 125–127).

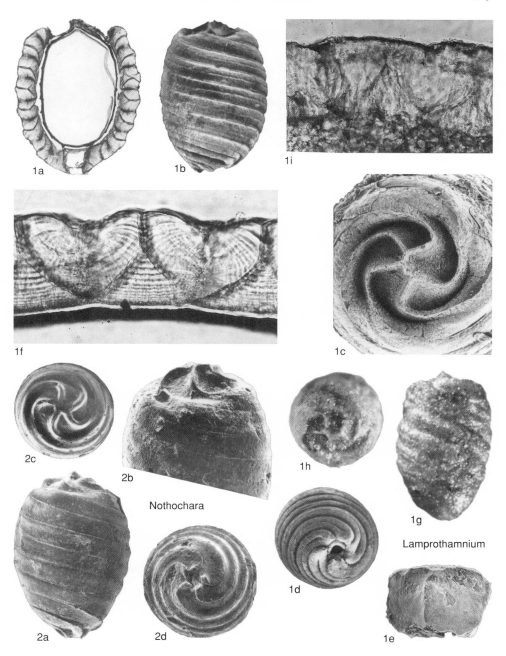

1a

1b

1i

1f

1c

2c

2b

Nothochara

1h

1g

Lamprothamnium

2a

2d

1d

1e

FIG. 68. Characeae (p. 127–136).

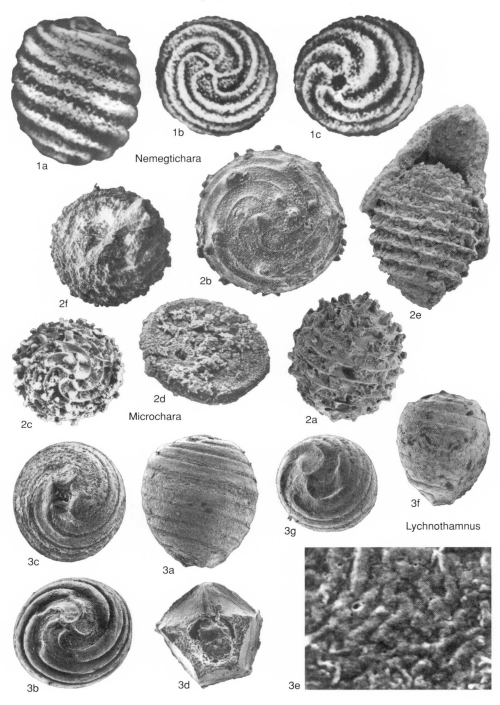

1a   1b   1c

Nemegtichara

2f   2b   2e

2c   2d   2a   3f

Microchara

3c   3a   3g   Lychnothamnus

3b   3d   3e

<small>Fig. 69. Characeae (p. 127–134).</small>

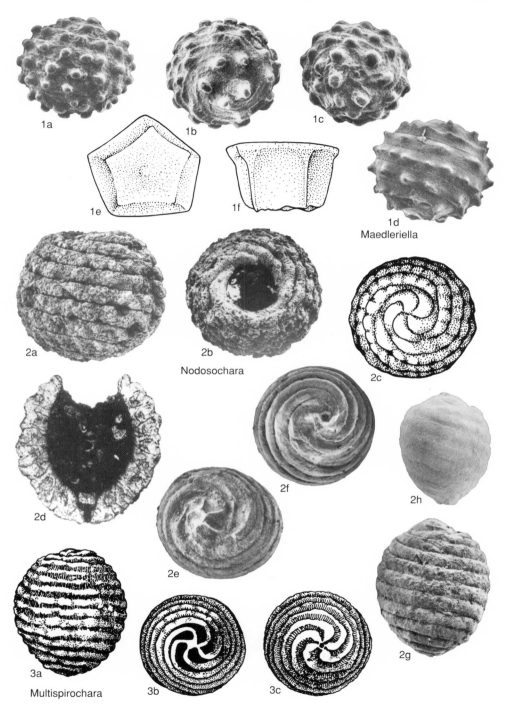

1a 1b 1c
1e 1f
1d
Maedleriella

2a 2b
Nodosochara
2c

2d 2f 2h

2e 2g

3a
Multispirochara 3b 3c

FIG. 70. Characeae (p. 127–136).

70,*1a–c.* **M. monolifera* (PECK & REKER) GRAMBAST, Paleocene or lower Eocene, Peru, topotypes; *a,* lateral view, C.1224-1; *b,* apical view, C.1224-2; *c,* basal view, C.1224-3, ×60 (new).——FIG. 70,*1d. M. cristellata* GRAMBAST, Paleocene–lower Eocene, France; lateral view, C.1108-6, ×60 (new).——FIG. 70,*1e–f. M. mangenoti* GRAMBAST; *e,* basal plate, lower side; *f,* basal plate, lateral view, ×300 (Grambast, 1957, fig. 3a–b).

Mesochara GRAMBAST, 1962b, p. 78 [**Praechara symmetrica* PECK, 1957, p. 39, pl. 7,*13–16;* OD] [=*Piriformachara* LIU & WU, 1985, p. 147 (type, *P. gumudiensis* LIU & WU, 1985, p. 148, pl. 3,*5–6,* OD)]. Apex psilocharoid, with apical spiral endings not enlarged or only slightly enlarged. General shape subprolate, with apex rounded or pointed and base thinner. Gyrogonites unornamented. Basal plate unknown. Size small to medium. [Differs from *Amblyochara* mainly in size and from *Chara* by absence of enlargement (or having only minor enlargement) of the apical spiral endings and having fewer convolutions. *Piriformachara* differs from *Mesochara* only by its spiral convexity, a character that may depend on the degree of calcification and cannot be alone considered as a generic criterion.] *Cretaceous:* USA, Argentina, France, Moldavia, Ukraine, China, Mongolia, Tanzania.——FIG. 71,*2a–b.* **M. symmetrica* (PECK) GRAMBAST, Lower Cretaceous, USA, topotypes; *a,* lateral view, C.1225-1; *b,* apical view, C.1225-1, ×80 (new). ——FIG. 71,*2c. M. fusiformis* FEIST, Upper Cretaceous, France, holotype; lateral view, ×80 (Feist, 1981, fig. 4g).

Microchara GRAMBAST, 1959b, p. 6 [**M. hystrix* GRAMBAST, 1959b, p. 7, fig. 1; OD] [=*Gobichara* KARCZEWSKA & ZIEMBIŃSKA-TWORZYDŁO, 1972, p. 72 (type, *G. deserta* KARCZEWSKA & ZIEMBIŃSKA-TWORZYDŁO, 1972, p. 73, pl. XIV, OD)]. Apex psilocharoid, with little or no modification. General shape subprolate, with apex rounded and base narrowed; in some species base projecting. Gyrogonites often with tubercles or crests, ornamentation reaching apex center. Basal plate very thin, not visible from exterior. Size generally small, in some species small to medium. [Gyrogonites of *Microchara* with tapered bases are difficult to distinguish from small specimens of *Harrisichara*. These resemblances may indicate a phylogenetic relationship between the two genera.] *Upper Cretaceous–Paleogene (middle Eocene):* Argentina, France, Spain, China, Mongolia, India.——FIG. 69,*2a–d.* **M. hystrix* GRAMBAST, lower Eocene, France; *a,* holotype, lateral view, C.63-4, ×80; *b,* apical view, C.2-4, ×110; *c,* basal view, C.63-7, ×80; *d,* basal plate, C.63-8, ×660 (new).——FIG. 69,*2e–f. M. vestita* CASTEL, lower Eocene, France; *e,* lateral view of specimen, tunicate in upper part around site of missing coronula cells, ×124; *f,* apical view, with remains of 3 coronula cells, ×105 (Feist-Castel, 1975, pl. II,*11,10*).

Mongolichara KYANSEP-ROMASCHKINA, 1975, p. 200; *emend.,* KARCZEWSKA & KYANSEP-ROMASCHKINA, 1979, p. 423 [**Tectochara gobica* KARCZEWSKA & ZIEMBIŃSKA-TWORZYDŁO, 1970, p. 137, pl. 33,*1–2;* OD]. Apex lamprothamnoid, with spirals narrowing and thinning on apex periphery, then slightly widening and thickening somewhat in apex center, without forming distinct nodules. General shape prolate spheroidal to subprolate, with apex center forming rounded or truncated cap; base rounded, in some species base slightly tapered. Spirals occasionally with surface ornamentation, especially secondary ridges or small cellular tubercles. Basal plate variable in thickness, generally thinner than wide. Size medium. [Differs from *Peckichara* in absence of apical nodules and weaker ornamentation.] *Upper Cretaceous–Paleogene (lower Eocene):* China, Mongolia.——FIG. 71,*3a–f.* **M. gobica* (KARCZEWSKA & ZIEMBIŃSKA-TWORZYDŁO) KARCZEWSKA & KYANSEP-ROMASCHKINA, Upper Cretaceous, Mongolia; *a,* holotype, lateral view; *b,* apical view; *c,* basal view; *d,* apical view, open summit, ×80 (Karczewska & Ziembińska-Tworzydło, 1970, pl. XXXIII,*1c,1a,1b,2*); *e,* longitudinal section, ×70 (Karczewska & Ziembińska-Tworzydło, 1981, pl. 35,*6*); *f,* lateral view, ×80 (Karczewska & Kyansep-Romaschkina, 1979, pl. 3,*4*).

Multispirochara HAO in HAO & others, 1983, p. 147 [**M. subovalis* HAO & others, 1983, p. 147, pl. 32,*9–10;* M]. Apex psilocharoid, without notable modifications. General shape prolate-spheroidal with apex truncated and base rounded. Convolutions numerous (11–14), without ornamentation. Basal plate unknown. Size small. Monospecific genus. *Upper Jurassic–Lower Cretaceous:* China.—— FIG. 70,*3a–c.* **M. subovalis* HAO, Upper Jurassic or Lower Cretaceous, holotype; *a,* lateral view; *b,* apical view, *c,* basal view, ×87 (adapted from Hao & others, 1983, pl. 32,*9a–c*).

Nanglingqiuchara TANG & DI, 1991, p. 99 [**N. columelaria* TANG & DI, 1991, p. 99, pl. 1,*9–13;* OD]. Rejected genus. Genus distinction based only on apical projections, which represent abnormal calcified apical cellular ends. Might be referable to *Chara.*

Neimongolichara LU & YUAN, 1991, p. 386 [**N. bayanhotensis* LU & YUAN, 1991, p. 386, pl. I,*7–11;* OD]. Rejected genus. Corresponds to nodoso-clavatoroid utricles, as recognized from the nodular surface and from the presence of gyrogonite cells inside (Lu & Yuan, 1991, pl. I,*11*).

Nemegtichara KARCZEWSKA & ZIEMBIŃSKA-TWORZYDŁO, 1972, p. 54 [**N. prima* KARCZEWSKA & ZIEMBIŃSKA-TWORZYDŁO, 1972, p. 54, pl. 7; OD]. Apex lamprothamnoid, with shallow periapical depression; in apex center, spirals thin and turn up, forming conical protuberance. General shape variable, oblate-spheroidal to prolate, apex pointed and base rounded or truncated. Spirals generally unornamented; however, some species have thick,

FIG. 71. Characeae (p. 132–134).

intercellular, prominent ridges. Basal plate twice as wide as high, generally visible from exterior. Size small. *Upper Cretaceous, Paleogene (?Paleocene):* China, Mongolia, India.——FIG. 69,*1a–c.* **N. prima* KARCZEWSKA & ZIEMBIŃSKA-TWORZYDŁO, Paleocene, Gobi desert; *a,* holotype, lateral view; *b,* apical view; *c,* basal view, ×70 (Karczewska & Ziembińska-Tworzydło, 1972, pl. VII,*3b,3a,3c*).

Neochara Z. WANG & LIN in Z. WANG, 1978b, p. 112 [**N. huananensis* Z. WANG & LIN in Z. WANG, 1978b, p. 113, pl. V,*21–24,40–45;* OD; holotype, NIGP PB5970, fig. 43–45]. Apex nitellopsidoid, with distinct periapical thinning and variable narrowing of spirals. General shape prolate to perprolate, with apex protruded and base tapered. Spirals generally smooth; in some species, spirals with wavy or nodular crest. Basal funnel present, basal plate thicker than half width, visible from exterior. Size small to medium. [Genus differs from *Stephanochara* in its periapical narrowing of the spirals. This character, however, is not strongly expressed in some species assigned to *Neochara,* such as *N. taikengensis* Z. WANG, LU, & ZHAO, 1985.] *Upper Cretaceous–Paleogene (Eocene):* China.——FIG. 71,*1a–d.* **N. huananensis* Z. WANG & LIN, lower Eocene; *a,* lateral view; *b,* lateral view; *c,* apical view; *d,* basal view, ×60 (new, courtesy of Wang Zhen).

Nitellopsis HY, 1889, p. 398 [*Chara obtusa DESVAUX in LOISELEUR-DESLONGCHAMPS, 1810, p. 136; OD] [=*Tectochara* L. GRAMBAST & N. GRAMBAST, 1954, p. 668 (type, *Chara meriani* BRAUN *ex* UNGER, 1850, p. 34); *Qinghaichara* YANG in HAO & others, 1983, p. 156 (type, *Q. ovalis* YANG in HAO & others, 1983, p. 156, pl. 36,*1–4,* OD)]. Apex nitellopsidoid; spirals with distinct periapical narrowing and thinning, with ends thickening and expanding, forming prominent central rosette. General shape prolate-spheroidal to subprolate and subovoidal, with apex prominent and base rounded or tapered. Spirals smooth or with tubercles. Basal pore flaring, pentagonal, or star shaped. Basal plate very thin, not visible from the exterior. Size medium to large. [KRASSAVINA (1971) established the identity of the extant *Nitellopsis obtusa* and of the Quaternary *Tectochara diluviana.* GRAMBAST and SOULIÉ-MÄRSCHE (1972) detailed the past history of *Nitellopsis* and established three subgenera, *Nitellopsis, Tectochara,* and *Campaniella.* FEIST-CASTEL (1977c) added a fourth subgenus, *Microstomella.*] *Paleogene (Paleocene)–Holocene:* worldwide.

N. (Nitellopsis) (HY, 1889, p. 398) GRAMBAST & SOULIÉ-MÄRSCHE, 1972, p. 3 [*Chara obtusa DESVAUX in LOISELEUR-DESLONGCHAMPS, 1810, p. 136; OD]. General shape prolate-spheroidal to subprolate; basal region rounded, with basal funnel poorly developed or absent. *Neogene (Pliocene)–Holocene:* scattered in Europe and Asia, rare in Africa (Mali, Sudan) and South America (Argentina).——FIG. 72,*1a–c.* **N. (N.) obtusa* (DESVAUX) J. GROVES, Holocene, France; *a,* lateral view; *b,* apical view, ×47 (Feist &

Grambast-Fessard, 1991, fig. 4a, 4e); *c,* basal view, CF.2953-4, ×47 (new).

N. (Campaniella) GRAMBAST & SOULIÉ-MÄRSCHE, 1972, p. 3 [*Chara helicteres BRONGNIART, 1822, p. 63, pl. VI,*3;* OD]. General shape prolate-spheroidal; basal part with protruding funnel surrounding basal pore. *Paleogene (Paleocene–lower Eocene):* Belgium, France, Spain.——FIG. 72,*3a–c.* **N. (C.) helicteres* (BRONGNIART) GRAMBAST & SOULIÉ-MÄRSCHE, lower Eocene, France; *a,* lateral view, C.7-1; *b,* apical view, C.6-10; *c,* basal view, C.6-11, ×30 (new).

N. (Microstomella) FEIST-CASTEL, 1977c, p. 117 [**M. aptensis* FEIST-CASTEL, 1977c, p. 118, pl. I,*1–8,* text-fig. 1; OD]. General shape subprolate; base rounded without distinct funnel, basal pore very small. *Paleogene (upper Eocene):* France, Spain.——FIG. 72,*2a–c.* **N. (M.) aptensis* FEIST-CASTEL, upper Eocene, France; *a,* holotype, lateral view; *b,* apical view; *c,* basal view, ×30 (Feist-Castel, 1977c, pl. I,*1,7,4*).

N. (Tectochara) (L. & N. GRAMBAST, 1954, p. 668) GRAMBAST & SOULIÉ-MÄRSCHE, 1972, p. 3 [*Chara meriani BRAUN, unpublished ms, *ex* UNGER, 1850, p. 34; OD; =*Chara meriani* BRAUN *ex* HEER,1855, p. 24, pl. IV,*3*] [=*Tectochara (Sulcosphaera)* MASLOV, 1966, p. 62 (type, *S. nethoiensis* MASLOV, 1966, p. 62, fig. 20)]. General shape subprolate, with contracted base and basal funnel well marked but not protruding. *Paleogene (Paleocene)–Neogene (Pliocene):* Mexico, Peru, Europe (widespread), China, India, Algeria, Senegal.——FIG. 72,*4a–e.* **N. (T.) meriani* (BRAUN *ex* UNGER) GRAMBAST & SOULIÉ-MÄRSCHE, Oligocene, Belmont, Switzerland, topotypes; *a,* holoneotype, designated herein, lateral view, C.1226-1, ×30 (new); *b,* apical view, ×30; *c,* basal view, ×30; *d,* longitudinal section of basal part of gyrogonite, ×120 (Castel, 1967, pl. XIX,*3,4,14*); *e,* basal plate, ×915 (Grambast, 1956b, text-fig. 3).——FIG. 72,*4f. N. (T.) morulosa* (FEIST-CASTEL) FEIST & GRAMBAST-FESSARD, middle Eocene, France; lateral view (Feist-Castel, 1972, pl. I,*5*).

Nodosochara MÄDLER, 1955, p. 276 [**Aclistochara clivulata* PECK & REKER, 1948, p. 88, pl. 21,*1–7;* OD] [=*Turbochara* Z. WANG, 1978a, p. 78 (type, *T. specialis* Z. WANG, 1978a, p. 78, pl. VI,*1–9,* OD)]. Apex nitellopsidoid; spirals with distinct periapical narrowing and thinning, thickening and expanding at ends to form prominent central rosette. General shape prolate-spheroidal to prolate; apex rounded, prominent in center, base tapered. Spirals smooth or with tubercles. Basal plate thick, at least as thick as half of width, to thicker than wide, not visible from exterior. Size small to large. [Differs from *Tectochara* mostly in the characters of the basal part and not by the presence of an ornamentation as stated in MÄDLER diagnosis. The presence of this genus in the Neogene is questionable, the apical structure of ?*N. globosa* S. WANG, 1961, being unknown, and thus its attribution to *Nodosochara* is

1b

1c

1a

Nitellopsis
(Nitellopsis)

2a

Nitellopsis
(Microstomella)

2b

2c

3b

3c

Nitellopsis
(Campaniella)

3a

4e

Nitellopsis
(Tectochara)

4b

4f

4c

4a

4d

Fig. 72. Characeae (p. 134).

uncertain.] *Upper Cretaceous–Paleogene (upper Eocene), ?Neogene:* USA, Peru, France, Spain, China.——FIG. 70,*2a–d.* *N. clivulata* (PECK & REKER) MÄDLER, middle Eocene, USA, topotypes; *a,* lateral view, C.1227-1, ×52 (new); *b,* apical view, open summit, C.1227-2, ×42 (adapted from Peck & Reker, 1948, pl. 21,*6*); *d,* longitudinal section, ×62 (Horn af Rantzien, 1959b, pl. IX,*12*).——FIG. 70,*2e–g. N. thevallensis* (DOLLFUS) RIVELINE, upper Eocene, France, topotypes; *e,* apical view, C.49-11; *f,* basal view, C.49-12; *g,* lateral view, C.49-10, ×32 (new).—— FIG. 70,*2h. N. (Turbochara) specialis* (Z. WANG) FEIST & GRAMBAST-FESSARD, ?lower Eocene, China; holotype, lateral view, NIGP PB 4509, ×37 (Z. Wang, 1978a, pl. VI,*2*).

Nothochara MUSACCHIO, 1973, p. 8 [*N. apiculata MUSACCHIO, 1973, p. 9, pl. II,*1,4–5,7–12;* M]. Apex psilocharoid; spirals convex, becoming concave with high, intercellular crests in apical zone and turning up in center. General shape prolate to subprolate, with apex strongly protruding; base rounded, with ends of spirals concave, sutures forming crests around pore. Spirals smooth. Basal plate nearly as thick as wide, generally visible from exterior. Size small. Monospecific genus. *Upper Cretaceous:* Argentina.——FIG. 68,*2a–d.* *N. apiculata* MUSACCHIO; *a,* holotype, lateral view, ×117; *b,* upper part of gyrogonite, ×150; *c,* apical view, ×100; *d,* basal view, ×117 (Musacchio, 1973, pl. II,*4,5,7,1*).

Peckichara GRAMBAST, 1957, p. 352 [*P. varians GRAMBAST, 1957, p. 352, pl. VIII,*1–8;* OD] [=*Sinochara* LIN & Z. WANG in S. WANG & others, 1982, p. 32 (type, *S. rudongensis* LIN & Z. WANG in S. WANG & others, 1982, p. 32, pl. 15,*5–9,* OD)]. Apex nitellopsidoid, with periapical furrow weakly marked and variable narrowing of spirals. Apical nodules present, generally elongated. General shape prolate spheroidal and often quadrangular, with rounded apex; base rounded or slightly tapering, with flaring funnel. Spirals generally with tubercles, rods, or crests. Basal plate as thick as about one-third width. Size small to large. [All the salient features of *Peckichara* are found in *Sinochara.* Only the apical tubercles of *Sinochara* are slightly more protruding. The differences in spiral ornamentation do not appear significant.] *Upper Cretaceous–Paleogene (Eocene, ?Oligocene):* USA, Peru, France, United Kingdom, Spain, Algeria, China, ?India, Mongolia.——FIG. 73,*1a–c.* *P. varians* GRAMBAST, lower Eocene, France, topotypes; *a,* lateral view, C.57-9; *b,* apical view, C.57-10; *c,* basal view, C.57-11, ×40 (new).——FIG. 73,*1d–e. P. pectinata* GRAMBAST, Upper Cretaceous, France; *d,* lateral view; *e,* apical view, ×46 (Grambast, 1971, text-fig. 9a–b).——FIG. 73,*1f. P. toscarensis* FEIST, Paleocene, Spain; longitudinal section, C.1124-8, ×40 (new).

Peckisphaera GRAMBAST, 1962b, p. 78 [*Chara verticillata* PECK, 1937, p. 84, fig. 30–33; OD] [=*Circonitella* WATSON, 1969, p. 214 (type, *Chara knowltoni* SEWARD, 1894, p. 13, text-fig. 1); *Retusochara* GRAMBAST, 1971, p. 28 (type, *R.*

macrocarpa GRAMBAST, 1971, p. 31, fig. 18, pl. XXIV–XXV, OD)]. Apex psilocharoid, without distinct apical modifications of spirals but with slight enlargement at ends. General shape prolate-spheroidal to subprolate with apex rounded. Spirals smooth. Basal plate thick, the thickness up to twice width, visible or not from exterior. Size small to large. [*Retusochara* and *Peckisphaera* have similar apical structures and thick basal plates; plate is sunken in *Retusochara* but in some species is still visible from the exterior.] *Upper Jurassic–Cretaceous:* USA, Argentina, France, Germany, Portugal, Spain, Ukraine, China, Lebanon.——FIG. 74,*1a–c.* *P. verticillata* (PECK) GRAMBAST, Upper Jurassic, USA, topotypes; *a,* lateral view, C.1228-1, ×80; *b,* basal view, C.1228-2, ×72; *c,* apical view, C.1228-3, ×72 (new).——FIG. 74,*1d. P. (Retusochara) macrocarpa* (GRAMBAST) FEIST & GRAMBAST-FESSARD, Upper Cretaceous, France; longitudinal section, ×40 (Grambast, 1971, pl. XXV,*8*).

Platychara GRAMBAST, 1962b, p. 76 [*Chara compressa KNOWLTON, 1888, p. 156, fig. 1–2; OD; *non* KUNTH, 1815]. Apex nitellopsidoid; periapical zone variably thinned and slightly or not narrowed. Apical nodes convex and elongated; in some species, apical nodes absent. General shape oblate, suboblate to oblate-spheroidal, with apex rounded or truncated; base similar or, in numerous instances, spirals turned downward around basal pore to form small cone or distinct column. Spirals smooth or with tubercles or crests. Basal plate slightly calcified, not visible from exterior. Size small to large. [Differs from *Gyrogona* in being distinctly wider than high, in having wide spirals, continuous periapical furrow, and frequently a basal extension. In species with a protruding base, gyrogonite height may equal width or slightly exceed width, such as *P. sahnii* BHATIA & MANNIKERI, 1976, from the Paleocene of India. Some species described as *Gyrogona* from the Upper Cretaceous of China are in fact representatives of *Platychara* (GRAMBAST & GRAMBAST-FESSARD, 1981).] *Upper Cretaceous–Paleogene (Paleocene):* Canada, Mexico, USA, Argentina, Bolivia, Jamaica, Peru, Belgium, France, Spain, China, India.——FIG. 74,*2a–e.* *P. compressa* (KNOWLTON) GRAMBAST, Upper Cretaceous, USA, topotypes; *a,* lateral view, C.1229-1, ×40; *b,* lateral view, C.1229-2, ×40; *c,* wall structure of spiral cells, C.1229-5, ×300; *d,* apical view, C.1229-3, ×40; *e,* basal view, C.1229-4, ×40 (new).——FIG. 74,*2f. P. complanata* GRAMBAST & GUTIÉRREZ, Upper Cretaceous, Spain, holotype; lateral view, ×78 (Grambast & Gutiérrez, 1977, pl. VI,*1*).——FIG. 74,*2g–h. P. stipitata* GRAMBAST & GUTIÉRREZ, Upper Cretaceous, Spain; *g,* lateral view, paratype; *h,* apical view, ×100 (Grambast & Gutiérrez, 1977, pl. VII,*5a–b*).

Pseudoharrisichara MUSACCHIO, 1973, p. 10 [*P. walpurgica* MUSACCHIO, 1973, p. 11, pl. III,*9–16,* pl. IV,*3,6;* OD]. Apex psilocharoid, with spirals somewhat thinned in apical zone, particularly on apex periphery. General shape prolate to subprolate, with apex rounded and base tapered; basal column

1a

Peckichara

1f

1b

1c

1d

1e

2f

Rhabdochara

2a

2e

2d

2c

2b

3

Saidakovskyella

4b

Songliaochara

4c

4a

FIG. 73. Characeae (p. 136–141).

1a
Peckisphaera
1c
1b
1d
2b
2a
2f
Platychara
2g
2e
2d
2h
2c

FIG. 74. Characeae (p. 136).

axis slightly curved with respect to polar axis. Spirals smooth or with nodular crests. Basal pore surrounded by distinct funnel. Basal plate wider than thick. Size small to medium. [Differs from *Harrisichara* in periapical thinning, oblique projecting base, and thicker basal plate.] *Upper Cretaceous:* Argentina, Spain.——FIG. 75,*1a.* **P. walpurgica* MUSACCHIO, Argentina; holotype, lateral view, ×67 (Musacchio, 1973, pl. III,*13*).——FIG. 75,*1b–d. P. isonae* FEIST, Spain; *b,* apical view; *c,* basal view; *d,* lateral view, holotype, ×46 (Feist & Colombo, 1983, pl. I,*10,9,6*).

1a

1b

Pseudoharrisichara

1c

1d

2a

2b

2c

2d

2e

Shandongochara

3a

3d

3b

3e

Pseudolatochara

3c

4c

4d

4a

Stylochara

4b

Fig. 75. Characeae (p. 136–142).

1a

1d

1e
Strobilochara

1b

1c

2b

2d
Psilochara

2a

2c

3b

3a

3d
Stephanochara

3c

FIG. 76. Characeae (p. 141–142).

Pseudolatochara Z. WANG, 1978a, p. 74 [*P. jianghanensis* Z. WANG, 1978a, p. 74, pl. V,*36–42;* OD] [=*Grambastiella* MASSIEUX in MASSIEUX & TAMBAREAU, 1978, p. 143 (type, *G. acuta* MASSIEUX in MASSIEUX & TAMBAREAU, 1978, p. 144, pl. 1,*1–* 6, OD)]. Apex lamprothamnoid, with peripheral spiral thinning weak or absent. In apex center, spiral endings abruptly arise and form projecting cone. General shape prolate–spheroidal with apex protruded and base rounded; in some species base tapered. Spirals smooth. Basal plate unknown. Size small. *Upper Cretaceous–Paleogene (Eocene):* France, China.——FIG. 75,*3a–b*. **P. jianghanensis* Z. WANG, Upper Cretaceous, China; *a,* holotype, lateral view; *b,* apical view, ×95 (Z. Wang, 1978a, pl. V,*38,40*).——FIG. 75,*3c–e*. *P. (Grambastiella) acuta* MASSIEUX, Paleocene, France; *c,* apical view, ×85; *d,* basal view, ×95; *e,* lateral view, holotype, ×85 (Massieux & Tambareau, 1978, pl. 1,*2,3,1*).

Psilochara GRAMBAST, 1959b, p. 10 [*Chara archiaci var. *undulata* DOLLFUS & FRITEL, 1919, p. 252, fig. 14; OD]. Apex psilocharoid, convex, without periapical modification; spiral ends slightly enlarged. General shape prolate-spheroidal to perprolate, with apex rounded or pointed and base rounded or tapered. Spirals smooth, in numerous instances with sinuous spiral sutures. Basal pore at same level as lower surface, in some species surrounded by flaring funnel. Basal plate slightly calcified, about one-third as thick as wide, with upper face hollow. Size medium to large. [Differs from *Grovesichara* in its lack of periapical thinning, a basal plate that is not visible from the exterior, and presence of sinuous spiral sutures.] *Paleogene (Eocene–Oligocene):* Belgium, France, United Kingdom, Spain, China.——FIG. 76,*2a–c.* **P. undulata* (DOLLFUS & FRITEL) GRAMBAST, middle Eocene, France, topotypes; *a,* lateral view, C.121-17; *b,* apical view, C.121-19; *c,* basal view, C.121-18, ×35 (new).——FIG. 76,*2d.* *P. bitruncata* (REID & GROVES) FEIST-CASTEL, upper Eocene, France; lateral view, C.F1509-6, ×50 (new).

Rhabdochara MÄDLER, 1955, p. 299; *emend.,* GRAMBAST, 1957, p. 357 [*Chara langeri ETTINGSHAUSEN, 1872, p. 162, pl. 1,*2–3;* OD]. Apex psilocharoid; apical zone thin but convex; weakly marked apical nodules rarely present. General shape subprolate to ellipsoidal with summit truncated and base somewhat tapered. Spirals generally concave, smooth or with transverse rods. Basal plate conical and hollow. Size variable. [Differs from *Stephanochara* and *Lychnothamnus* in lacking periapical depression and having strongly developed nodules, hollow basal plate, and ornamentation consisting of rods instead of tubercles.] *Paleogene (?lower Eocene, upper Eocene)–Neogene (Miocene):* Europe (widespread), China.——FIG. 73,*2a–d.* **R. langeri* (ETTINGSHAUSEN) MÄDLER, lower Miocene; *a,* lateral view, ×40 (adapted from Ettingshausen, 1872, pl. I,*3*); *b,* lateral view, France, ×47 (Feist & Ringeade, 1977, pl. 23,*9*); *c,* basal view, France, C.536-9; *d,* apical view, France, C.536-8, ×40 (new).——FIG. 73,*2e. R. stockmansi* GRAMBAST, lower Oligocene, France; lateral view, ×50 (Grambast, 1957, text-fig. 6).——FIG. 73,*2f. R. praelangeri* CASTEL, upper Oligocene, France; longitudinal section, basal part, ×50 (Castel, 1967, pl. XX,*11*).

Saidakovskyella SHAIKIN, 1976, p. 83 [**S. corpulenta* SHAIKIN, 1976, p. 84, fig. 14–19; M]. Apex psilocharoid, with apical ends of spirals thickened. General shape spheroidal with apex pointed and base rounded. Spirals smooth. Basal funnel present.

Basal plate moderately thick. Size medium to large. Genus monotypic. *Lower Cretaceous:* Ukraine.——FIG. 73,*3.* **S. corpulenta* SHAIKIN; holotype, lateral view, ×33 (adapted from Shaikin, 1976, text-fig. 14).

Shandongochara XINLUN in WANG Shui & others, 1978, p. 46 [**S. decorosa* XINLUN in WANG Shui & others, 1978, p. 46, pl. 21,*1–7,* pl. 22,*1–2,* pl. 23,*2;* OD; lectotype, NIGP 390133, pl. 21,*1a–c,* designated FEIST & GRAMBAST-FESSARD herein]. Apex psilocharoid, with distinct periapical narrowing and thinning; apical ends of spirals slightly pointed in center, without nodules. General shape prolate-spheroidal to prolate; apex nearly flat to broadly conical, base truncated. Spirals flat to slightly convex with elongated, tumorlike decorations. Basal plate nearly twice as wide as thick, visible from exterior. Size large. *Paleogene (Oligocene):* China.——FIG. 75,*2a–e.* **S. decorosa* XINLUN; *a,* lectotype, lateral view; *b,* lateral view; *c,* basal view; *d,* apical view, ×34; *e,* longitudinal section, basal part, ×68 (Wang Shui & others, 1978, pl. 21,*1b,2b,2c,2a,6a*).

Songliaochara Z. WANG, LU, & ZHAO, 1985, p. 64 [**S. heilongjiangensis* Z. WANG, LU, & ZHAO, 1985, p. 65, pl. XXVIII,*2–8;* OD; holotype, NIGP 9836, fig. 3a–c]. Apex nitellopsidoid, with shallow periapical groove; apical nodules rounded, moderately thick. General shape ovoid with apex rounded, projecting above apical level. Spirals generally convex, smooth. Base tapering, sometimes forming well-marked basal column. Basal pore small; basal funnel absent. Basal plate multipartite (LU & LUO, 1990), as wide as thick, not visible from exterior. Size small. Immature specimens reminiscent of *Aclistochara*. [The recognition of the basal plate structure shows that *Songliaochara* can no longer be considered a synonym of *Nodosochara* (FEIST & GRAMBAST-FESSARD, 1991).] *Upper Cretaceous:* China.——FIG. 73,*4a–c.* **S. heilongjiangensis* Z. WANG, LU, & ZHAO, lower Upper Cretaceous, holotype; *a,* lateral view; *b,* apical view; *c,* basal view, ×120 (Z. Wang, Lu, & Zhao, 1985, pl. XXVIII,*3b,3a,3c*).

Stephanochara GRAMBAST, 1959b, p. 8 [**S. compta* GRAMBAST, 1959b, fig. 3; OD] [=*Croftiella* HORN AF RANTZIEN, 1959b, p. 104 (type, *Chara escheri* UNGER, 1850, p. 34); *Eotectochara* HU & ZENG, 1982, p. 562 (type, *E. hunanensis* HU & ZENG, 1982, p. 562, pl. 372,*1–7,* OD); *Dongmingochara* ZHAO & HUANG, 1985, p. 13 (type, *D. concinna* ZHAO & HUANG, 1985, p. 13, pl. I,*4–10,* pl. II,*7–9,* OD)]. Apex nitellopsidoid, with deep depression and no constrictions at apical periphery; apical nodules strongly developed. General shape prolate-spheroidal to prolate and perprolate with apex protruding and base tapered. Spirals smooth or with tubercles. Basal funnel star shaped, sometimes absent. Basal plate variable in thickness, about half as thick as wide. Size medium to large. [FEIST-CASTEL (1977c) documented the nonvalidity of *Croftiella*.] *Upper Cretaceous–Neogene (Miocene):* Europe (widespread), Mongolia, China.——FIG. 76,*3a–c.* **S. compta* GRAMBAST, lower Oligocene, United

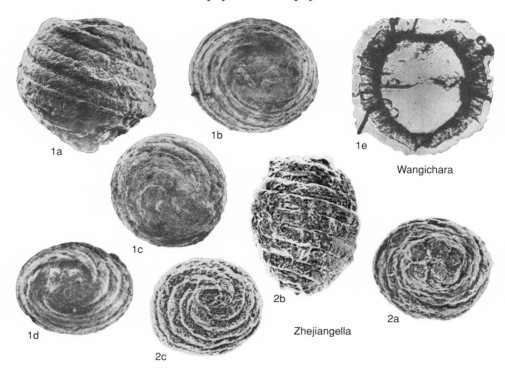

1a
1b
1e

Wangichara

1c

2b

2a

1d

Zhejiangella

2c

FIG. 77. Characeae (p. 142–143).

Kingdom; *a,* holotype, lateral view; *b,* paratype, apical view, C.1230-2; *c,* paratype, basal view, C.1230-3, ×40 (new).——FIG. 76,*3d. S. berdotensis* FEIST, lower Miocene, western France; holotype, lateral view, ×43 (Feist & Ringeade, 1977, pl. XIII,*1*).

Strobilochara GRAMBAST, 1975, p. 72 [*S. viallardi* GRAMBAST, 1975, p. 73, text-fig. 3, pl. II; OD]. Apex psilocharoid, with spirals unmodified at apex. General shape prolate-spheroidal to subprolate; apex rounded or truncated, central part variably prominent; base tapering to point or column. Spirals smooth or with tubercles. Basal plate thicker than wide, not visible from exterior. Size medium to large. [Differs from *Hornichara* in having apical zone normally calcified, thicker basal plate, larger size, and possible ornamentation.] *Upper Cretaceous:* Spain.——FIG. 76,*1a–c. *S. viallardi* GRAMBAST, topotypes; *a,* lateral view, C.1057-29; *b,* apical view, C.1057-30; *c,* basal view, C.1057-31, ×30 (new).——FIG. 76,*1d–e. S. diademata* GRAMBAST & GUTIÉRREZ; *d,* holotype, lateral view, ×53; *e,* longitudinal section, ×80 (Grambast & Gutiérrez, 1977, pl. X,*1,* pl. XV,*5*).

Stylochara JIANG & ZHANG in JIANG, ZHANG, & MENG, 1985, p. 162 [*S. xitanlouensis* JIANG, ZHANG, & MENG, 1985, p. 163, pl. II,*1–9;* M; holotype,

BGMRH Y00043, pl. II,*1a–c*]. Apical zone sunken. General shape cylindrical with apex and base truncated. Spirals smooth, clearly widened and thickened in upper and lower parts. Basal plate multipartite, thick. Size small. Genus monotypic. [The swelling of apical and basal parts may represent a calcification anomaly. In spite of strong differences concerning the gyrogonite shape, *Stylochara* has been put in synonymy with *Aclistochara* by LU & LUO (1990).] *Lower Cretaceous:* China.——FIG. 75,*4a–d. *S. xitanlouensis* JIANG & ZHANG; *a,* holotype, lateral view, ×86; *b,* longitudinal section, ×82; *c,* apical view, ×86; *d,* basal view, ×86 (Jiang, Zhang, & Meng, 1985, pl. II,*1b,9,1a,1c*).

Wangichara LIU & WU, 1985, p. 144 [*W. tanshanensis* LIU & WU, 1985, p. 144, pl. 2,*1–4;* OD; holotype, BIG0225, pl. 2,*1a–c*]. Apex lamprothamnoid, with apical rosette in well-marked depression bearing slightly convex nodules in center. General shape of gyrogonite ovoid with truncated summit and tapering base. Spirals smooth, flat to convex. Size small. Basal plate nearly as wide as thick. [Differs from *Aclistochara* mainly by the presence of distinct apical nodules and from *Stephanochara* in its smaller size and apex not projecting above the general surface.] *Lower Cretaceous:* China.——FIG. 77,*1a–e.

W. tanshanensis LIU & WU; *a–c,* holotype, lateral, apical, basal views; *d,* apical view; *e,* longitudinal section, ×80 (Liu & Wu, 1985, pl. II,*1b,1a,1e,2a,4*).

Zhejiangella LIN, 1989, p. 5 [**Z. tongxiangensis* LIN, 1989, p. 5, pl. III,*1–10;* OD; holotype, NIGP PB1029, pl. III,*1*]. Apex nitellopsidoid, with slight narrowing and no depression of spiral cells in periapical zone. Apical nodules prominent, grouped into apical rose. Gyrogonite ellipsoid, with apex rounded and base tapering. Size small to medium. Basal plate wider than thick, visible from exterior. [Differs from *Neochara* by the absence of periapical depression.] *Upper Cretaceous:* China.——FIG. 77,*2a–c.* **Z. tongxiangensis* LIN; *a,* holotype, apical view; *b,* lateral view; *c,* basal view, ×80 (Lin, 1989, pl. III,*1–3*).

Subfamily NITELLOIDEAE Braun, 1890

[*nom. correct.* FEIST & GRAMBAST-FESSARD, herein, *pro* subfamily Nitelleae BRAUN in MIGULA, 1890 in 1890–1897, p. 94]

Gyrogonite of Characeae with basal plate multipartite, except in *Sphaerochara* where basal plate is undivided. Uncalcified oogonia of *Nitella* and *Tolypella* are only occasionally fossilized. Extant species with 10 small uncalcified coronula cells in 2 tiers. Thallus not corticated, uncalcified. *Jurassic–Holocene.*

The Nitelloideae represent the tolypelloid morphological type (FEIST & GRAMBAST-FESSARD, 1982). This subfamily is characterized by gyrogonites with a prominent apex, either rounded or pointed, and without any periapical depression, except immediately around apical nodules when present, as in some *Sphaerochara* species. The origin of the Nitelloideae seems to go back to the Lower Devonian, as suggested by vegetative remains of *Palaeonitella* KIDSTON & LANG, resembling the extant *Nitella.*

Nitella AGARDH, 1824, p. 123; *emend.,* BRAUN, 1847, p. 5; VON LEONHARDI, 1863, p. 69 [**N. opaca* AGARDH, 1824, p. 125; SD HORN AF RANTZIEN & OLSEN, 1949, p. 99] [=*Nitellites* HORN AF RANTZIEN, 1957, p. 12 (type, *N. sahnii* HORN AF RANTZIEN, 1957, p. 12, pl. I,*1–5,* pl. II,*1–2,* OD)]. Enveloping cells do not secrete calcite, thus gyrogonites do not occur. Oogonia and oospore small, laterally compressed, with 3 basal sister cells. [The only substantiated fossil records of the genus are silicified materials. The oldest one is *Palaeonitella* KIDSTON & LANG (1921) from the Lower Devonian Rhynie Chert of Scotland, with uncorticated thallus very

similar to the extant *Nitella.* This structure is visible in the section given by TAYLOR, REMY, and HASS (1992, fig. 1). In *Nitellites* HORN AF RANTZIEN (1957), from the Jurassic of India, the resemblance with *Nitella* is in the reticulate membrane sculpture of the oospore.] *Jurassic–Holocene:* worldwide.——FIG. 78,*2a–d.* **N. opaca* AGARDH, Holocene, France, oospore; *a,* lateral view, CF.2955-1; *b,* apical view, CF.2955-2; *c,* basal view, CF.2955-3, ×96 (new); *d,* oogonium, without coronula, CF.2955.4, ×73 (new).——FIG. 78,*2e. N. tenuissima* (DESVAUX in LOISELEUR) KÜTZING; *emend.,* WOOD & IMAHORI, Holocene, France, oospore; lateral view, ×225 (Soulié-Märsche, 1987, fig. 4A).

Sphaerochara MÄDLER, 1952, p. 6; *emend.,* SOULIÉ-MÄRSCHE, 1989, p. 172 [**Chara hirmeri* RÁSKY, 1945, p. 36, pl. I,*10–12;* OD] [=*Maedlerisphaera* HORN AF RANTZIEN, 1959b, p. 100 (type, *Chara ulmensis* STRAUB, 1952, p. 470, pl. A,*19,* OD); ?*Raskyaechara* HORN AF RANTZIEN, 1959b, p. 146 (type, *Aclistochara pecki* RASKY, 1945, pl. II,*13–15*); *Tolypella* section *Rothia* R. D. WOOD, 1962, p. 23 (type, *Chara intricata,* TRENTEPOHL *ex* ROTH, 1797, p. 125, OD)]. Apex curved, with central rosette. In well-calcified specimens, spirals become thinner in periapical zone, then recover thickness at ends. General shape spheroidal to prolate-spheroidal. Spirals in most instances with granulate surface. When present, ornamentation consisting of constrictions and irregular, elongated nodules. Basal plate undivided, as thick as wide, with upper and lower faces commonly stellate, visible from exterior. Size generally small. [Identity of *Maedlerisphaera* and *Sphaerochara* established by HORN AF RANTZIEN & GRAMBAST (1962). *Raskyaechara* doubtfully assigned to *Sphaerochara* as gyrogonite structure incompletely known (GRAMBAST, 1962b).] *Cretaceous–Holocene:* worldwide.——FIG. 78,*1a.* **S. hirmeri* (RÁSKY) MÄDLER, upper Oligocene, Hungary, topotype; lateral view, ×70 (adapted from HORN AF RANTZIEN, 1959b, pl. XVI,*1*).——FIG. 78,*1b. S. hirmeri* ssp. *longiuscula* GRAMBAST & PAUL, upper Oligocene, France; longitudinal section, basal part with basal plate in situ, ×150 (Castel, 1968, pl. XXI,*3b*).——FIG. 78,*1c–e. S. intricata* (TRENTEPOHL *ex* ROTH) FEIST & GRAMBAST-FESSARD var. *intricata* f. *prolifera* R. D. WOOD, Holocene, Uruguay; *c,* lateral view, ×90; *d,* apical view, ×100; *e,* basal view, ×100 (Soulié-Märsche, 1989, pl. XLIII,*2,4,7*).——FIG. 78,*1f. S. labellata* FEIST, upper Eocene, France; paratype, lateral view, ×95 (Feist & Ringeade, 1977, pl. XI,*4*).——FIG. 78,*1g. S. senonensis* FEIST, Upper Cretaceous, France; internal view of gyrogonite with microscopic waving of spiral cell walls, ×370 (Feist & Freytet, 1983, pl. I,*14*).

Tolypella (BRAUN, 1849) BRAUN, 1857, p. 338; *emend.,* SOULIÉ-MÄRSCHE, 1989, p. 171 [**Conferva nidifica* MÜLLER, 1778, p. 761; OD] [=*Tolypella* section *Tolypella* WOOD, 1962, p. 23, obj.]. In extant species, oogonia uncalcified, not laterally compressed,

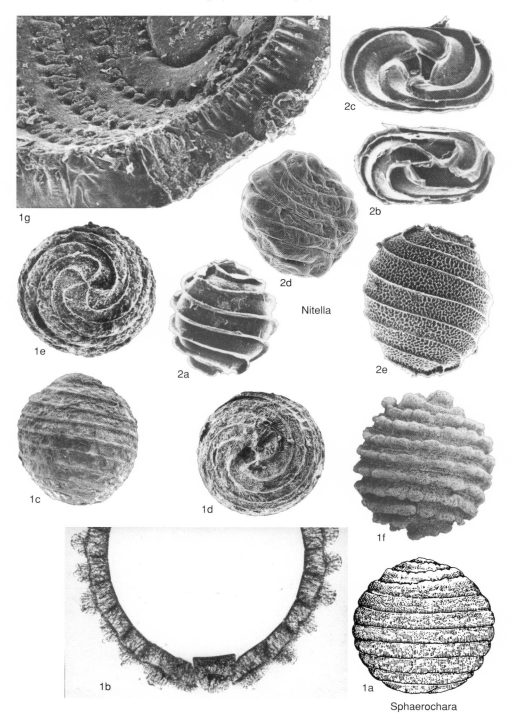

1g

2c

2b

2d

Nitella

1e

2a

2e

1c

1d

1f

1b

1a

Sphaerochara

FIG. 78. Characeae (p. 143).

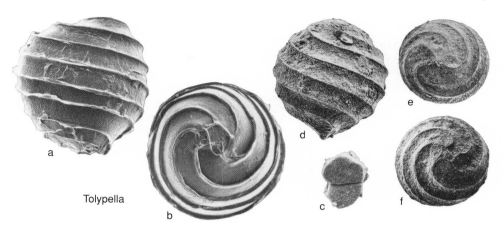

Tolypella

FIG. 79. Characeae (p. 143–145).

with 3 basal sister cells. In fossil species, uncalcified forms unknown; calcified gyrogonites with bipartite or tripartite basal plate. Apex without distinct modifications. General shape spheroidal with apex and base pointed. Spirals concave, smooth. Size very small. [Species with external characters of *Tolypella* but with basal plate unknown are questionably assigned to this genus, such as the Upper Jurassic *T. harrisi* MÄDLER, 1952.] *Upper Cretaceous–Holocene:* Alaska, Argentina, Belgium, France, Germany, *Upper Cretaceous–lower Oligocene* (calcified); worldwide, *Holocene* (not calcified).——FIG. 79*a–b.* **T. nidifica* (O. MÜLLER) BRAUN, Holocene, Sweden; *a,* lateral view; *b,* basal view, ×120 (Soulié-Märsche, 1989, pl. XLI,*2,1*).——FIG. 79*c–f. T. pumila* GRAMBAST in STOCKMANS, upper Eocene, Belgium; *c,* isolated multipartite basal plate, ×325; *d,* lateral view, ×110 (Feist & Grambast-Fessard, 1991, fig. 5e, 5d); *e,* apical view, C.1231-2; *f,* basal view, C.1231-3, ×110 (new).

NOMINA DUBIA AND GENERIC NAMES WRONGLY ATTRIBUTED TO CHAROPHYTES

Monique Feist and Nicole Grambast-Fessard

[Université Montpellier II, France]

NOMINA DUBIA

Algites Seward, 1894. Nomen nudum.

Astrocharas Stache, 1872. Nomen nudum (Groves, 1933).

Barrandeina Stur, 1881. Vascular plant (Groves, 1933).

Bechera Sternberg, 1825. An artificial genus, conceived to include unlike charophyte plants (Groves, 1933).

Characeites Tuzson, 1913. Nomen nudum.

Cristatella Stache, 1889. Nomen nudum.

Kosmogyra Stache, 1889. Nomen nudum.

Kosmogyrella Stache, 1889. Nomen nudum.

Palaeoxyris Brongniart. Probably not vegetal (Groves, 1933).

Spirangium Schimper, 1869. Probably not vegetal (Groves, 1933).

GENERIC NAMES WRONGLY ATTRIBUTED TO CHAROPHYTES

Uncatoella Li & Cai, 1978. Dasycladales (Kenrick & Li, 1998).

Munieria Deecke, 1883. Dasycladales (Feist, Génot, & Grambast-Fessard, 2003).

Umbella Maslov in Bykova & Polenova, 1955; *emend.,* Poyarkov, 1965, and related genera. Microproblematica (Peck, 1974).[1]

[1]New data on the utricles of the Sycidiales suggest that some umbellids could correspond to charophytes (Feist, Monique, Liu Junying, & Paul Tafforeau. In press. New insights on Paleozoic charophyte morphology and phylogeny. American Journal of Botany (in press).

RANGES OF TAXA

The stratigraphic distribution of the Charophyta recognized in this volume is shown graphically in the range chart (Table 9).

Because of the very long stratigraphic ranges of many higher taxa of Charophyta, ranges in the chart are rather broad in order to ensure that all periods are included. For more detailed stratigraphic information, refer to the systematic section of the volume, p. 92–145.

The following chart was compiled using software developed for the Paleontological Institute by Kenneth C. Hood and David W. Foster.

It must be emphasized that the order of taxa in this chart is governed entirely by their stratigraphic range and, within that, by alphabetical order and differs in some cases from the taxonomic order in the systematic part of the volume. No taxonomic conclusions should be drawn from the position of taxa in this chart.

Explanation for Table 9	
PHYLUM	▬▬▬
CLASS	▬▬▬
ORDER SUBORDER	▬▬
FAMILY SUBFAMILY	▬▬
Genus Subgenus	▬
Occurrence questionable	????
Occurrence inferred	- - -

TABLE 9. *Stratigraphic Distribution of the Charophyta.*

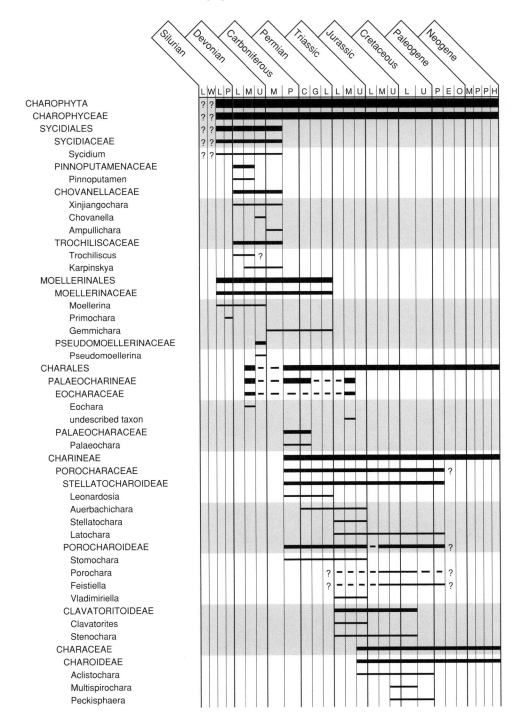

TABLE 9. *(Continued).*

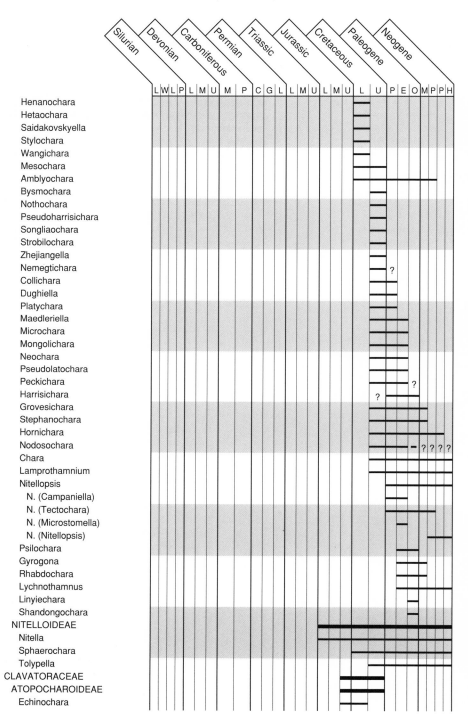

TABLE 9. *(Continued).*

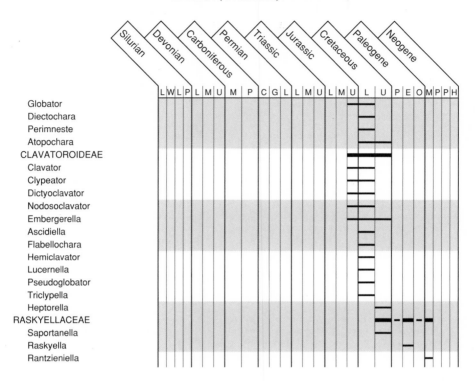

REFERENCES

Agardh, Carl Adolf. 1824. Systema Algarum. Literis Berlingianis. Lund. 312 p. Characeae, p. XXVII–XXVIII & 123–130.

Alvarez, Luis W., Walter Alvarez, Frank Asaro, & Helen V. Michel. 1980. Extraterrestrial cause for the Cretaceous-Tertiary extinctions. Science 208:1,095–1,108.

Anadón, Pedro, & Monique Feist. 1981. Charophytes et biostratigraphie du Paléogène inférieur du bassin de l'Ebre oriental. Palaeontographica (Abt. B) 178(4/6):143–168, 4 pl.

Anadón, Pedro, Monique Feist, Jean-Louis Hartenberger, Carla Muller, & José de Villalta-Comella. 1983. Un exemple de corrélation biostratigraphique entre échelles marines et continentales dans l'Eocène: La coupe de Pontils (bassin de l'Ebre, Espagne). Bulletin de la Société Géologique de France (série 7) 25(5):747–755.

Antunes, Miguel T., Ingeborg Soulié-Märsche, Pierre Mein, & Jaime Pais. 1992. Le gisement de Asseiceira, Portugal (Miocène Supérieur). Données complémentaires sur Freiria de Rio Maior. Ciencias da Terra (UNL), Lisboa 11:219–253, 7 pl.

Babinot, J.-F., P. Freytet, M. Amiot, M. Bilotte, F. de Broin, F. Colombo, J.-P. Durand, M. Feist, M. Floquet, M. Gayet, B. Lange-Badré, A. Masriera, M. Massieux, J. Médus, Y. Tambareau, J. Ullastre, & J. Villatte. 1983. Le Sénonien supérieur continental de la France méridionale et de l'Espagne septentrionale: État des connaissances biostratigraphiques. Géologie méditerranéenne 10(3–4):145–268.

Baldwin, Bruce G., Michael J. Sanderson, J. Marc Porter, Martin F. Wojciechowski, Christopher S. Campbell, & Michael J. Donoghue. 1995. The ITS region of nuclear ribosomal DNA: A valuable source of evidence on angiosperm phylogeny. Annals of the Missouri Botanical Garden 82:247–277.

de Bary, Anton. 1875. Zur Keimungsgeschichte der Charen. Botanische Zeitung 23:377–385, 393–401, 409–420, pl. V–VI.

Bathurst, Robin G. C. 1971. Carbonate Sediments and Their Diagenesis, Developments in Sedimentology, vol. 12. Elsevier. Amsterdam, New York. 620 p.

Becker, Damien, Laurent Picot, & Jean-Pierre Berger. 2002. Stable isotopes (d¹³C and d¹⁸O) of charophyte gyrogonites; example from the Brochene Fluh section (late Oligocene–early Miocene, Switzerland). Geobios 35:89–97.

Bell, W. A. 1922. A new genus of Characeae and new Merostomata from the Coal Measures of Novia Scotia. Transactions of the Royal Society of Canada 3(16):159–162, 1 pl.

Benton, Michael J. 1993. The Fossil Record 2. Chapman & Hall. London. 945 p. Charophyta, p. 16–19.

Berger, Jean-Pierre. 1985. La transgression de la molasse marine supérieure (OMM) en Suisse occidentale. Münchner Geowissenschaftliche (Abhandlungen A) 5:1–208.

———. 1986. Biozonation préliminaire des charophytes oligocènes de Suisse occidentale. Eclogae Geologicae Helvetiae 79(3):897–912.

———. 1990. Floral changes in the molasse of western Switzerland (Oligo–Miocene): Paleoclimatic implications. In E. Knobloch & Z. Kvacek, eds., Proceedings of the Symposium Paleofloristic and Paleoclimatic Changes in the Cretaceous and Tertiary, Prague 1989. Geological Survey Publications. Prague. p. 189–194.

Berggren, William A., Dennis V. Kent, Marie-Pierre Aubry, & Jan Hardenbol. 1995. Geochronology, Time Scales and Global Stratigraphic Correlation. SEPM (Society for Sedimentary Geology) Special Publication number 54. Society for Sedimentary Geology. Tulsa, Oklahoma. 386 p.

Bharathan, S. 1980. Studies on Characeae. Ph.D. dissertation. University of Madras. Madras. 143 p.

Bhatia, Shashi B., & M. S. Mannikeri. 1976. Some Charophyta from the Deccan Intertrappean Beds near Nagpur, central India. Geophytology 6(1):75–81.

———. 1977. Callovian Charophyta from Jaisalmer, Western India. Geologica et Palaeontologica 11:187–196.

Bhatia, Shashi B., & Rajendra S. Rana. 1984. Palaeogeographic implications of the Charophyta and Ostracoda of the Inter-trappean beds of peninsular India. Mémoires de la Société Geologique de France (new series) 147:29–35.

Bignot, Gérard, & Louis Grambast. 1969. Sur la position stratigraphique et les charophytes de la Formation de Kozina (Slovénie, Yougoslavie). Comptes Rendus des Séances de l'Académie des Sciences, Paris (series D) 269:689–692.

Bilan, Wieslaw. 1988. The epicontinental Triassic charophytes of Poland. Acta Palaeobotanica 28(1,2):63–161, 12 pl.

Birina, L. M. 1948. Nouvelles espèces d'algues calcaires et de foraminifères des limites du Dévonien. Sovetskaya Geologiya, Sbornik 28:154–160.

Blindow, Irmgard. 1994. Sällsynta och hotade kransalger i Sverige. Svensk Botanisk Tidskrift 88:65–73. In Swedish, English summary.

Blindow, Irmgard, & Anders Langangen. 1995. Kransalgen Lamprothamnium papulosum i Sverige [The charophyte Lamprothamnium papulosum in Sweden]. Svensk Botanisk Tidskrift 89:171–174.

Blow, W.-H. 1969. Late middle Eocene to recent planktonic biostratigraphy. In P. Brönnimann & H. H. Renz, Proceedings of the 1st International Conference on Planktonic Microfossils, Geneva, 1967, vol. 1. E. J. Brill. Leiden. p. 199–422.

Bold, Harold C., & Michael J. Wynne. 1985. Introduction to the Algae, 2nd ed. Prentice-Hall, Inc. Englewood Cliffs, NJ. 720 p.

Braun, Alexander. 1847. Übersicht der Schweizerischen Characeen. Ein Beitrag zur Flora der Schweiz. Neue Denkschriften der Schweizerische Gesellschaft der Naturwissenschaften 10(3):1–23.

———. 1849. Charae Australes et Antarticae, or characters and observations on the Characeae of Australia and the southern circumpolar regions. Hooker's Journal of Botany and Kew Garden Miscellany 1:193–203.

———. 1857. Über Parthenogenesis bei Pflanzen. Abhandlungen der Königlichen Preussischen Akademie der Wissenschaften zu Berlin für das Jahr 1856:311–376.

Braun, Alexander, & Otto Nordstedt. 1882. Fragmente einer Monographie der Characeen. Nach den hinterlassenen Manuskripten A. Braun's herausgegeben von Dr. Otto Nordstedt. Abhandlungen der königlichen Akademie der Wissenschaften zu Berlin 1882:1–211, pl. 1–7.

Bremer, Kåre. 1985. Summary of green plant phylogeny and classification. Cladistics 1:369–385.

Breuer, Roswitha. 1988. Zur taxonomischen Gliederung der Familie Porocharaceae (Charophyta). Paläontologische Zeitschrift 62(1/2):3–10.

Breuer, Roswitha, & Monique Feist. 1986. Biostratigraphisch bedeutsame Charophyten aus dem Alttertiär von Erdölfeldern des Oberrheingrabens. Newsletters on Stratigraphy 16(3):139–147.

Briggs, John C. 1995. Global Biogeography. Developments in Palaeontology and Stratigraphy, No. 14. Elsevier. Amsterdam. 552 p.

Brongniart, Adolphe. 1822. Sur la classification et la distribution des végétaux fossiles. Mémoires Museum National d'Histoire Naturelle 8:1–91.

Burne, R. V., J. Bauld, & Patrick De Decker. 1980. Saline lake charophytes and their geological significance. Journal of Sedimentary Petrology 50:281–293.

Bykova, E. V., & E. N. Polenova. 1955. Foraminifery radilyarii i ostracody Devona Volgo-Ural'skoi oblasti [Foraminifera, Radiolaria and Ostracoda of the Devonian of the Volga-Ural district]. Trudy Vsesoi ushoro neftognaznovo N. I. Geologorazvednovo Instituta (new series) 87:5–190.

Carpenter, William, B. 1869. Philosophical Transactions of the Royal Society of London.

Casanova, Michelle T. 1997. Report on instream flora survey for Department of Natural Resources, Queensland. University of New England. Armidale. 3 p., 1 map.

Castel, Monique. 1967. Charophytes de l'Oligocène supérieur de Marseille. Bulletin de la Société Géologique de France (series 7) 9(4):514–519, 3 pl.

———. 1968. Zones de charophytes pour l'Oligocène d'Europe Occidentale. Comptes Rendus Sommaires de la Société Géologique de France 4:121–122.

———. 1969. Sur des charophytes de l'Eocène inférieur de Provence. Comptes Rendus des Séances de l'Académie des Sciences, Paris (series D) 268:1,589–1,592.

Castel, Monique, & Louis Grambast. 1969. Charophytes de l'Eocène des Corbières. Bulletin de la Société Géologique de France 11(7):936–943, 3 pl.

Cavelier, Claude, & Charles Pomerol. 1986. Stratigraphy of the Palaeogene. Bulletin de la Société géologique de France (8ème série) II(2):255–265.

Chapman, Russel L., Mark A. Buchheim, Charles F. Delwiche, Thomas Friedl, Volker A. R. Huss, Kenneth G. Karol, Louise A. Lewis, James Manhart, Richard M. McCourt, Jeanine L. Olsen, & Debra A. Waters. 1998. Molecular systematics of the green algae. *In* D. E. Soltis, P. S. Soltis, & J. J. Doyle, eds., Molecular Systematics of Plants II. Kluwer Academic Publishers. Boston. p. 508–540.

Chapman, Russel L., & Debra A. Waters. 2002. Green algae and land plants—An answer at last? Journal of Phycology 38:237–240.

Charrière, André, Françoise Depêche, Monique Feist, Nicole Grambast-Fessard, Michel Jaffrezo, Bernard Peybernes, & Miguel Ramalho. 1994. Microfaunes, microflores et paléoenvironnements successifs dans la formation d'El Mers (Bathonien ? Callovien) du synclinal de Skoura (Moyen Atlas, Maroc). Geobios 27:157–174.

Chen Zhong-Liang, & Yang Hua-ming. 1992. The discovery of *Sycidium* fossils in the Yezhutang formation in Xichang. Regional Geology of China 2:229–232.

Choi Sun Ja. 1989. Les charophytes du bassin potassique catalan (Nord Est de l'Espagne) à la limite Eocène-Oligocène. Paléobiologie continentale 16:1–67, 16 pl.

Choquette, George B. 1956. A new Devonian charophyte. Journal of Paleontology 30:1,371–1,374.

Choubert, B. 1932. Sur la présence d'algues dévoniennes dans le niveau du "Calcaire rose" du système du Kundelungu du Katanga. Académie Royale de Belgique, Bulletin de la Classe des Sciences (série 5) 17:1,421–1,431.

Cimino, Matthew T., & Charles F. Delwiche. 2002. Molecular and morphological data identify a cryptic species complex in endophytic members of the genus *Coleochaete* Bréb. (Chlorophyta: Coleochaetaceae). Journal of Phycology 38:1,213–1,221.

Cimino, Matthew T., Kenneth G. Karol, & Charles F. Delwiche. 2000. An artifact in the small subunit rDNA sequence of *Chaetosphaeridium globosum* (Charophyceae, Streptophyta). Journal of Phycology 36:440–442.

Conkin, James E., & Barbara M. Conkin. 1977. North American primitive Paleozoic charophytes and descendents. Geobotany 1977:173–193.

———. 1992. Late Silurian (Ludlovian) charophyte *Moellerina laufeldi* n. sp., from the Karma beds of the Isle of Gotland, Sweden. University of Louisville Notes in Paleontology and Stratigraphy J:1–21, 6 pl.

Conkin, James E., & Barbara M. Conkin, G. S. Gregory, & A. T. Hotchkiss. 1974. Revision of the charophyte genus *Moellerina* Ulrich 1886 and suppression of the genus *Karpinskya* (Croft 1952) Grambast 1962. University of Louisville Studies in Paleontolology and Stratigraphy 3:1–15, 2 pl.

Cope, John C. W., Keith L. Duff, Colin F. Parsons, Hugh S. Torrens, William A. Wimbledon, & John K. Wright. 1980. A correlation of Jurassic rocks in the British Isles. Part Two: Middle and Upper Jurassic. Geological Society of London, Special Report 15:1–109.

Corillion, Robert. 1957. Les Charophycées de France et d'Europe occidentale. Bulletin de la Société Scientifique de Bretagne 32(fascicule hors série):499 p., 35 pl., 64 maps.

———. 1975. Flore et Végétation du Massif Armoricain, volume IV, Flore des Charophytes (Characées) du Massif armoricain et des contrées voisines d'Europe occidentale. Jouve. Paris. 216 p., 16 pl., 18 maps.

———. 1982. Les Characées des îles Kerguelen (Terres australes et antartiques françaises). Bulletin de la Société des Etudes Scientifique d'Anjou (new series) 11:47–64.

———. 1994. Les Characées de la baie d'Audierne. Penn Ar Bed 152:1–19.

Corillion, Robert, & Micheline Guerlesquin. 1973. Remarques sur les Characées d'Afrique intertropicale. International Association of Theoretical and Applied Limnology, Proceedings 18(3):1,380–1,384.

Croft, William N. 1952. A new *Trochiliscus* (Charophyta) from the Downtonian of Podolia. Bulletin of the British Museum (Natural History), Geology 1(7):189–220, 2 pl.

Dalechamps, Jacques. 1587. Historia Generalis Plantarum, vol. 1. G. Rouillium. Lyon. p. 1,070.

Dawson, John W. 1883. Palaeontological notes. *Saccammina?* (Calcisphaera) Eriana. Canadian Naturalist and Quarterly Journal of Sciences (new series) 10:5–8.

Deecke, W. 1883. Über einige neue Siphoneen. Neues Jahrbuch für Geologie und Palaeontologie 48:1–14.

Delwiche, Charles F., Kenneth G. Karol, Matthew T. Cimino, & Kenneth J. Sytsma. 2002. Phylogeny of the genus *Coleochaete* (Coleochaetales, Charophyta) and related taxa inferred by analysis of the chloroplast gene *rbcL*. Journal of Phycology 38:394–403.

Demin, V. M. 1967. Kharovye vodorosli iz pestrotsvetnykh otlozhenii Donskoï Luki [Taxonomic Characters of Fossil Charophytes. Fossil Algae from USSR]. Izdat Nauk SSSR. Moscow. p. 23–29.

Detraz, M., & Pierre-Olivier Mojon. 1989. Evolution paléogéographique de la marge jurassienne de la Téthys du Tithonique-Portlandien au Valanginien: Corrélations biostratigraphique et séquentielle des faciès marins à continentaux. Eclogae Geologicae Helvetiae 82(1):37–112.

Dollfus, Gustave F., & Paul H. Fritel. 1919. Catalogue raisonné des characées fossiles du bassin de Paris. Bulletin de la Société géologique de France (4ème série) 19:243–261.

Donze, Pierre. 1955. Nouvelles espèces de charophytes dans les niveaux de la limite jurassico-crétacé du Jura, des Alpes-Maritimes et de la Provence. Bulletin de la Société Géologique de France (6ème série) 5:287–290, pl. xiii.

Ducreux, Georges. 1975. Corrélations et morphogenèse chez le *Chara vulgaris* L. cultivé in vitro. Revue générale de Botanique 82:215–357.

Dumortier, Barthelemy C. 1822. Commentationes botanicae. Observations dédiées à la Société d'Horticulture de Tournay. Ch. Casterman-Dieu. Tournay. 117 p.

Dyck, Lawrence A. 1970. Morphological, chemical and developmental studies of *Chara* oosporangial walls. Ph.D. dissertation. Washington University. Missouri. 207 p.

Edwards, David S., & A. Geoffrey Lyon. 1983. Algae from the Rhynie Chert. Botanical Journal of the Linnean Society 86:37–55.

Ehrenberg. 1858. Über fortschreitende Erkenntnis massenhafter mikroskopischer Lebensformen in den untersten silurischen Thonschichten bei Petersburg. Monatsberichte der Königlichen Preussischen Akademie der Wissenschaften zu Berlin 5:295–311 (Band 1859).

Ettingshausen, Constantin Frieherr von. 1872. Die fossile Flora von Sagor in Krain. 1 Theil. Denkschriften der Kaiserlichen Akademie der Wissenschaften. Kaiserlich-Koeniglichen Hof- und Staatsdruckerei, Wien. Mathematisch-naturwissenschaftliche classe, Band 32, Abtheilung 1:159–199, 10 pl.

Feist, Monique. 1979. Charophytes at the Cretaceous/Tertiary boundary. New data and present state of knowledge. *In* W. Kegel Christensen & T. Birkelund, eds., Cretaceous Tertiary Boundary events Symposium, University of Copenhagen, II Proceedings. Copenhagen. p. 88–94.

———. 1981. Charophytes du Crétacé moyen et données nouvelles sur l'évolution des Clavatoracées. Cretaceous Research 2:319–330.

Feist, Monique, Shashi B. Bhatia, & P. Yadagiri. 1991. On the oldest representative of the family Characeae and its relationships with the Porocharaceae. Bulletin de la Société Botanique de France, Actualités Botaniques 138:25–32.

Feist, Monique, & Elisabeth Brouwers. 1990. A new *Tolypella* from the Ocean Point dinosaur locality, Northslope, Alaska, and the Late Cretaceous to Paleocene nitelloid charophytes. U.S. Geological Survey Bulletin 1990-F:1–7, 1 pl.

Feist, Monique, & Fernando Colombo. 1983. La limite Crétacé-Tertiaire dans le nord-est de l'Espagne, du point de vue des charophytes. Géologie Méditerranéenne 10(3–4):303–326.

Feist, Monique, & René Cubaynes. 1984. Découverte de charophytes dans le Lias du Sud de la France. Implications paléo-écologiques et phylogénétiques. Comptes Rendus de l'Académie des Sciences de Paris 299:593–596.

Feist, Monique, & Raimund Feist. 1997. Oldest record of a bisexual plant. Nature 385:401.

Feist, Monique, & Pierre Freytet. 1983. Conséquences stratigraphiques de la répartition des charophytes dans le Campanien et le Maastrichtien du Languedoc. Géologie Méditerranéenne 10(3–4):291–301.

Feist, Monique, Patrick Génot, & Nicole Grambast-Fessard. 2003. Ancient Dasycladales and Charophyta: Convergences and differences, with special attention to *Munieria baconica* Deecke. Phycologia 42:123–132.

Feist, Monique, & Nicole Grambast-Fessard. 1982. Clé de détermination pour les genres de charophytes. Paléobiologie continentale 13(2):1–28.

———. 1984. New Porocharaceae from the Bathonian of Europe: Phylogeny and palaeoecology. Palaeontology 27(2):295–305.

————. 1985. Questions sur la nature et l'habitat des charophytes paléozoïques. Actes 110ème Congrès National des Sociétés Savantes (Section Science) 5:65–75.

————. 1991. The genus concept in Charophyta: Evidence from Palaeozoic to recent. *In* R. Riding, ed., Calcareous Algae and Stromatolites. Springer-Verlag. Berlin, New York. p. 189–203.

Feist, Monique, Robert D. Lake, & Christopher J. Wood. 1995. Charophyte biostratigraphy of the Purbeck and Wealden of southern England. Palaeontology 38:407–442.

Feist Monique, & Michel Ringeade. 1977. Etude biostratigraphique et paléobotanique (charophytes) des formations continentales d'Aquitaine, de l'Eocène supérieur au Miocène inférieur. Bulletin de la Société Géologique de France (series 7) 19(2):341–354, pl. x–xiii.

Feist, Monique, & Zhen Wang. 1995. The species concept in Clavatoraceae (fossil Charophyta) reviewed. Taxon 44:351–361.

Feist-Castel, Monique. 1971. Sur les charophytes fossiles du bassin tertiaire d'Alès. Géobios 4:157–172, 3 pl.

————. 1972. Charophytes éocènes de la région montpelliéraine. Paléobiologie continentale 3(1):1–22, 6 pl.

————. 1973. Observations nouvelles sur la paroi des fructifications chez les charophytes. Geobios 6(4):239–242, 3 pl.

————. 1975. Répartition des charophytes dans le Paléocène et l'Eocène du bassin d'Aix-en-Provence. Bulletin de la Société de Géologie de France (series 7) 17(1):88–97.

————. 1977a. Evolution of the charophyte floras in the upper Eocene and lower Oligocene of the Isle of Wight. Palaeontology 20(1):143–157.

————. 1977b. Description du nouveau genre *Krassavinella* (charophytes, Characeae) et répartition de *K. lagenalis* (Straub) dans l'Oligocène Supérieur de la Molasse suisse. Eclogae Geologicae Helvetiae 70(3):771–775, 1 pl.

————. 1977c. Etude floristique et biostratigraphique des charophytes dans les séries du Paléogène de Provence. Géologie Méditerranéenne 4(2):109–138.

Flajs, Gerd. 1977. Die Ultrastrukturen des Kalkalgenskeletts. Palaeontographica (Abt. B) 160(4–6):69–128.

Gadek, Paul, Peter G. Wilson, & Christopher J. Quinn. 1996. Phylogenetic reconstruction in Myrtaceae using *matK*, with particular reference to the position of *Psiloxylon* and *Heteropyxis*. Australian Systematic Botany 9:283–290.

Gaillon, Benjamin. 1833. Aperçu d'histoire naturelle et observations sur les limites qui séparent le règne végétal du règne animal. Imprimerie Le Roy-Mabille. Boulogne. 35 p., 1 pl.

Galbrun, Bruno, Monique Feist, Fernando Colombo, Robert Rocchia, & Yvette Tambareau. 1993. Magnetostratigraphy and biostratigraphy of Cretaceous-Tertiary continental deposits, Ager Basin, Province of Lerida, Spain. Palaeogeography, Palaeoclimatology, Palaeoecology 102:41–52.

Garbary, David J., Karen Renzaglia, & Jeffrey G. Duckett. 1993. The phylogeny of land plants: A cladistic analysis based on male gametogenesis. Plant Systematics and Evolution 188:237–269.

Gao Qin-qin, Du Pin-de, Huang Zhi-bin, Wu Xin-ying, Li Meng, & Tan Ze-jin. 2002. Early Carboniferous charophytes from northern and central Tarim Basin. Acta Micropalaeontologica Sinica 19(3):288–300. In Chinese, English abstract.

Gebhardt, Ute, & Jörg Schneider. 1985. *Stomochara* aus den Mansfelder Schichten (Stefan) der Saale-Senke und der erste sichere Nachweis von Characeen Thalli in Paläozoikum. Freiberger Forschungshefte (series C) 400:37–43.

Gensel, Patricia G., & Dianne Edwards. 2001. Plants Invade the Land: Evolutionary & Environmental Perspectives. Columbia University Press. New York. 304 p.

Gess, R. W., & N. Hiller. 1995. Late Devonian charophytes from the Witteberg group, South Africa. Review of Palaeobotany and Palynology 89:417–428.

Gmelin, Carl C. 1826. Flora Badensis Alsatica et confinium regionum cis et transrhenana plantes a lacu Bodamico usque ad confluentem Mosellae et Rheni sponte nascentes exhibens secundum systema sexuale cum iconibus ad naturam delineatis, vol. IV. Müller. Carlsruhe. 708 p.
Chara, p. 643–647.

Gradstein, F. M., F. P. Agterberg, J. O. Ogg, J. Hardenbol, P. Van Veen, J. Thierry, & Huang Z. 1994. A Mesozoic time scale. Journal of Geophysycal Research 99(B12):24,051–24,074.

Graham, Linda E. 1993. Origin of Land Plants. John Wiley & Sons. New York. 287 p.

Grambast, Louis. 1956a. La plaque basale des Characées. Comptes Rendus des Séances de l'Académie des Sciences, Paris (series D) 242:2,585–2,587.

————. 1956b. Le genre *Gyrogona* Lmk. (Characeae). Comptes Rendus Sommaires des Séances de la Société géologique de France 14:278–280.

————. 1956c. Sur la déhiscence de l'oospore chez *Chara vulgaris* L. et la systématique de certaines *Characeae* fossiles. Revue générale de Botanique 63:331–336.

————. 1957. Ornementation de la gyrogonite et systématique chez les charophytes fossiles. Revue générale de Botanique 64:339–362, 4 pl.

————. 1958. Etude sur les charophytes tertiaires d'Europe Occidentale et leurs rapports avec les formes actuelles. Unpublished Master's thesis. University of Paris. Paris. 286 p.

————. 1959a. Tendances évolutives dans le phylum des charophytes. Comptes Rendus des Séances l'Académie des Sciences, Paris (series D) 249:557–559.

————. 1959b. Extension chronologique des genres chez les *Charoideae*. Société des éditions Technip. Paris. p. 1–12.

————. 1961. Remarques sur la systématique et la répartition stratigraphique des Characeae prétertiaires. Comptes Rendus Sommaires des Séances de la Société géologique de France 7:200–201.

———. 1962a. Sur l'intérêt stratigraphique des charophytes fossiles: Exemples d'application au Tertiaire parisien. Comptes Rendus Sommaires de la Société Géologique de France 7:207–209.

———. 1962b. Classification de l'embranchement des charophytes. Naturalia Monspeliensia (série Botanique) 14:63–86.

———. 1963. Charophytes du Trias. Etat des connaissances acquises, intérêt phylogénétique et stratigraphique. Mémoires du Bureau de Recherches Géologiques et Minières 15:567–569.

———. 1966a. Un nouveau type structural chez les Clavatoracées; son intérêt phylogénétique et stratigraphique. Comptes Rendus des Séances l'Académie des Sciences, Paris (series D) 262:1,929–1,932.

———. 1966b. Structure de l'utricule et phylogénie chez les Clavatoracées. Comptes Rendus des Séances de l'Académie des Sciences, Paris (series D) 262:2,207–2,210, 3 pl.

———. 1966c. Remarques sur le genre *Nodosoclavator* Maslov emend. (charophytes). Comptes Rendus Sommaires de la Société Géologique de France 1966(7):269–270.

———. 1967. La série évolutive *Perimneste-Atopochara* (charophytes). Comptes Rendus des Séances de l'Académie des Sciences, Paris (series D) 264:581–584, 4 pl.

———. 1968. Evolution of the utricle in the charophyte genera *Perimneste* Harris and *Atopochara* Peck. Journal of the Linnean Society of London (Botany) 61(384):5–11, 3 pl.

———. 1969. La symétrie de l'utricule chez les Clavatoracées et sa signification phylogénétique. Comptes Rendus des Séances de l'Académie des Sciences, Paris (series D) 269:878–881, 4 pl.

———. 1970. Origine et évolution des *Clypeator* (charophytes). Comptes Rendus de l'Académie des Sciences, Paris (series D) 271:1,964–1,967, 4 pl.

———. 1971. Remarques phylogénétiques et biochronologiques sur les *Septorella* du Crétacé terminal de Provence et les charophytes associées. Paléobiologie continentale 2(2):1–38, 29 pl.

———. 1972a. Etude sur les charophytes tertiaires d'Europe Occidentale. I. Genre *Tectochara*. Paléobiologie continentale 3(2):1–30, 8 pl.

———. 1972b. Principes de l'utilisation stratigraphique des charophytes. Application au Paléogène d'Europe Occidentale. Colloque d'Orsay 1970. Mémoires du Bureau des Recherches Géologiques et Minières 77(1):319–328.

———. 1974. Phylogeny of the Charophyta. Taxon 23:463–481.

———. 1975. Charophytes du Crétacé supérieur de la région de Cuenca. *In* Caja Provincial de Ahorros de Cuenca, ed., Reunión de campo sobre el Cretácico de la Serranía de Cuenca. Symposium sobre el Cretácico de la Cordillera Ibérica 1974, Cuenca. Cuenca. Imprenta Magerit, Coslada. Madrid. p. 67–83, 6 pl.

———. 1977a. Étude sur les charophytes tertiaires d'Europe Occidentale. II. Espèces nouvelles de l'Éocène inférieur. Paléobiologie continentale 8(1):1–27, 7 pl.

———. 1977b. Rôle possible de la multiplication végétative dans l'histoire de certains groupes: L'exemple des charophytes au Crétacé terminal. Bulletin de la Société botanique de France 124:149–152.

Grambast, Louis, & Nicole Grambast. 1954. Sur la position systématique de quelques charophytes tertiaires. Revue Générale de Botanique 61:665–671.

———. 1955. Les Raskyelloideae, sous-famille fossile des Characeae. Comptes Rendus de l'Académie des Sciences 240:999–1,001.

Grambast, Louis, & Nicole Grambast-Fessard. 1981. Etude sur les charophytes tertiaires d'Europe Occidentale. III. Le genre *Gyrogona*. Paléobiologie continentale 12(2):1–35, 6 pl.

Grambast, Louis, & Guillermo Gutierrez. 1977. Espèces nouvelles de charophytes du Crétacé supérieur terminal de la province de Cuenca (Espagne). Paléobiologie continentale 8(2):1–34, 15 pl.

Grambast, Louis, & Jacob Lorch. 1968. Une flore de charophytes du Crétacé inférieur du Proche-Orient. Naturalia monspeliensia (série Botanique) 19:47–56, 6 pl.

Grambast, Louis, & Ingeborg Soulié-Märsche. 1972. Sur l'ancienneté et la diversification des *Nitellopsis* (charophytes). Paléobiologie continentale 3(3):1–14.

Grambast-Fessard, Nicole. 1980. Les charophytes du Montien de Mons (Belgique). Review of Palaeobotany and Palynology 30:67–88.

———. 1986. Deux nouveaux représentants du genre *Ascidiella* (Clavatoraceae, Charophyta). Geobios 19(2):255–260.

Grambast-Fessard, Nicole, Monique Feist, & Zhen Wang. 1989. Concerning rejected proposal 781 to conserve *Trochiliscus* (fossil Charophyta). Taxon 38(4):641–643, fig. 1–4.

Grambast-Fessard, Nicole, & Miguel Ramalho. 1985. Charophytes du Jurassique supérieur du Portugal. Revue de Micropaléontologie 28(1):58–66, 2 pl.

Gray, Samuel F. 1821. A natural arrangement of British plants according to their relations to each other. London. vol. 1, 824 p., vol. 2, 760 p.

Groves, James. 1916. On the name *Lamprothamnus* Braun. Journal of Botany 54:336–337.

———. 1924. *Clavator* Reid et Groves. Journal of Botany 62:116–117.

———. 1926. Charophyta. *In* E. M. Reid & M. E. J. Chandler, eds., The Bembridge Flora. I. Catalogue of Cainozoic Plants. British Museum, Natural History. London. p. 165–173.

———. 1933. Charophyta. *In* W. Jongmans, ed., Fossilium Catalogus II, Plantae, pars 19. Junk. Berlin. p. 1–74.

Groves, James, & G. R. Bullock-Webster. 1920. The British Charophyta, vol. 1. The Ray Society. London. 141 p., 20 pl.

———. 1924. The British Charophyta, vol. 2. The Ray Society. London. 129 p., 45 pl.

Guerlesquin, Micheline. 1984. Nombres chromosomiques et ploïdie chez les charophytes. Cryptogamie Algologie 5:115–126.

———. 1986. *Lamprothamnium papulosum* (Wallr.) J. Gr., Characée, espèce halophile en régression. Cryptogamie Algologie 7(3):182–183.

Hacquaert, Armand L. 1932. Notes sur les genres *Sycidium* et *Trochiliscus*. Bulletin Musée Royal Histoire Naturelle, Belgique 8(30):1–22.

Hao Yichun, Ruan Peihua, Zhou Xiugao, Song Qishan, Yang Guodong, Cheng Shuwei, & Wei Zhenxin. 1983. [Middle Jurassic–Tertiary deposits and Ostracod-Charophyta fossil assemblages of Xining and Minhe basins]. Earth Science, Journal of the Wuhan College of Geology 23:1–219, 44 pl. In Chinese with English abstract, p. 177.

Hardenbol, Jan, Jacques Thierry, Martin B. Farley, Tierry Jacquin, Pierre-Charles de Graciansky, & Peter R. Vail. 1998. Mesozoic and Cenozoic chronostratigraphic framework of European Basins. Special Publication, Society for Sedimentary Geology 60:3–13.

Harris, Thomas M. 1939. British Purbeck Charophyta. British Museum (Natural History). London. 83 p., 17 pl.

Heckel, Philip. 1972. Recognition of ancient shallow marine environments. *In* J. Keith Rigby & William K. Hamblin, eds., Recognition of Ancient Sedimentary Environments. SEPM Special Publication 16:226–286.

Heer, Oswald. 1855. Flora Tertiaria Helvetiae I. Winterthur. Wurster. p. 1–117, 50 pl.

Hennings, P. 1897. Beitrage zur Pilzflora Südamerikas, II. Hedwigia 36:190–246.

Hillis, David M., Craig Moritz, & Barbara K. Mable. 1996. Molecular Systematics. Sinauer Associates, Inc. Sunderland, Massachusetts. 600 p.

Horn af Rantzien, Henning. 1954. Middle Triassic Charophyta of south Sweden. Opera Botanica 1(2):1–83, 7 pl.

———. 1956a. An annotated check-list of genera of fossil Charophyta. Micropaleontology 2(3):243–256.

———. 1956b. Morphological terminology relating to female charophyte gametangia and fructifications. Botaniska Notiser 109(2):212–259.

———. 1957. Nitellaceous charophyte gyrogonites in the Rajmahal Série (Upper Gondwana) of India, with notes on the flora and stratigraphy. Stockholm Contributions in Geology I(1):1–29, 3 pl.

———. 1959a. Recent charophyte fructifications and their relation to fossil charophyte gyrogonites. Arkiv for Botanik 4(2):165–332, 19 pl.

———. 1959b. Morphological types and organ-genera of Tertiary charophyte fructifications. Stockholm Contributions in Geology IV(2):45–197, 21 pl.

Horn af Rantzien, Henning, & L. Grambast. 1962. Some questions concerning recent and fossil charophyte morphology and nomenclature. Stockholm Contributions in Geology IX(3):135–144.

Horn af Rantzien, Henning, & Sigurd Olsen. 1949. A suggested starting-point for the nomenclature of Charophyta. Svensk Botanisk Tidskrift 43:98–106.

Hoshaw, Robert W., & James R. Rosowski. 1973. Isolation and purification methods for microscopic algae. *In* J. R. Stein, ed., Handbook of Phycological Methods, vol. 1. Cambridge University Press. Cambridge. p. 53–68.

Hu Jimin, & Zeng Denim. 1982. The palaeontological atlas of Hunan. Charophyta. Geological Memoirs 2(1):543–595, 952–967, pl. 359–394.

Hutchinson, G. Evelyn. 1975. A Treatise on Limnology, vol. 3, Limnological Botany. John Wiley & Sons. New York. 660 p.

Hy, Félix C. 1889. Sur les modes de ramification et de cortication dans la famille des Characées et les caractères qu'ils peuvent fournir à la classification. Bulletin de la Société botanique de France 36:393–398.

———. 1913. Les Characées de France. Bulletin de la Société botanique de France 60(26):1–47.

Imahori, Kozo. 1954. Ecology, phytogeography and taxonomy of the Japanese Charophyta. Kanazawa University. Kanazawa, Japan. 234 p., 66 fig., 41 pl.

Ishchenko, T. A., & A. A. Ishchenko. 1982. Novaia nakhodka kharofitov v verkhniem silure Podolii [New finds of Charophyta in the upper Silurian of Podolia]. *In* J. V. Teslenko, ed., Sistématika i èvolutsia drevnik rastenii Ukraini. Naukowa Dumka. Kiev. p. 21–32, pl. 5–6. In Ukrainian.

Ishchenko, T. A., & L. Ya. Saidakovsky. 1975. Nakhodka kharofitov v Silure Podolii [Charophyte finds in the Silurian deposits of Podolia]. Doklady Akadademii Nauk SSSR 220(1):1–80, pl. I–XV. In Ukrainian.

Iyengar, M. O. P. 1958. *Nitella terrestris* sp. nov., a terrestrial charophyte from south India. Bulletin of the Botanical Society of Bengal 12:85–90.

Jeppsson, Lennart. 1998. Silurian oceanic events: Summary of general characteristics. *In* E. Landing & M. E. Johnson, eds., Silurian Cycles. New York State Museum Bulletin 491:239–257.

Jiang Yuan, Zhang Zerun, & Meng Xiangsong. 1985. [Early Cretaceous charophyte flora from southern Henan and its stratigraphical significance]. Acta Micropaleontologica Sinica 2(2):161–168. In Chinese with abstract and table of contents in English.

John, David M., & Jenny A. Moore. 1987. An SEM study of the oospore of some *Nitella* species (Charales, Chlorophyta) with descriptions of wall ornamentation and an assessment of its taxonomic importance. Phycologia 26:334–355.

John, David M., Jenny A. Moore, & Dawn R. Green. 1990. Preliminary observations on the structure and ornamentation of the oosporangial wall in *Chara* (Charales, Charophyta). British Phycological Journal 25:1–24.

Johnson, Leigh A., & Douglas E. Soltis. 1994. *MatK* DNA sequences and phylogenetic reconstruction in *Saxifragaceae* s. str. Systematic Botany 19:143–156.

———. 1995. Phylogenetic inference in Saxifragaceae *sensu stricto* and *Gilia* (Polemoniaceae) using *matK* sequences. Annals of the Missouri Botanical Garden 82:149–175.

Jones, Timothy P., Steven M. Fortier, Allan Pentecost, & Margaret E. Collinson. 1996. Stable carbon and oxygen compositions of recent charophyte oosporangia and water from Malham Tarn, U.K. Biogeochemistry 34:99–112.

Jost, Ludwig. 1895. Beiträge zur Kenntniss der Coleochaeteen. Berichte der Deutschen Botanischen Gesellschaft 8:433–452.

Judd, Walter S., Christopher S. Campbell, Elisabeth A. Kellogg, Peter F. Stevens, & Michael J. Donoghue. 2002. Plant Systematics: A Phylogenetic Approach, 2nd ed. Sinauer. Sunderland, Massachusetts. 576 p.

Karczewska, Jawiga, & N. P. Kyansep-Romaschkina. 1979. Revision of the late Cretaceous genus *Mongolichara* Kyansep-Romaschkina. Acta Palaeontologica Polonica 24(4):423–427, 2 pl.

Karczewska, Jadwiga, & Maria Ziembińska-Tworzydło. 1970. Upper Cretaceous Charophyta from the Nemegt basin, Gobi Desert. Palaeontologica Polonica 21(1970):121–144, 5 pl.

———. 1972. Lower Tertiary Charophyta from the Nemegt Basin, Gobi Desert. Palaeontologica Polonica 27:51–81, 20 pl.

———. 1981. New Upper Cretaceous Charophyta from the Nemegt basin, Gobi Desert. Palaeontologica Polonica 42:97–146, 18 pl.

Karol, Kenneth G., Richard M. McCourt, Matthew T. Cimino, & Charles F. Delwiche. 2001. The closest living relatives of plants. Science 294:2,351–2,353.

Karpinsky, A. P. 1906. Die Trochilisken. Mémoires du Comité Géologique (new series) 27:1–86, 3 pl. In Russian, German translation, p. 87–166.

Katsuhara, M., & Masashi Tazawa. 1986. Salt tolerance in *Nitellopsis obtusa.* Protoplasma 135:155–16.

Kenrick, Paul, & Peter R. Crane. 1997. The Origin and Early Diversification of Land Plants. Smithsonian Institution Press. Washington, D.C. 441 p.

Kenrick, Paul, & Li Cheng-Sen. 1998. An early, non-calcified, dasycladalean alga from the Lower Devonian of Yunnan Province, China. Review of Palaeobotany and Palynology 100:73–88.

Khan, Mahmood, & Y. S. R. K. Sarma. 1984. Cytogeography and cytosystematics of Charophyta. *In* D. E. G. Irvine & D. M. John, eds., Systematics Association Special Volume Number 27, Systematics of the Green Algae. Academic Press. London and Orlando. p. 303–330.

Kidston, Robert, & William H. Lang. 1921. On old red sandstone plants showing structure, from the Rhynie Chert Bed, Aberdeenshire. Part V. The Thallophyta occurring in the peat-bed; the succession of the plants throughout a vertical section of the bed, and the conditions of accumulation and preservation of the deposit. Transactions of the Royal Society of Edinburgh 52(part IV, no. 33):855–902, 1 fig., 10 pl.

Kisielevsky, Franciszek J. 1967. Novye dannye o Triasovykh Kharophytakh Prikaspiïskoï vpadiny [New data on the Lower Triassic charophytes from the Caspian Depression]. Voprosy Geologii Yuzhnogo Urala i Povolzh'ya. Saratovskogo Universiteta Saratov 4:37–44. In Russian.

———. 1980. Novye vidy Verkhnepermskikh Kharophitov [New species of Charophyta from the upper Permian]. Voprosy Geologii Yuzhnogo Urala i Povolzh'ya. Saratovskogo Universiteta Saratov 19:3–11. In Russian.

———. 1993a. Biostratigrafiia verkhnepermskika otlozheniï vostoka Vostochnoevropeïskoï Platformy po charophytam [Biostratigraphy of upper Permian deposits from the east of the eastern European platform after charophytes]. Nedra Povolzhia i Prikaspia, p. 16–18. In Russian.

———. 1993b. Kharophity iz Inderskovo gorizonta Prikaspiïskoï Vpadiny [Charophyta from the Inder horizon of the Caspian depression]. Paleontologicheskii Zhurnal 1:87–94. In Russian.

———. 1993c. Kharophity iz verkhnepermskikh otlozheniï vostochnoï chasti Vostochno Evropeïskoï Platformy [Permian Charophyta from the east of the Eastern European Platform]. Paleontologicheskii Zhurnal 3:97–109, 2 pl. In Russian.

———. 1996. Kharophyty. *In* N. K. Esaulova, V. R. Lozovsky, & A. Yu Rozanov, eds., Stratotypy i opornye razrezy verkhneï Permi Povolzh'ia [Stratotypes and Reference Sections of the Upper Permian of Regions of the Volga and Kama Rivers]. University of Kazan. Kazan. p. 294–300, pl. 5.6-1 and 5.6-2. In Russian.

Kiss, John Z., & Andrew Staehelin. 1993. Structural polarity in the *Chara* rhizoid, a reevaluation. American Journal of Botany 80(3):273–282.

Knoll, Andrew H. 1984. Patterns of extinction in the fossil record of vascular plants. *In* Matthew H. Nitecki, ed., Extinctions. University of Chicago Press. Chicago. p. 21–68.

Knowlton, F. H. 1888. Description of a new fossil species of the genus *Chara.* Botanical Gazette 13:156–157.

Kozur, Heinz. 1973. Beiträge zur Stratigraphie und Paläontologie der Trias. Geologische und Paläontologische Mitteilungen Innsbruck 3(1):1–37.

Kranz, Harold D., & Volker A. R. Huss. 1996. Molecular evolution of pteridophytes and their relationship to seed plants: Evidence from complete 18S rRNA gene sequences. Plant Systematics and Evolution 202:1–11.

Krassavina, L. K. 1966. Charophyta fossilia nova et curiosa e sedimentis quaternariis regionis in fluxu medio fluminis kama jacentis. Novitatis Systematica Plantarum non vascularium 3:115–125. In Russian and Latin.

———. 1971. Sravnitel'noie' isuchenie sovremennykh i iskopaemykh kharofitov: Plodonoshenyia *Nitellopsis obtusa* i guiroguonity vidov *Tectochara* [A comparative study of recent and fossil Charophyta: Of the fructification in *Nitellopsis obtusa* and of the gyrogonites in the species of *Tectochara*]. Botanicheskii Zhurnal 56(1):106–117. In Russian.

———. 1978. Interesnye nakhodki iskopaemykh kharovykh vodorosleï iz Vostochnoï Sibiri [Interesting records of the fossil Charophyta from eastern Siberia]. Botanicheskii Zhurnal 63:226–233, 2 pl. In Russian.

Krause, Werner. 1984. Rote Liste der Armleuchteralgen (Charophyta). *In* J. Blab, E. Nowak, & W.

Trautmann, eds., Rote Liste der gefährdeten Tiere und Pflanzen in der Bundesrepublik Deutschland. Kilda-Verlag. Greven. p. 184–187.

Kunth, Carol S. 1815. *In* Aimé Bonpland & Alexander von Humboldt, eds., Nova genera et species plantarum, quas in peregrinatione ad plagam aequinoctialem orbis novi collegerunt, descripserunt, partim adumbraverunt A. Bonpland et A. de Humboldt. Ex schedis autographis Amati Bonplandi in ordinem digessit C. S. Kunth, accedunt Alexandri de Humboldt notationes ad geographiam plantarum spectantes. Sumtibus Librariae Graeco-Latino-Germanicae. Lutetiae. Paris. vol. 1, 377 p.
Characeae Richard, p. 38.
7 vol., 1815-1825.

Kützing, Friedrich, T. 1843. Phycologia Generalis, oder Anatomie, Physiologie und Systemkunde der Tange. Brockhaus. Leipzig. XXXII + 459 p., 80 pl.
Charae, p. 313–321, pl. 38–39.

Kyansep-Romaschkina, N. P. 1974. Znachenié kharovykh vodorosleï dlya stratigrafiï Mezozoïskikh otlozheniï Fergany i paleolimnologuicheskikh rekonstruktsiï [Importance of charophytes for the stratigraphy of Mesozoic sediments from Fergana and for the palaeolimnologic reconstitutions]. Probl issled drtevnikh ozer evrazii L. Nauka. Leningrad. p. 21–37, fig.125–126, pl. I–III.

———. 1975. Nekotorye pozdneiurkie i melovye kharophity Mongolii [Some charophytes from the Upper Jurassic and Cretaceous of Mongolia]. Iskoppaemaya Fauna Flora i Mongolii. Sovmestnaya sovestsko-Mongolyskaya paleontologicheskaya ekspediskaya. Trutsy 2:181–204, 6 pl.
In Russian.

———. 1980. Pozdnemelovye kharovye vodorosli iz ozernykh otlozhenii Mongolii i Zakavkaz'ia [Charophytes from Upper Cretaceous lacustrine deposits of Mongolia and Transcaucasia]. *In* G. G. Martinson & N. P. Kyansep-Romaschkina, Limnobios drevnikh ozernykh basseinov Evrazii. Nauka. Leningrad. p. 71–90, fig. 123–124, 2 pl.
In Russian.

de Lamarck, Jean Baptiste P. A. de Monet. 1801. Système des Animaux Sans Vertèbres. Published by the author. Paris. 432 p.

———. 1804. Suite des mémoires sur les fossiles des environs de Paris. Annales du Museum d'Histoire Naturelle 5:349–357.
Gyrogona, p. 355–356.

———. 1822. Histoire Naturelle des Animaux Sans Vertèbres, vol. 1. Verdière. Paris. 711 p.
Gyrogonites medicaginula, p. 614.

Langangen, Anders. 1974. Ecology and distribution of Norwegian charophytes. Norwegian Journal of Botany 21:31–52.

———. 1979. *Chara canescens* reported from Spitsbergen. Phycologia 18(4):436–437.

Langer, Wolfhart. 1976. Neufunde von *Sycidium* G. Sandberger (nova class., Charophyta?) aus dem Devon der Eifel. Paläontologische Zeitschrift 50(3/4):209–221.

———. 1991. Über Charophyta und einige Foraminiferen aus dem westdeutschen Mitteldevon.

Neues Jahrbuch für Geologie und Paläontologie, Monatshefte 1991(5):307–318.

Leitch, Andrew R. 1989. Formation and ultrastructure of a complex, multilayered wall around the oospore of *Chara* and *Lamprothamnium* (Characeae). British Phycological Journal 24:229–236.

———. 1991. Calcification of the charophyte oosporangium. *In* R. Riding, ed., Calcareous Algae and Stromatolites. Springer-Verlag. Berlin. p. 204–216.

Leitch, Andrew, R., David M. John, & Jenny A. Moore. 1990. The oosporangium of the Characeae (Chlorophyta, Charales). Progress in Phycological Research 7:213–261.

Leman, S. 1812. Note sur la gyrogonite. Nouveau Bulletin des Sciences, Société Philomatique 3(2):208–210, fig. 5, pl. 2.

von Leonhardi, Herman Freiherrn. 1863. Über die böhmischen Characeen. Lotos 13:55–62, 69–80, 110–111, 124–132.

Li Xing-Xue, & Cai Chong-Yang. 1978. [A type-section of Lower Devonian strata in southwestern China with brief notes on the succession and correlation of its plant assemblages.] Acta Geologica Sinica 52:1–12.
In Chinese, with English abstract.

Liere, K., & G. Link. 1995. RNA-binding activity of the matK protein encoded by the chloroplast *trnK* intron from mustard (*Sinapis alba* L.). Nucleic Acids Research 23:917–921.

Lin Huanan. 1989. Cretaceous–early Tertiary charophytes from the Mid-Hebei Province and its adjacent regions. Petroleum Industry Press. p. 1–106, pl. 1–40.

Lin Xiaodong. 1989. [Cretaceous fossil charophytes in Zhejiang]. Editorial office of Geology of Zhejiang. Hangzhou, Zhejiang. p. 1–11, 6 pl.
In Chinese.

Lindley, John. 1836. A Natural System of Botany, 2nd ed. Longman, Rees, Orme, Brown, Green, and Longman. London. 526 p.
Charales, p. 414.

Linnaeus [Linné, von Linnaeus], Carl. 1753. Species plantarum, exhibentes plantas rite cognitas, ad genera relatas, cum differentiis specificis, nominibus trivialibus, synonymis selectis, loci natalibus, secundum sexuale digestas, vol. 2. Impensis Laurentii Salvii. Stockholm. vol. 2, p. 561–1,200.
Chara p. 1,156–1,157.

Liu Junying. 1982. [Jurassic charophytes from Sichuan province]. Bulletin of the Institute of Geology, Chinese Academy of Geological Sciences 5:97–110, 2 pl.
In Chinese.

Liu Junying, & Chen Zhongliang. 1992. Discovery of fossil charophytes from the Late Triassic Xujiahe Formation and Early Jurassic Lower Yimen Formation, Sichuan Province, and its significance. Acta Geologica Sinica 66:73–81, 1 pl.

Liu Junying, & Wu Xinying. 1985. [Charophytes from Tugulu group of the Junggar basin]. Bulletin of the Institute of Geology Chinese Academy of Geological Sciences 11:139–153, 4 pl.
In Chinese with English abstract, p. 151.

Liu Xiao-feng, & Zhang Rong-fu. 1994. Charophytes in the Lower Carboniferous of Liaoning Province. Liaoning Geology 1–2:165–171.

Loeblich Jr., Alfred R., & Helen Tappan. 1961. Suprageneric classification of the Rhyzopodea. Journal of Paleontology 35:245–330.

Loiseleur-Deslongchamps, Jean Louis Auguste. 1810. Notice sur les plantes à ajouter à la Flore de France. (Flora Gallica); avec quelques corrections et observations. Sajou. Paris. 172 p., 6 pl. Characeae, p. 135–139.

Lu Hui-nan. 1997. On charophyte genera named by Chinese authors. Acta Micropalaeontologica Sinica 14(4):391–404.
In Chinese, English abstract.

Lu Hui-Nan, & Luo Q. X. 1984. Upper Permian and Triassic fossil charophytes from Xinjiang, with special reference to the development of upper Paleozoic to lower Mesozoic charophyte floras. Acta Micropaleontologica Sinica 1(2):155–169, 3 pl.

———. 1990. [Fossil charophytes from the Tarim Basin, Xinjiang]. Scientific and Technical documents Publishing House. Beijing. 261 p., 48 pl.
In Chinese, English abstract, Latin descriptions.

Lu Huinan, I. Soulié-Märsche, & Wang Qifei. 1996. [Evolution and classification of Palaeozoic charophytes]. Acta Micropaleontologica Sinica 13(1):1–12.
In Chinese, English abstract.

Lu Huinan, & Yuan Xiaoqi. 1991. [Jurassic and Early Cretaceous charophytes from the Bayan hot basin and its neighborhood]. Acta Micropaleobotanica Sinica 8:373–394.
In Chinese, English summary.

Lu Huinan, & Zhang Shanzen. 1990. [New Palaeozoic charophytes of China]. Acta Micropalaeontologica Sinica 7(1):9–17, 1 pl.
In Chinese, English summary.

Lyell, Charles. 1826. On a recent formation of freshwater limestone in Forfarshire and on some recent deposits of freshwater marl. Transactions of the Geological Society of London 2(2):73–96. Appendix on the *Chara* and on its seed-vessel, the gyrogonite, p. 90–94, pl. xii–xiii.

Mädler, Karl. 1952. Charophyten aus dem Nordwestdeutschen Kimmeridge. Geologisches Jahrbuch 67:1–46, 2 pl.

———. 1955. Zur taxonomie der tertiären charophyten. Geologisches Jahrbuch 70:265–328, 4 pl.

Mädler, Karl, & Ulrich Staesche. 1979. Fossile charophyten aus dem Känozoikum (Tertiär und Quartär) der Türkei. Geologisches Jahrbuch B33:81–157, 9 pl.

Magniez, Guy, Pierre Rat, & Henri Tintant. 1960. Découverte d'oogones de charophytes dans le Bathonien marin près de Dijon. Comptes Rendus de l'Académie des Sciences (series D) 250:1,692–1,694.

Mamet, Bernard, Alain Roux, Martine Lapointe, & Louise Gauthier. 1992. Algues ordoviciennes et siluriennes de l'Ile Anticosti (Québec, Canada). Revue de Micropaléontologie 35:211–248.

Margulis, Lynn, John O. Corliss, Michael Melkonian, & David J. Chapman, eds., Heather I. McKhann, editorial coordinator. 1990. Handbook of Protoctista. The structure, cultivation, habitats and life histories of the eukaryotic microoorganisms and their descendants exclusive of animals, plants and fungi. Jones & Bartlett Publishers. Boston. 914 p.

Martin-Closas, Carles. 1988. Découverte de la plaque basale chez les Clavatoraceae (Charophyta). Implications phylogénétiques. Comptes Rendus de l'Académie des Sciences de Paris 306(2):1,131–1,136.

———. 1996. A phylogenetic system of Clavatoraceae (fossil Charophyta). Review of Palaeobotany and Palynology 94:259–293.

Martin-Closas, Carles, R. Bosch, & J. Serra-Kiel. 1999. Biomechanics and evolution of spiralization in charophyte fructifications. In M. H. Kurmann & A. R. Hemsley, eds., The Evolution of Plant Architecture. Royal Botanic Gardens, Kew. London. p. 399–421.

Martin-Closas, Carles, & Nicole Grambast-Fessard. 1986. Les charophytes du Crétacé inférieur de la région de Maestrat (Chaîne ibérique–Catalanides, Espagne). Paléobiologie continentale 15:1–66, 10 pl.

Martin-Closas, Carles, & Michael E. Schudack. 1991. Phylogenetic analysis and systematization of post-Paleozoic charophytes. Bulletin de la Société botanique de France, Actualités botaniques 138(1):53–71.

———. 1997. On the concept of species in fossil Charophyta. A reply to Feist & Wang. Taxon 46:521–525.

Martin-Closas, Carles, & Josep Serra-Kiel. 1991. Evolutionary patterns of Clavatoraceae (Charophyta) in the Mesogean basins analysed according to environmental change during Malm and Lower Cretaceous. Historical Biology 5:291–307.

Martin-Closas, C., J. Serra-Kiel, P. Busquets, & E. Ramos-Guerrero. 1999. New correlation between charophyte and larger foraminifera biozones (middle Eocene, southeastern Pyrenees). Geobios 32:5–18.

Martini, Erlend. 1971. Standard Tertiary and Quaternary calcareous nannoplankton zonation. Proceedings of the 2nd International Congress on Planktonic Microfossils, Rome, 1970. Tecnoscienza 2:739–785.

Maslov, Vladimir Petrovich. 1961. Ne iavliaiutsia li Sitsidii i Khovanelly utrikulami kharophytov? [Are *Sycidium* and *Chovanella* not the utricles of charophytes?]. Doklady Akademii Nauk SSSR 138(3):677–680.
In Russian.

———. 1963a. Vvedenie v izuchenie iskopaemykh kharovykh vodoroslei [Introduction to the study of fossil charophytes]. Trudy Geologicheskogo Instituta, Akademiya Nauk SSSR 82:1–104.
In Russian.

———. 1963b. Prorastanie oospory i iskopaemykh kharophytov i novyi organ-pod [Germination of the oospore in fossil charophytes and a new organ-genus]. Doklady Akademiya Nauk SSSR 152(2):443–445, fig. 1–2.
In Russian.

———. 1966. Nekotorye Kainozoïskie kharophyty Iuga SSSR i metodika ikh izucheniia [Certain Ceno-

zoic charophytes in the south of the USSR and the methods of their studies]. *In* V. P. Maslov & V. A. Vakhrameev, eds., Iskopaemye kharophyty SSSR [Fossil charophytes of the USSR]. Trudy Geologicheskogo Instituta SSSR 143:10–92.
In Russian.

Massieux, Michèle, & Yvette Tambareau. 1978. Charophytes thanétiennes et infra-ilerdiennes des Pyrénées Centrales. Revue de Micropaléontologie 21(3):140–148.

Mattox, Karl R., & Kenneth D. Stewart. 1984. Classification of the green algae: A concept based on comparative cytology. *In* D. E. G. Irvine & D. M. John, eds., Systematics of the Green Algae, The Systematics Association Special Volume Number 27. Academic Press. London and Orlando, Florida. p. 29–72.

Maynard Smith, J. 1978. The Evolution of Sex. Cambridge University Press. Cambridge. 222 p.
Reprinted in 1990.

McCourt, Richard M. 1995. Green algal phylogeny. Trends in Ecology and Evolution 10:159–163.

McCourt, Richard M., Kenneth G. Karol, Michelle T. Casanova, & Monique Feist. 1999. Monophyly of genera and species of Characeae based on *rbc* L sequences, with special reference to Australian and European *Lychnothamnus barbatus* (Characeae: Charophyceae). Australian Journal of Botany 47:361–369.

McCourt, Richard M., Kenneth G. Karol, Micheline Guerlesquin, & Monique Feist. 1996. Phylogeny of extant genera in the family Characeae (Charales, Charophyceae) based on *rbc* L sequences and morphology. American Journal of Botany 83:125–131.

McCourt, Richard M., Susan Meiers, Kenneth G. Karol, & Russell L. Chapman. 1996. Molecular systematics of the Charales. *In* D. B. Chaudhary & S. B. Agrawal, eds., Cytology, Genetics and Molecular Biology of Algae. SPB Publishing. Amsterdam. p. 323–336.

Mebrouk, Fateh, Mahamed Mahboubi, Mustapha Bessedik, & Monique Feist. 1997. L'apport des charophytes à la stratigraphie des formations continentales paléogènes de l'Algérie. Geobios 30:171–177.

Médus, Jacques, Monique Feist, Robert Rocchia, David J. Batten, Daniel Boclet, Fernando Colombo, Yvette Tambareau, & Juliette Villatte. 1988. Prospects for recognition of the palynological Cretaceous/Tertiary boundary and an iridium anomaly in nonmarine facies of the eastern Spanish Pyrenees: A preliminary report. Newsletters on Stratigraphy 18:123–138.

Meiers, Susan, T., Vernon W. Proctor, & Russell L. Chapman. 1999. Phylogeny and biogeography of *Chara* (Charophyta) inferred from 18S rDNA sequences. Australian Journal of Botany 47:347–360.

Meiers, Susan T., W. L. Rootes, Vernon W. Proctor, & Russell L. Chapman. 1997. Phylogeny of the Characeae (Charophyta) inferred from organismal and molecular characters. Archiv für Protistenkunde 148:308–317.

Mein, P. 1989. Updating of MN zones. *In* E. Lindsay, V. Fahlbusch, & P. Mein, eds., European Neogene mammal chronology. NATO ASI Series A, Life Sciences 180:73–90.

Meyen, F. 1827. Beobachtung und Bemerkungen über die Gattung *Chara*. Linnaea 2(1):55–81, pl. 2–3.

Michaux-Ferrière, Nicole, & Ingeborg Soulié-Märsche. 1987. The quantities of DNA in the vegetative nuclei of *Chara vulgaris* and *Tolypella glomerata* (Charophyta). Phycologia 26(4):435–442, 3 fig., 4 tables.

Migula, Walter. 1897. Die Characeen. *In* G. L. Rabenhorst, ed., 1890–1897, Kryptogamen-flora von Deutschland, Oesterreichs und der Schweiz, Bd. 5. Edward Kummer. Leipzig. 765 p., 149 fig.

Mishler, Brent D., & Steven P. Churchill. 1985. Transition to a land flora: Phylogenetic relationships of the green algae and bryophytes. Cladistics 1:305–328.

Mohr, G., P. S. Perlman, & A. M. Lambowitz. 1993. Evolutionary relationships among group II intron-encoded proteins and identification of a conserved domain that may be related to maturase function. Nucleic Acids Research 21:4,991–4,997.

Mojon, Pierre-Olivier. 1989. Charophytes et Ostracodes laguno-lacustres du Jurassique de la Bourgogne (Bathonien) et du Jura septentrional franco-suisse (Oxfordien). Remarques sur les discontinuités émersives du Kimmeridgien du Jura. Revue de Paléobiologie (volume spécial) 3:1–18.

Mojon, Pierre-Olivier, & André Strasser. 1987. Microfaciès, sédimentologie et micro-paléontologie du Purbeckien de Bienne (Jura Suisse occidental). Eclogae Geologicae Helvetiae 80(1):37–58.

Moore, Jenny A. 1986. Charophytes of Great Britain and Ireland. Handbook number 5. Botanical Society of the British Isles. London. 140 p.

———. 1991. *Lamprothamnium papulosum*, a pioneer in the conservation of Characeae and their habitats. Bulletin de la Société botanique de France, Actualités botaniques 138(1):73–74.

Müller, Otto Friedrich. 1778. Flora danica, vol. V, no. 13. Published by the author. Copenhagen. pl. 721–780.
Conferva nidifica, pl. 761.

Musacchio, Eduardo A. 1971. Charophytas de la formación La Amarga (Cretácico inferior), Provincia de Neuquén, Argentina. Revista del Museo de La Plata (new series) 6(Paleontología 37):19–38, 3 pl.

———. 1973. Charophytas y Ostracodos no marinos del grupo Neuquén (Cretácico Superior) en algunos afloramientos de las provincias de Río Negro y Neuquén, República Argentina. Revista del Museo de la Plata (new series) 8(Paleontología 48):1–32, 7 pl.

Nötzold, T. 1965. Die Präparation von Gyrogoniten und Kalkigen Charophyten-Oogonien aus festen Kalksteinen. Monatsberichte Deutschen Akademie Wissenschaften zu Berlin 7(3):216–221.

Nordstedt, Otto. 1889. De Algis et Characeis 4. Über die Hartschale der Characeenfrüchte. Lunds Universitet Årsskrift 25:2–17, fig. 7–44, pl. 1.

Oliver, Daniel. 1877. Flora of Tropical Africa, vol. III, Umbelliferæ to Ebenaceæ. L. Reeve. London. 544 p.

Olsen, Sigurd. 1944. Danish Charophyta. Chorological, ecological and biological investigations. Det Kongelige Danske Videnskabernes Selskab Biologiske Skrifter 3(1):1–240.

Ooi, K. A., Y. Endo, J. Yokoyama, & N. Murakami. 1995. Useful primer designs to amplify DNA fragments of the plastid gene *matK* from angiosperm plants. Journal of Japanese Botany 70:328–331.

Pal, B. P., B. C. Kundu, V. S. Sundaralingam, & G. S. Venkataraman. 1962. Charophyta. Monographs on Algae. India Council of Agricultural Research. New Delhi. 130 p., 296 fig.

Pander, Christian H. 1856. Monographie der fossilen Fische des Silurischen Systems des russisch-baltischen Gouvernements. Geognostische Beeschreibung der russisch-baltischen gouvernements. Kaiserliche Akademie der Wissenschaften. St. Petersburg. x + 91 p., 8 pl.

Papenfuss, George F. 1946. Proposed names for the phyla of Algae. Bulletin of the Torrey Botanical Club 73:217–218.

Peck, Raymond E. 1934a. The North American trochiliscids, Paleozoic Charophyta. Journal of Paleontology 8:83–119.

———. 1934b. Late Paleozoic and early Mesozoic Charophyta. American Journal of Science (series 5) 27:49–55, 1 pl.

———. 1936. Structural trends of the Trochiliscaceae. Journal of Paleontology 10:764–768.

———. 1937. Morrison Charophyta from Wyoming. Journal of Paleontology 11(2):83–90, 1 pl.

———. 1938. A new family of Charophyta from the Lower Cretaceous Texas. Journal of Paleontology 12:173–176, fig. 1, pl. 28.

———. 1941. Lower Cretaceous Rocky Mountain nonmarine microfossils. Journal of Paleontology 15:285–304, p. 42–44.

———. 1957. North American Mesozoic Charophyta. Geological Survey Professional Paper 294-A. United States Government Printing Office. Washington, D.C. 44 p., 8 pl.

———. 1974. On the systematic position of the umbellids. Journal of Paleontology 48(2):409–412.

Peck, Raymond E., & Jerome A. Eyer. 1963a. Representatives of *Chovanella,* a Devonian charophyte in North America. Micropaleontology 9(1):97–100.

———. 1963b. Pennsylvanian, Permian and Triassic Charophyta of North America. Journal of Paleontology 37:835–844, 1 pl.

Peck, Raymond E., & Gustavo A. Morales. 1966. The Devonian and lower Mississippian charophytes of North America. Micropaleontology 12:303–324.

Peck, Raymond E., & Carl C. Reker. 1947. Cretaceous and lower Cenozoic Charophyta from Peru. American Museum Novitates 1369:1–6.

———. 1948. Eocene Charophyta from North America. Journal of Paleontology 22(1):85–90, pl. 21.

Pia, Julius. 1927. Thallophyta. *In* M. Hirmer, ed., Handbuch der Paläobotanik. I. R. Oldenbourg. München, Berlin. p. 31–136.

Poyarkov, Budimir Vladimirovich. 1965. O systematicheskoy polozhenii umbell [Status of *Umbella*]. Doklady Akademiya Nauk SSSR 163:728–730. In Russian.

Prevost, Constant. 1826. Sur une nouvelle gyrogonite ou capsule de *Chara* fossile très abondante dans les meulières d'eau douce dans les environs de Paris. Nouveau Bulletin Société Philomatique 2(3):186–188.

Proctor, Vernon W. 1962. Viability of *Chara* oospores taken from migratory water birds. Ecology 43:528–529.

Racki, Grzegorz. 1982. Ecology of the primitive charophyte algae: A critical review. Neues Jahrbuch für Geologie und Paläontologie, Abhandlungen 162(3):388–399.

Racki, Grzegorz, & Maria Racka. 1981. Ecology of the Devonian charophyte algae from the Holy Cross Mts. Acta Geologica Polonica 31(3/4):213–222, 2 pl.

Racki, G., & J. Sobon-Podgorska. 1992. Givetian and Frasnian calcareous microbiotas of the Holy Cross Mountains. Acta Palaeontologica Polonica 37(2/4):255–289.

Rafinesque, Constantine S. 1815. Analyse de la Nature, ou Tableau de l'Univers et des corps organisés. Published by the author. Palermo. 224 p. Characias, p. 209.

Rásky, Klara. 1945. Fossile Charophyten-Früchte aus Ungarn. Ungarischen Naturwissenschaftlichen Museums 2:1–75, 3 pl.

Reid, Clement R., & James Groves. 1916. Preliminary report on the Purbeck Characeae. Proceedings of the Royal Society of London (series B) 89:252–256, 1 pl.

———. 1921. The Charophyta of the Lower Headon Beds of Hordle (Hordwell) Cliffs (South Hampshire). Quarterly Journal of the Geological Society 77:175–192, 3 pl.

Reitlinger, E. A., & M. V. Jarzewa. 1958. Novye Kharofity verkhnefamenskikh otlozhenii Russkoi Platformy [New charophytes of the upper Famennian deposits of the Russian platform]. Doklady Akademiya Nauk SSSR 123(6):1,113–1,116, 1 pl. In Russian.

Richard, L. Cl. 1815. *See* Kunth, 1815.

Ridley, Henry N. 1930. The dispersal of plants throughout the world. L. Reeve & Co. Ashford, Kent. 744 p.

Riveline, Jeanine. 1986. Les charophytes du Paléogène et du Miocène inférieur d'Europe occidentale. Cahiers de Paléontologie. Centre National de la Recherche Scientifique. Paris. 227 p., 38 pl.

Riveline, J., J.-P. Berger, M. Feist, C. Martin-Closas, M. Schudack, & I. Soulié-Märsche. 1996. European Mesozoic-Cenozoic charophyte biozonation. Bulletin de la Société Géologique de France 167(3):453–468.

Riveline, Jeanine, & Michel Perreau. 1979. Les Characées à incrustation calcaire du gisement de Mutigny (Marne). Revue de Micropaléontologie 22(1):37–43.

Roth, A. G. 1797. Catalecta Botanica quibus plantae novae et minus cognitae describuntur atque illustrantur, vol. I. G. Mülleriano. Lipsiae. viii + 244 + 10 p., 8 pl.

Ruprecht, F. J. 1845. Distributio cryptogarum vascularum in imperio Rossico. Beiträge zur Pflanzenkunde des Russischen Reiches, fasc. 3. Kaiserlichen Academie der Wissenschaften. St. Petersburg. 56 p.

Sahni, B., & S. R. Naranaya Rao. 1943. On *Chara sausari,* sp. nov. a *Chara* (*sensu stricto*) from the intertrappean cherts at Sausar in the Deccan. Proceedings of the National Academy of Sciences of India 13:215–223.

Saidakovsky, L. Ya. 1960. Biostratigraphichna skhema nizhnogo Triasi Dnieprovsko-Donetskoï Zapadini [Biostratigraphical scheme of the Lower Triassic from the Dniepr-Donetz depression]. Akademiya Nauk Ukraïni RSR, Geologiczeski Zhurnal 20(6):50–57. In Ukrainian.

———. 1962. Kharophity iz Triasovykh pestrotsvetov Bol'shovo Dombassa [Charophytes du Trias bigarré du Grand Donbass]. Doklady Akademiya Nauk SSSR 145(5):1,141–1,144, pl. 1. In Russian.

———. 1966. Biostratigraphiia Triasovykh Otlozheniï Iuga Russkoi Platformy [Biostratigraphy of the Triassic deposits of the south of the Russian Platform]. *In* V. P. Maslov & V. A. Vakhrameev, Iskopaemye kharophyty SSSR [Fossil charophytes of the USSR], Trudy Geologicheskogo Instituta SSSR 143:93–144, 4 pl. In Russian.

———. 1968. Kharofity iz triasa prikaspiyskoy vpadiny [Charophyta from the Triassic of the Caspian depression]. Paleontologicheskii Zhurnal 2:95–110, 1 pl. In Russian; translated in Paleontological Journal 1968, 2(2):324–347, 1 pl.

———. 1971. Novyi rod Triasovykh Kharophytov [A new genus of Triassic charophytes]. Geologiczeski Zhurnal SSSR 31(3):121–122. In Russian.

———. 1989. Kharofity iz verkhnekamennougol'nykh i permskikh otlozheniï Evropeïskoï chasti SSSR [Charophytes in deposits from Upper Carboniferous and Permian in the European part of USSR]. Paleontologicheskii Zhurnal 1989:84–94, 1 pl. In Russian.

———. 1993. Permskie i Triasovskie Charophyta zemnoho shara [Permian and Triassic Charophyta of the world]. Algologiya 3(2):76–82. In Russian, abstract in English.

Samoilova, R. B. 1955. Ob Ozersko-Khovanskikh Trokhiliskakh [Les *Trochiliscus* d'Ozerki-Khovansk]. Doklady Akademiya Nauk SSSR 103(5):909–911. In Russian.

———. 1961. Pervaya Nakhodka Trokhiliskov podrola Karpinskya Croft v Devonskikh otlozheniyakh Russkoy Platformy [First discovery of *Trochiliscus* of the genus *Karpinskya* Croft in the Devonian deposits of the Russian Platform]. Doklady Akademiya Nauk SSSR 139(1):206–207. In Russian.

Sandberger, Guido. 1849. Eine neue Polypen-Gattung *Sycidium* aus der Eifel. Neues Jahrbuch für Mineralogie, Geognosie, Geologie und Petrefakten-Kunde 20:671–672, 1 pl.

Sanders, Erin R., Kenneth G. Karol, & Richard M. McCourt. 2003. Occurrence of *matK* in a *trnK* group II intron in charophyte green algae, and phylogeny of the Characeae. American Journal of Botany 90:628–633.

Sawa, Takashi, & Paul W. Frame. 1974. Comparative anatomy of Charophyta. I. Oogonia and oospores of *Tolypella,* with special reference to the sterile oogonial cell. Bulletin of the Torrey Botanical Club 101(3):136–144.

Schimper, W. P. 1869. Traité de Paléontologie végétale. J. B. Baillère. Paris. Vol. I, text, 738 p. Characeae: p. 215–232, pl. V. Atlas published in 1874, 110 pl.

Schellwien, Ernst. 1898. Die fauna des Karnischen Fusulinenkalks. Theil II: Foraminifera. Palaeontographica XLIV:237–282, pl. 17–24. *Möllerina* (Foraminifer): p. 238, 281.

Schmidt-Kittler, Norbert E., ed. 1987. International Symposium on mammalian biostratigraphy and palaeoecology of the European Paleogene. München Geowissenschaften (Abhandlungen A) 10:1–312.

Schreber, Johan C. D. 1759. Lithographia Halensis: Exhibens lapides circa Halam Saxonum reperiundas, systematice digestos secundum classes et ordines, genera et species cum synonymis selectis et descriptionibus specierum; cum figuris aeneis. Curt. Halae (Halle an der Saale, Germany). xxiv + 80 p.

Schudack, Michael. 1986. Zur Nomenklatur der Gattungen *Porochara* Mädler 1955 (syn. *Musacchiella* Feist & Grambast-Fessard 1984) und *Feistiella* n. gen. (Charophyta). Paläontologische Zeitschrift 60(1/2):21–27.

———. 1987. Charophytenflora und fazielle Entwicklung der Grenzschichten mariner Jura/Wealden in den Nordwestlichen Iberischen Ketten (mit Vergleichen zu Asturien und Kantabrien). Palaeontographica (Abt. B) 204:1–180, 9 pl.

———. 1989. Charophytenfloren aus den unterkretazischen Vertebraten-Fundschichten bei Galve und Uña (Ostspanien). Berliner Geowissenschaftliche (abhandlungen A) 106:409–443.

———. 1990. Bestandsaufnahme und Lokalzonierung der Charophyten aus der Oberjura und Unterkreide des Nordwestdeutschen Beckens. Berliner Geowissenschaftliche (abhandlungen A) 124:209–245, 4 pl.

———. 1993a. Möglichkeiten palökologischer Aussagen mit Hilfe von fossilen Charophyten. Festschrift Professor W. Krutzsch. Museum für Naturkunde. Berlin. p. 39–58, 2 pl.

———. 1993b. Die Charophyten in Oberjura und Unterkreide Westeuropas. Mit einer phylogenetischen Analyse der Gesamtgruppe. Berliner geowissenschaftliche Abhandlungen E8:209 p., 20 pl.

———. 1999. Some charophytes from the Middle Dinosaur Member of the Tendaguru Formation (Upper Jurassic of Tanzania). Mitteilungen aus dem Museum für Naturkunde Berlin, Geowissenschaftliche Reihe 2:201–205.

Schudack, Michael, C. Turner, & F. Peterson. 1998. Biostratigraphy, paleoecology, and biogeography of charophytes and ostracodes from the Upper Jurassic Morrison Formation, Western Interior, USA. Modern Geology 22:379–414.

Schwarz, J., & Th. W. Griessemer. 1992. Charophyten-Massenvorkommen aus den Oberen Pechelbronn-Schichten (Unteroligozän) von Merkwiller-Pechelbronn im Elsaß (Frankreich, Dépt. Bas-Rhin). Paläontologische Zeitschrift 66(1/2):23–37.

Scotese, Christopher R. 1997. Paleogeographic Atlas, Paleomap progress Report 90-0497. Department of Geology, University of Texas. Arlington, Texas. 45 p.

Seward, Albert C. 1894. Catalogue of the Mesozoic Plants in the Department of Geology, British Museum (Nat. Hist.). The Wealden Flora. I, Thallophyta and Pteridophyta. British Museum (Natural History). London. x + 179 p.
Algites, p. 4, pl. 1,*1–2.*

Shaikin, I. M. 1966. Characeae (kharofity) verkhnevo Karbona Dombasa [Characeae of the Upper Carboniferous in the Donez bassin]. Trudy Geologicheskogo Instituta Akademiya Nauk SSR 143:154–160, 1 pl. In Russian.

———. 1976. Novye svedenia po Biostratigrafii Iurskikh i Melovykh otlozhenii Preddobrudzhinskogo proggiba (po Dannym Izuchenia Kharophitov) [New data on biostratigraphy of the Jurassic and Cretaceous deposits of the Fore-Dobrogean trough (by the data of studies in Charophyta)]. Geologiczeski Zhurnal 36(2):77–86, 2 pl. In Russian.

———. 1977. Kharophity v produktivnoï tovshchi Boltis'koï Zappadini [Charophyta from productive strata of Boltishka depression]. Materiali do paleontologii Kainozoyu Ukraïni [The materials of the Cenozoic paleontology of Ukraine] C:107–110. In Ukrainian.

———. 1987. Chapter 5: Kharovye vodorloli (Charaphyta). *In* V. N. Dubatolov, ed., Iskopaemye izvestkovye vodorosli. Morphologia, sistematika, Metody i zucheniya [Methods, morphology, and systematics of fossil calcareous Algae]. Akademiya Nauk SSSR, Sibirskoe otdelenie, Novosibirsk 674:140–160, fig. V1–V7, pl. XXIII–XXIV. In Russian.

Shaw, G. 1971. The chemistry of sporopollenin. *In* J. Brooks, P. R. Grant, M. Muir, P. Van Gijzel, & G. Shaw, eds., Sporopollenin, Proceedings of a Symposium held at the Geology Department, Imperial College, London, 23–25 September, 1970. Academic Press. London, New York. p. 306–348.

Shu Zhiqing & Zhang Zerun. 1985. [Early Cretaceous charophytes from the Hetao area of Inner Mongolia]. Selected papers of the 1st National Fossil Algal Symposium. Beijing. p. 63–74, 2 pl. In Chinese.

Simons, Jan, Marieke Ohm, Remko Daalder, Peter Boers, & Winnie Rip. 1994. Restoration of Botshol (The Netherlands) by reduction of external nutrient load: recovery of a characean community, dominated by *Chara connivens.* Hydrobiologia 275/276:243–253.

Sirna, Giuseppe. 1968. The Lower Cretaceous Charophyta and the paleogeography of Mediterranean basin. Atti dell' Accademia Nazionale dei Lincei 44:566–573, 2 pl.

Sluiman, Hans J., & Caroline Guihal. 1999. Phylogenetic position of the *Chaetosphaeridium* (Chlorophyta), a basal lineage in the Charophyceae inferred from 18S rDNA sequences. Journal of Phycology 35:395–402.

Smith, Gilbert M. 1938. Algae and Fungi, vol. 1. *In* Cryptogamic Botany. McGraw-Hill. New York. 545 p.
Charophyceae, p. 127–135.

———. 1950. The Fresh-Water Algae of the United States. McGraw-Hill Book Company. New York. 719 p.

Sohn, I. G. 1961. Techniques for preparation and study of fossil ostracods. *In* R. C. Moore, ed., Treatise on Invertebrate Paleontology, Part Q. Geological Society of America & The University of Kansas Press. New York & Lawrence, Kansas. p. 64–70.

Sommer, Friedrich W. 1954. Contribuçao à paleofitografia do Paraná. *In* F. W. Lange, ed., Paleontologia do Paraná. Volume Comemorativo do 1 Centenário do Estado do Paraná. Commissão de Comemorações do Centenário do Paraná. Paraná, Brazil. p. 175–194, pl. 15–20.

Soulié-Märsche, Ingeborg. 1979. Origine et évolution des genres actuels des Characeae. Bulletin du Centre de Recherches, de Production, d'Exploration et de Production d'Elf-Aquitaine 3(2):821–831.

———. 1981. Palaeoflora. *In* N. Petit-Maire & J. Riser, Holocene lake deposits and palaeoenvironments in central Sahara, northeastern Mali. Palaeogeography, Palaeoclimatology, Palaeoecology 35:45–61.

———. 1987. Les charophytes. *In* J. C. Misovsky, ed., Géologie de la Préhistoire: Méthodes, techniques, applications (GEOPRE). Société géologique de France. Paris. p. 669–683.

———. 1989. Etude comparée de gyrogonites de charophytes actuelles et fossiles et phylogénie des genres actuels. Imprimerie des Tilleuls. Millau, France. 237 p., 45 pl.

———. 1991. Charophyte remains from Wadi Howar as evidence for deep mid-Holocene freshwater lakes in the eastern Sahara of northwest Sudan. Quaternary Research 36:210–223.

———. 1999. Chirality in charophytes: Stability and evolution from 400 million years to present. *In* G. Pályi, C. Zucchi, & L. Caglioti, eds., Advances in BioChirality. Elsevier. Amsterdam. p. 191–207.

Stache, Guido. 1872. Über neue Characeenreste aus der oberen Abteilung der Liburnische Stufe bei Isino in Istrien. Verhandlungen der Geologischen Reichsanstalt, Wien. p. 316–319.
Astrocharas, p. 316.

———. 1880. G., Die Liburnische Stufe. Verhandlung der Kaiserlichen und Königlichen geologischen Reichsanstalt 12:195–209.

———. 1889. Die Liburnische Stufe. Abhandlungen der Kaiserlich Königlichen geologischen Reichsanstalt 13(1):1–170, 6 pl.

Steele, Kelly P., & Rytas Vilgalys. 1994. Phylogenetic analyses of Polemoniaceae using nucleotide sequences of the plastid gene *matK*. Systematic Botany 19:126–142.

Sternberg, Kaspar. 1825. Versuch einer geognotisch-botanischen Darstellung der Flora der Vorwelt, vol. IV. Fleischer. Regensburg. 48 p.
Bechera, p. XXX–XXXI.

Stockmans, François. 1960. Initiation à la paléobotanique stratigraphique de la Belgique et notions connexes: Guide de la salle des végétaux fossiles. Naturalistes belges. Bruxelles. 222 p.
Charophytes, p. 62.

Straub, E.W. 1952. Mikropaläontologishe Untersuchungen im Tertiär zwischen Ehingen und Ulm an der Donau. Geologisches Jahrbuch 66:433–524

Strauss, René, & Jeannine Lepoint. 1966. Influence des chlorures alcalins sur la nutrition et la croissance des Characées. Comptes Rendus des Séances de l'Académie des Sciences, Paris (series D) 263:40–43.

Stroede, W. 1933. Über die Beziehungen der Characeen zu den chemischen Faktoren der Wohngewässer und des Schlammes. Archiv für Hydrobiologie 25:192–223.

Stur, D. 1881. Die Silur-Flora der Etage H-h in Böhmen. Sitzungsbericht der Akademie der Wissenschaften 84(1):330–391.
Barrandeina, p. 362.

Summerson, G. H. 1958. Arenaceous Foraminifera from the Middle Devonian limestones of Ohio. Journal of Paleontology 32(3):544–558, pl. 81–82.

Talent, J. A., R. Mawson, J. C. Aitchison, R. T. Becker, K. N. Bell, M. A. Bradshaw, C. J. Burrow, A. G. Cook, G. Dargan, M. Feist, G. Playford, A. J. Wright, & Zhen Y. Z. 2000. Devonian palaeobiogeography of Australia and adjoining regions. Memoirs of the Association of Australian Palaeontologists 23:167–257.
Charophyta, p. 222–223.

Tambareau, Yvette, Monique Feist, Carla Gruas-Cavagnetto, & Marco Murru. 1989. Caractérisation de l'Ilerdien continental dans le domaine ouest-méditerranéen. Comptes Rendus des Séances de l'Académie des Sciences de Paris (series D) 308(2):689–695.

Tang Lunhe, & Di Hengshu. 1991. [Fossil charophytes from Qaidam basin, Qinghai]. Ke xue ji shu wen xian chu ban she. Beijing. 220 p., 79 pl.
In Chinese with abstract and table of contents in English.

Tappan, Helen. 1980. The Paleobiology of Plant Protists. W. E. Freeman and Company. San Francisco. 1,028 p.

Taylor, Thomas N., Winfried Remy, & Hagen Hass. 1992. Parasitism in a 400-million year-old green alga. Nature 357:493–494.

Thaler, Louis. 1965. Une échelle de zones biochronologiques pour les mammifères du Tertiaire d'Europe. Comptes Rendus Sommaires de la Société Géologique de France 4:118.

Traverse, Alfred F. 1955. Pollen analysis of the Brandon lignite of Vermont. United States Bureau of Mines, Report of Investigations 5,151:108 p.

Turmel, Monique K., Megumi Ehara, Christian Otis, & Claude Lemieux. 2002. Phylogenetic relationships among streptophytes inferred from chloroplast small and large subunit rDNA gene sequences. Journal of Phycology 38:364–375.

Tuttle, A. H. 1926. The location of the reduction divisions in a charophyte. University of California Publications in Botany 13:227–235, 2 pl.

Tuzson, J. 1909. Zur Phyletisch-paläontologischen Entwicklungsgeschichte des Pflanzenreichs, vol. XVIII, no. 5. Engler's Botanisches Jahrbuch. Leipzig. p. 461–473.
Charales, p. 470.

———. 1913. Adatok Magyarorszag Fosszilis Flórájához (Addimenta ad floram fossilem Hungariae III). Magyar Földtani XXI(8):208–234, pl. XIII–XXI.

Uliana, M. A. & Eduardo A. Musacchio. 1978. Microfosiles calcareos no-marinos del Cretacico superior en Zampal, provincia de Mendoza, Argentina. Ameghiniana 15:111–135.

Ulrich, Edward O. 1886. Description of new Silurian and Devonian fossils. Contributions to American Paleontology 1:3–35, 3 pl.

UNESCO. 1981. Background papers and supporting data on the Practical Salinity Scale 1978. UNESCO Technical Papers in Marine Science 37:1–144.

Unger, Franz. 1850. Genera et Species Plantarum Fossilium. Published by the author. Vindobonae. 627 p.
Characeae, p. 31–36.

Vaillant, S. 1719. Caractères de quatorze genres de plantes. Mémoires de l'Académie royale des Sciences de Paris pour 1719:17–20.

Van Raam, Joop C. 1995. The Characeae of Tasmania. Nova Hedwigia, Beiheft 110:1–80.

Wallroth, F. G. 1833. Flora cryptogamia Germaniae. Pars posterior—Continens Algas et Fungos. *In* M. J. Bluff & C. A. Fingerhuth, Compendium florae Germanicae. Sectio II plantae cryptogamicae sine cellulosae. Tomus IV. J. L. Schrag. Norimbergae. lvi + 923 p.

Walter Lévy, Léone, & René Strauss. 1968. Sur l'absorption du strontium par *Chara fragilis* Desvaux. Comptes Rendus des séances de l'Académie des Sciences Paris (série D) 266:1,486–1,489.

———. 1974 . Résistance des characées aux effets toxiques des ions Pb^{2+}. Comptes Rendus des séances de l'Académie des Sciences Paris (series D) 278:2,023–2,026, 1 fig.

Wang Qifei, Yang J.-L., & Lu H.-N. 2003. Late paleozoic charophyte assemblages of China. Acta Micropalaeontologica Sinica 20:199–211, 4 pl., 1 map.

Wang Shui. 1961. Tertiary Charophyta from Chaidamu (Tsaidam) Basin, Qinghai (Chinghai) Province. Acta Palaeontologica Sinica 9(3):183–209, 7 pl.
In Chinese with English summary, p. 209–219.

Wang Shui, & Chang Shan-zen. 1956. On the occurrence of *Sycidium melo* var. *pskowensis* Karpinsky from the Devonian of Northern Szechuan. Acta Palaeontologica Sinica 4(3):381–386, 1 pl.
In Chinese, English summary.

Wang Shui, Huang Renjin, Wang Zhen, Lin Xiaodong, Zhang Zerun, & Xu Xilin. 1982. [Cretaceous and Cenozoic charophytes from Jiangsu]. Geological Publishing House. Beijing. 66 p., 28 pl. In Chinese with English abstract.

Wang Shui, Huang Renjin, Yang Chenqiong, & Li Huanan. 1978. Early Tertiary charophytes from coastal region of Bohai, vol 1. Science Press. Beijing. 49 p., 23 pl. In Chinese with English abstract.

Wang Zhen. 1976. [Middle Devonian *Sycidium* and *Chovanella* from southwestern China]. Acta Palaeontologica Sinica 15(2):175–186, 3 pl. In Chinese with English abstract.

———. 1978a. [Cretaceous charophytes from the Yangtze-Han river basin with a note on the classification of Porocharaceae and Characeae]. Memoirs Nanjing Institute of Geology and Palaeontology, Academia Sinica 9:61–88, 8 pl. In Chinese with English abstract.

———. 1978b. [Paleogene charophytes from the Yangtze-Han River basin]. Memoirs Nanjing Institute of Geology and Palaeontology, Academia Sinica 9:101–120, 5 pl. In Chinese with English abstract.

———. 1984. [Two new charophyte genera from the upper Permian and their bearing on the phylogeny and classification of Charales and Trochiliscales]. Acta Micropalaeontologica Sinica 1(1):49–60, 2 pl. In Chinese with English abstract.

Wang Zhen, J. E. Conkin, Huang Ren-jin, & Lu Huinan. 1980. Early and Middle Devonian charophytes of eastern Guangxi, China. University of Louisville Studies, Paleontology and Stratigraphy 13:1–16, 3 pl.

Wang Zhen, & Huang Renjin. 1978. [Triassic charophytes of Shaanxi]. Acta Palaeontologica Sinica 17(3):267–276, 2 pl. In Chinese with English abstract.

Wang Zhen, Huang Renjin, & Wang Shui. 1976. [Mesozoic and Cenozoic Charophyta from Yunnan Province]. Mesozoic Fossils of Yunnan, vol. 1. Nanjing Institute of Geology and Palaeontology Science Press. Nanjing. 65–86, 6 pl. In Chinese.

Wang Zhen, & Lu Huinan. 1980. [New discovery of Devonian charophytes from southern China with special reference to classification and gyrogonite orientation of Trochiliscales and Sycidiales]. Acta Paleontologica Sinica 19(3):190–200, 2 pl. In Chinese with English abstract.

———. 1982. [Classification and evolution of Clavatoraceae, with notes on its distribution in China]. Bulletin Nanjing Institute of Geology and Paleontology, Academia Sinica 4:77–104, 4 pl. In Chinese with English abstract.

Wang Zhen, Lu Huinan, & Zhao Chanben. 1985. [Cretaceous charophytes from Songliao basin and adjacent areas]. Tectonic & Scientific Press of Hi Long Jiang. Haerbin. 84 p., 30 pl. In Chinese with English abstract.

Wang Zhen, & Wang Ren-nong. 1986. [Permian charophytes from the southeastern area of the North China platform]. Acta Micropaleontologica Sinica 3(3):273–278, 1 pl. In Chinese with English summary.

Watson, Joan. 1969. A revision of the English Wealden Flora-I, Charales-Ginkgoales. Bulletin of the British Museum (Natural History), Geology 17(5):207–254, pl. I–VI.

Westphal, M., & J. P. Durand. 1990. Magnétostratigraphie des séries continentales fluvio-lacustres du Crétacé supérieur dans le synclinal de l'Arc (région d'Aix-en-Provence, France). Bulletin de la Société géologique de France (série 8) 6:609–620.

Wiley, E. O. 1978. The evolutionary species concept reconsidered. Systematic Zoology 27:17–26.

Williamson, W. C. 1880. On the organization of the fossil plants of the coal-measures. Part X. Including an examination of the supposed radiolarians of the Carboniferous rocks. Philosophical Transactions of the Royal Society of London 171(2):493–539, pl. 14–21.

Winter, Ursula, & Gunter O. Kirst. 1991. Partial turgor pressure regulation in *Chara canescens* and its implications for a generalized hypothesis of salinity response in charophytes. Botanica Acta 104:37–46.

Winter, Ursula, Ingeborg Soulié-Märsche, & Gunter O. Kirst. 1996. Effects of salinity on turgor pressure and fertility in *Tolypella* (Characeae). Plant, Cell and Environment 19:869–879.

Wium-Andersen, Soten, U. Anthoni, C. Christophersen, & G. Houen. 1982. Allelopathic effects on phytoplankton by substances isolated from aquatic macrophytes (Charales). Oikos 39:187–190.

Womersley, H. B. S., & I. L. Ophel. 1947. *Protochara,* a new genus of Characeae from Western Australia. Transactions of the Royal Society of South Australia 71:311–317, 2 fig.

Wood, Richard D. 1962. New combinations and taxa in the revision of Characeae. Taxon 11:7–25.

———. 1972. Characeae of Australia. Nova Hedwigia 22:1–120, 17 pl.
Also separately printed the same year by J. Cramer, Lehre, 120 p.

———. 1978. Cryptogams. *In* O. A. Leistner, ed., Flora of Southern Africa, vol. 9. Botanical Research Institute, Department of Agricultural Technical Services. Pretoria. 56 p.

Wood, Richard D., & Kozo Imahori. 1959. Geographical distribution of Characeae. Bulletin of the Torrey Botanical Club 86(3):172–183.

———. 1964–1965. A revision of the Characeae. J. Cramer. Weinheim. Part 1: Monograph, 1965: 904 p., Part 2: Iconograph, 1964: 395 pl.

Wood, Richard D., & R. Mason. 1977. Characeae of New Zealand. New Zealand Journal of Botany 15:87–180.

Woodruff, Fay, Samuel M. Savin, & Robert G. Douglas. 1981. Miocene stable isotope record: A detailed deep ocean study and its paleoclimatic implications. Science 212:665–668.

Yang Chenqiong. 1987. New materials of charophytes from the Paleogene Shahejie Formation of the Dong Ying depression and their environment. Reports on the Redbeds and Palaeontology in Gas and Petroleum Areas 1:156–164, 4 pl.
In Chinese with English abstract.

Yang Guodong, & Zhou Xingao. 1990. [Discovery of lower Carboniferous charophytes in the northern part of the Tarim basin and their importance]. Dizhi lunping 36:269–276, 2 pl.
In Chinese.

Zaneveld, Jacques S. 1940. The Charophyta of Malaysia and adjacent countries. Blumea 4(1):1–223.

Zeng De-nim, & Hu Ji-min. 2001. Discussion about the charophyte fossils during Middle Devonian period and its living environment. Hunan Geology 20(2):89–91.

Zhang Jie-fang, Lu Hui-nan, Zhang Zhen-lai, & Gao Qin-qin. 1978. Charophyta. Palaeontological Atlas of Southern Central China 4:325–382, 710–722.

Zhao Zhiqing & Huang Ren-jin. 1985. Early Tertiary charophytes from the upper part of the Shahejie Formation in Puyang, Henan. Selected Papers on Micropalaeontology of China, p. 11–18, pl. III.

INDEX